Shifting Educational Behaviours

Don Passey

Shifting Educational Behaviours

The Real Impact of Digital Technologies

Springer

Don Passey
Department of Educational Research
Lancaster University
Lancaster, UK

ISBN 978-3-032-18941-7 ISBN 978-3-032-18942-4 (eBook)
https://doi.org/10.1007/978-3-032-18942-4

This Springer imprint is published by the registered company Springer Nature Switzerland AG
The registered company address is: Gewerbestrasse 11, 6330 Cham, Switzerland

I dedicate this book to Petra

Preface

The uses of digital technologies have continued to not only blur boundaries, but to encourage communication and discussion across those boundaries. Whether those boundaries are considered as country or state boundaries, or school or home boundaries, we see increased forms of communication. Those increased forms of communication might be through social media, emails, or the sharing of documents, but in all cases the boundary itself becomes blurred as it is seen to become more seamless. Educators in one country now communicate online with educators in other countries through videoconferencing, for example, while parents and guardians may use email or social media to increasing extents, to communicate with the school where their children are supported. Teachers also increasingly find that communication with their learners may now involve more online interaction. The ideas of 'hard boundaries' are being questioned and reduced by the uses of communication technologies.

This being the case, if behaviours are shifting, and if the future of those shifting behaviours is to be adequately considered, then a view across those boundaries needs to be taken. In this way, a systemic approach is needed when exploring the current and future contexts of educational practices and development.

In this book, a systemic approach is taken. Whilst teaching and learning behaviours that are influenced by digital technology uses are at the core of this concern, the ways that those behaviours involve and are influenced by those who support teaching and learning also need to be taken into account. To consider this systemic perspective, educational behaviours of parents and guardians and advisers and policy makers are explored. Behaviours are not therefore limited to learning and teaching, to learners and teachers, but also concern support and policy behaviours that relate to parents and guardians and advisers and policymakers. An aspect of education that is not explored in this text is assessment; in itself, this aspect is worthy of in-depth exploration that goes beyond the realms of this text.

In this book, Chaps. 1–4 provide an introduction and explore how learning and teaching behaviours are currently conceived and described, considering the impacts of emerging technologies on educational behaviours, the impacts of past and present digital technologies on educational behaviours, and the theoretical perspectives that underlie the approaches taken to learning and teaching. Chapters 5–9 explore educational behaviours from different perspectives, from the learner and from learning, from the teacher and from teaching, from the parent and guardian and from the home support, from the peer and from the online, and from the policymaker and guidance perspectives. Chapters 10 and 11 focus more on the implications of wider systemic behaviours that are emerging, and they consider how these behaviours can support individuals and what features are identified as crucial to accommodate what the future might hold.

The author recognises that there are major differences across the world in terms of digital access and the potential for digital uses in schools and in homes. This text looks at the current and future nature of education by considering educational behaviours that are seen to be developed when digital technologies are used (and sometimes this involves using a wide range of different digital technologies). The text highlights specific forms of digital technology and how their uses have influenced and do influence shifts in educational behaviours. If educational stakeholders have access to specific ranges of digital technologies, then it is hoped that the effect of those digital technologies can be recognised in this text and that the future for those contexts might be considered as wider digital technology access becomes available.

Lancaster, UK Don Passey

Acknowledgements

This text gathers evidence from a wide variety of sources—from an exploration and review of my own past and current experiences, from observations of classroom practices, from many discussions with teachers and senior leaders, and from a reflection on texts previously written. Where examples and vignettes are provided, these are in large part drawn from those observations and discussions.

I am deeply indebted to the very many individuals who have been willing to share their practices and ideas with me, sometimes sharing concerns and at other times successes. Viewing practices and gathering responses have, over the years, involved learners as well as teachers, senior leaders in schools as well as parents and guardians, advisers and policy makers, and other researchers. Without the generosity of this vast number of informants, this text could not have been conceived and written.

I would particularly like to thank those individuals who have supported my work recently: Petra Hobrecht, who has offered me insights into examples of leading school-based practices using digital technologies over many years; Peter Claxton, who enabled school-based practice to be seen from a digital development perspective; Prof. John Anderson, who has shared wide and notable practice from across Northern Ireland; Gavin Hawkins, who has developed support and innovative resources that make a difference to young people and their ways of working; and Anthony Wong, who has opened up international opportunities to work with individuals endeavouring to develop the sorts of practices that are presented in this text.

Contents

List of Figures

List of Tables

Chapter 1
Learning and Teaching Behaviours: What They Are and Are Not, and Why They Are Important

Abstract Learning is the fundamental concern of education, and it is clear from existing research that uses of digital technologies are shifting the ways that learners and those supporting them are engaging with and gaining from educational practices and activities. Digital technologies are influencing and affecting the ways that individuals tackle educational activities. These shifts are affecting learning behaviours, the ways that learners approach learning activities and learning needs. Learning behaviours that involve the uses of digital technologies can be exemplified, their importance can be demonstrated and has often been researched, and their impact on learning engagement can be observed. It is clear that different digital technologies affect and influence learning behaviours in a variety of ways. The breadth of ways suggests that the behaviours of those involved in educational support and guidance, whether teachers, parents and guardians, or advisers and policy makers, are shifting to more systemic-wide engagement.

Keywords Educational digital technologies · Learning and digital technologies · Teaching and digital technologies · Defining learning behaviours · Learning behaviours and the individual · Learning behaviours · Learning engagement

1.1 An Initial Starting Point

Learning is a fundamental concern of education, so this is where this exploration of behaviours will begin. Learning behaviours using digital technologies are sometimes reduced to a focus on digital skills, but another way of considering learning behaviours is to view digital skills as an element of influence rather than providing the whole picture.

When considering learning behaviours, a key question for me that raises an important consideration and further questions is: do I use the software Microsoft (MS) Word in the same way as a colleague in my same institution? The answer to this question is—no. So, does this mean that either my colleague or I lack digital or learning skills in some way? The answer to that question is—not as far as I can see. So, does this

D. Passey, *Shifting Educational Behaviours*,
https://doi.org/10.1007/978-3-032-18942-4_1

mean that my colleague or I do not understand how we adopt and accommodate different learning approaches or a range of digital competencies? The answer to that question is—not as far as I can see. So, does this mean that my colleague or I do not have adequate understanding of learning approaches or digital agency? The answer to that question again is—not as far as I can see. So, why is there a difference, when our uses are not the same, but we appear to be as competent as each other and as successful as each other in supporting learning? It is possible to address this question by exploring an important concept, of learning behaviours—which are considered and argued here as needing to be viewed as individual, rather than being regarded as a set of generic skills or competencies that all learners or users should possess.

This text focuses on how uses of digital technologies in education, to provide support for learning, have introduced practices where learning behaviours are shifting—and that those shifted and shifting behaviours are important, not just for learners, but also for teachers and those supporting educational practice (particularly parents and guardians, peers and policy makers). In a context of educational practice, learning and teaching behaviours should not be considered as an alternative to other areas of focal interest within this sphere, i.e., areas of concern such as digital skills, digital competencies, and digital agency. But learning and teaching behaviours are distinguished from these other areas by the fact that they are much more specific to the individual, as behaviours meet specific needs and interests, and they are applied to specific contexts, as they are not a set of general skills and approaches that are felt should be inherently accessible for all individuals to meet all situations.

Whilst there are some digital skills that could be regarded as ubiquitous for users, such as the ability to use a mouse or a keyboard, it is also arguable that for some individuals, such as those with visual or physical disability or impairment, the practices of using a mouse or a keyboard are distinctly different from those for individuals who do not have these same disabilities or impairments (Gür et al., 2020). Learning behaviours associated with this more individual contextual concern then relate to ways that individuals approach learning with digital technologies. In this way, this text considers the area of focus from an individual perspective, rather than from a perspective where individuals are generalised through concerns for an identification of specific generic skills, competencies or functions.

Some might argue that attempting to consider the needs of the individual within group settings is either not easy or not possible (Spratt & Florian, 2015). However, as this text will show, there are examples of how this has been achieved, as individualised learning behaviours can complement learning and teaching activity, rather than creating barriers. Indeed, in the final chapter, specific features associated with how behaviours can positively support the effectiveness of future educational contexts where individualised learning might be supported more will be identified.

1.2 An Introduction

Uses of digital technologies are not new to those in education, whether in the school, further education (FE), technical education, or training, vocational or higher education (HE) sectors, having been introduced in the 1980s to many educational institutions in many countries (Howard & Mozejko, 2015). But what difference digital technologies have made and make to learning and teaching, and the extent of those differences, has long been debated and sought (Butler, n.d.). This text draws evidence showing that using digital technologies to support teaching and learning effectively and successfully requires behaviours that can accommodate adaptability, change and flexibility. In some respects, this assertion may seem to contradict some of the current accepted theories and practices in education. For example, regarding applying social constructivism theory to teaching practices, Saleem et al. (2021) state that: "It is the teacher's responsibility to use learner-centered and collaborative teaching approaches" (p. 403). This would suggest that didactic approaches concerned with direct presentation and lectures, or even listening and watching video material, might be excluded. But in this text, evidence indicates how uses of digital technologies affect the need to be 'inquisitive', to not exclude possibilities, but to consider options that support shifting behaviours, for learning, for teaching, and for positively supporting the individual and the group, both in the home, when working with other peers and through policy maker actions. The text provides not just a view of the past to substantiate these claims, but a view of the future, which, some researchers claim, will additionally be likely to offer increasing prospects for those who do not always succeed in more traditional environments.

Whilst there are texts that have explored behaviours related to uses of digital technologies (for example, Asotić, 2023), these have not necessarily specifically focused on the educational field. Some previous texts have explored behaviours related to practices such as self-regulation (Cowley, 2021) in the early years sector, or behaviours in a more general sense (Ellis & Tod, 2018). This text focuses on and explores educational, learning and teaching behaviours in the context of digital technologies, from a systemic perspective (i.e., a perspective that considers the involvement and potential influence within and beyond the school, of parents and guardians, working with peers, and of advisers and policy makers). Some previous texts have considered rethinking pedagogies (Sharpe et al., 2010) when using digital technologies, while other journal articles have explored learning behaviours in specific contexts when using digital technologies. For example, a specific context has been explored in a fairly recent paper (Younas et al., 2022) that focused on the HE sector, while another relates to the online context (Zhang, 2021), and a further article relates to the development of digital literacy (Chiu et al., 2022). This text takes a wider perspective than these texts, exploring the formal, non-formal and informal blending of access and uses, and educational support, learning and teaching behaviours from a systemic perspective; that is, that learning and teaching behaviours can and are influenced not just by the individual, but by all stakeholders within the educational community: learners; teachers; parents and guardians; peers; and advisers and policy makers.

Whilst this text will provide an academic perspective, arising from a research background (and hence will be focused on a key audience of academics and researchers), it will nonetheless be relevant to practitioners and professionals, whether they be lecturers and tutors in initial teacher education, teachers in the compulsory sector, advisers or policy makers in education, or parents and guardians.

1.3 Digital Technologies and Learning and Teaching

Over the past 40 years, digital technologies have continued to be developed in a range of ways (Roser, 2023). Those digital technologies have rarely been developed for specific educational purposes, but innovative practices have led to many digital technologies being integrated into educational practices, both for teaching and for learning, as well as for management and governance (Male, 2016).

In this text, to fully explore the ways that digital technologies have influenced behaviours in learning and teaching, it is necessary to consider the full range of digital technologies that have become available over the years. Figure 1.1 shows an outline illustration of the forms of digital technologies that will be explored in this text, across a range of levels and actors involved, where levels indicate specific ranges of digital technologies, and where actors may choose specific digital technologies to support their needs (educational in the context of this text, albeit accepting that social choices outside the school and at home also can affect educational choices).

Considering the levels shown in Fig. 1.1, there are four distinct levels and groupings of digital technologies:

- The underlying infrastructure is concerned with connectivity and networking, involving uses of WiFi and the Internet, for example.

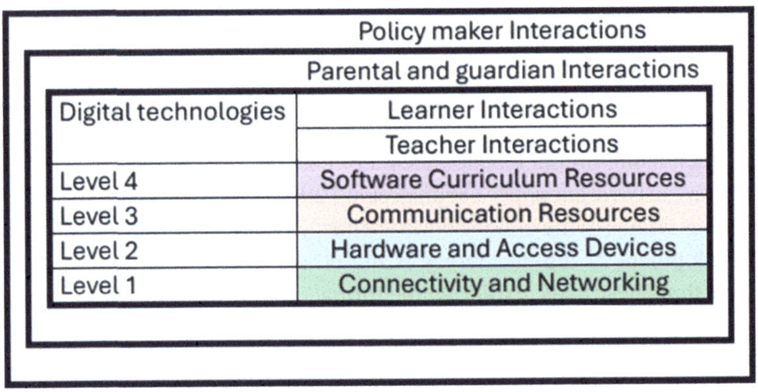

Fig. 1.1 Levels of infrastructure and use relating to the individual or learner groups

- To access this infrastructure, hardware and digital devices such as desktop computers, laptops, tablets, or mobile devices are used.
- Through these devices, communication is made possible through resources such as email, social media, or learning and conference management systems such as Microsoft (MS) Teams,[1] Office 365,[2] Google Classroom,[3] Moodle[4] or Blackboard.[5]
- For more specific needs or purposes, more focused software is used, which can range from the use of chatbots and YouTube where specific details through those resources are sought, to uses of subject orientated software such as Mathletics[6] or Accelerated Reader.[7]

Beyond the digital technologies, taking the actors into consideration, different actors may select from across this range of digital technologies:

- Learners may well focus on the latter of the levels in Fig. 1.1, without perhaps paying much attention to the provision of the other levels that underly this layer.
- Teachers may also focus on the latter levels, but they will additionally be concerned with the possibilities that might be provided by all levels (for example, with a learner group, uses of an electronic whiteboard rather than using a desktop computer), as well as the secure and safe provision of access through any of these levels.
- Parents may be more concerned about the former levels, and they are perhaps likely to have less experience with using the higher levels or how their young people might be accessing and using those higher levels.
- Policy makers may be more concerned about the lower levels, ensuring that learners and teachers have continuous and safe access to the resources that they need, when and as they need them.

Hence, already, it is clear to see that whilst all of these levels of digital technologies are important for educational practice, the focus on them is not necessarily the same for all actors involved in engagement with practice. When considering the ways that access to and uses of digital technologies can lead to learning outcomes, and hopefully successful outcomes, it is clear that the focus of the different stakeholders are all important and play their parts within a wide systemic configuration.

---

[1] https://www.microsoft.com/en-gb/microsoft-teams/group-chat-software#:~:text=Plan%20events%2C%20share%20photos%2C%20and%20connect%20with%20your,people%2C%20plus%20Microsoft%20365%20apps%20and%20advanced%20security.?msockid=2b77ea2bd6f969ec2cf4fc8bd7676857.

[2] https://www.microsoft.com/en-gb/microsoft-365?msockid=2b77ea2bd6f969ec2cf4fc8bd7676857.

[3] https://edu.google.com/intl/de/workspace-for-education/products/classroom/.

[4] https://moodle.org/?lang=en.

[5] https://help.blackboard.com/blackboard_app/quick_start.

[6] https://knowledgebase.mathletics.com/.

[7] https://www.renaissance.com/products/practice-instruction/accelerated-reader/.

1.4 Learning Behaviours and Digital Technologies

In a wide systemic educational arena, a learning behaviour can be defined as actions that are deployed or are necessary for a learner to learn effectively in an educational setting, whether that be in a classroom, a small discussion group, or through individual learning outside an education institutional setting (Ellis & Todd, 2018). Traditionally, it is perhaps felt that teachers have been mainly responsible for supporting learners in gaining and using effective learning behaviours. However, it is also clear that parents and guardians have played roles in this respect, and that advisers and policy makers have also contributed to this picture. More recently, the concern for a learning development focus on self-regulated, metacognitive activity of learners has also highlighted attention to the roles that the learners themselves play in developing effective learning behaviours. Digital technologies have in the research literature been identified as actors themselves, often described or defined as elements within a learning ecosystem (Schiavetto & Schnaider, 2024). It is through an exploration from the digital technologies' perspectives that this text explores the role that the digital technologies play in supporting learning behaviours that are seen to be effective and successful for positive learning outcomes.

Detailed examples and explanations of learning behaviours associated with each of the digital technologies related to the different levels will be explored further in subsequent chapters. Offering a summary overview at this stage:

- Level 1 digital technologies, the underpinning infrastructure concerned with networking and connectivity, have already shaped learning behaviours in a range of ways. Since the advent of the Internet, learners, teachers, parents and guardians, and advisers and policy makers have used abilities to gain wider access in a range of ways, enabling ad hoc research, often independent of time and place.
- Level 2 digital technologies, the hardware and digital devices concerned with gaining access, have continued to shape learning behaviours as increased uses of mobile devices have enabled access to be more independent of time and place.
- Level 3 digital technologies, concerned with communication through online resources, have enabled wider communication beyond local, regional and national boundaries, faster communication that becomes more real-time, and selective communication, depending on the needs and interests of the individual, whether learners, teachers, parents and guardians, or advisers and policy makers.
- Level 4 digital technologies, concerned with specific software and resources to support specific needs and interests, have enabled individuals to engage with subject and topic areas more widely, as resources have continued to be developed and made available, sometimes at a financial cost and sometimes without costs incurred.

Learners have been able to take advantage of each of these levels of digital technologies, and indeed learners often now are rarely without networking and communication access, have access through one or more devices (often mobile), enjoy wide communication, and can select software and resources related to specific needs at specific times. For learners, 'homework' has often changed in nature (highlighted at early stages of digital development in schools by, for example, Passey, 2000), and learning opportunities can be gained at times outside of institutional timetables and at places where the learner is located (highlighted as informal learning by, for example, Dron & Anderson, 2023). As a consequence, learning behaviours have either changed already or have the potential to change.

Teachers have also been able, through access to the four levels of digital technologies, to take advantage of widening teaching possibilities, at times to suit them and in places to suit them. Take the experiences of many teachers during the Covid-19 pandemic, for example, where online and remote emergency teaching, or hybrid teaching in some instances, became a norm (Sato et al., 2023). Some teachers have persisted with uses of these practices, even though classroom attendance is now more possible. Teaching behaviours have changed or have the chance to change as a result, and these can impact learners and learning behaviours. However, the impact can still rely heavily upon the shift of learning behaviours (as shown by Kamoyo et al., 2025).

Parents and guardians have been able to take advantage of access to, in many cases, the first three levels of digital technologies, enabling them to communicate more often with teachers in schools and colleges, at times to suit them and in places wherever they are located (Passey, 2024). Parental and guardian behaviours are now reported to have changed, so that awareness, understanding and knowing more detail about the practices that are happening in their children's schools has become a norm in some places, and these have also affected the learning behaviours of children and young people (Woodhouse et al., 2024).

Advisers and policy makers have been able to take advantage of these levels of digital technologies, enabling them to gain from sharing and contact to greater extents. As a consequence, policy makers report that they feel more able to understand and make policy decisions that are based on a wider appreciation and accommodation of detail (Lloyd, 2020). Advisory and policy making behaviours have changed, or have the opportunity to change, which can in turn and subsequently influence and affect learning behaviours.

1.5 What Learning Behaviours Are Not

Behaviours can be considered in terms of a simple stimulus–response. That is, if a stimulus is provided or experienced, then a particular response occurs or is likely to occur (Rong, 2024). This simplistic definition or concept of a behaviour is not what should be accepted as intended practice when learning and teaching behaviours in education are considered and discussed.

Learning should always be considered in terms of arising from thinking, and thinking should involve the development of exploring options, and making and taking decisions (Dawson et al., 2024). For learning or teaching behaviours, these should be based on a self-exploration and self-review that may lead to learning and teaching behaviours that are personal rather than necessarily generically applicable.

In this text, learning and teaching behaviours will be explored as practices that may apply to the individual but also to the individual's concern with working with wider groups. In the context of learning situations, learning and teaching behaviours can be influenced, of course, not only by specific digital technologies and actors, but also by subjects or topics of interest or focus. This variety of factors and influences can lead to a range of possibilities and approaches that are found to suit the individual in terms of needs and abilities to engage and to gain from educational interactions.

1.6 Why Learning Behaviours Are Important

In essence, learning and teaching behaviours are important because they can support the individual in their educational endeavours, although behaviours are likely to be influenced by a range of factors, including subject topic and discipline (Smyth et al., 2017). We hear of learners who, for example, choose to engage with learning at certain times of the day, while others do not (Muhammad et al., 2020). Similarly, we hear that some learners are supported when learning by having background music being played, while others are not (Tamim Faruq et al., 2023). In similar ways, learners and teachers can select digital technologies that accommodate their specific needs and interests, and the approaches that work most effectively for them.

Just as learning and teaching behaviours can be developed and selected by the individual, this aligns with the concept that digital technologies can support personalisation of learning (FitzGerald et al., 2018). Whilst some would argue that personalisation is difficult to achieve when a teacher is confronted by 30 or so learners in a classroom, it is also the case that engagement with learning can now happen at times and in places beyond that classroom. Learners (and teachers) have the chance to accommodate their learning (and teaching) in ways that were much more difficult in the past. The development of digital technologies to support educational practices over the past 40 or more years has led us to a time when more options become possible, not just at the individual learner and teacher level, but also at the institutional and policy levels. This possibility will be explored in more detail in subsequent chapters.

1.7 Learning Behaviours and Learning Engagement

It is important at this point to consider the differences between what are described as learning behaviours, compared to other forms of learning engagement—learning approaches, learning styles and learning skills, for example. Learning behaviours are described in this text as behaviours that individuals develop and adopt to address their specific needs and interests; these are therefore considered from learner, teacher, peer, parent or guardian, and adviser and policy maker perspectives in subsequent specific areas of the text. Whilst learning behaviours are related to the individual, this does not mean that the individual is not aware of others and how their behaviours can engage with others to support their learning.

Learning approaches are described as the ways that learners engage with specific areas of learning in order to gain educationally; these approaches are often described generically (see, for example, Urhahne, 2020), from the perspective of the focus of what the learner is engaged with (Entwistle, 2012). For example, for reviewing a subject topic one learner might make a list of notes, while another learner might view an online video.

Learning styles is a term with a longer history; these are described often in sensory terms, relating to the sensory routes that might be adopted when a learner engages with specific learner activities. Learning styles are again described in generic terms, usually through the lens of sensory engagements (Romanelli et al., 2009). Whilst the concept of learning styles has been quite widely contested (for example, Hattie & O'Leary, 2025), it is the application of the ways that learning styles have been used in practice that is particularly highlighted in challenges to the term. To argue that an individual learns through a single learning style (i.e. sensory route) or that learning styles cannot be developed over time is certainly problematic. Nevertheless, individuals can hold and select learning approaches that are informed by the ways in which they feel they might gain most effectively in adopted sensory routes through sensory inputs and sensory outputs. For example, an individual might feel for some data that they can accumulate detail from a graph rather than from a data table, or from an audio transcript rather than from a video. But for an individual, the range of chosen sensory routes can differ according to context and subject content. It is in this sense that learning styles are considered in this text.

Learning skills, on the other hand, are those applications and functions that a learner should acquire in order to gain access to learning materials. Again, these are described in generic terms, as specific skills that are seen to be independent of the individual (Higgins et al., 2007). In the context of learning behaviours, metacognitive skills are certainly those that are seen to support ways that learners can effectively manage their learning.

Trying to describe a relationship between these concepts is not easy, and any attempt would certainly be open to discussion and critique. However, Fig. 1.2 provides one way in which possible relationships between these terms might be considered. In Fig. 1.2, learning behaviours are held as conceptions and practices that can be brought to bear when the user is involved in forms of learning practice. These learning behaviours can be adapted according to subject and topic, enabling appropriate skills to be highlighted so that they can be applied in those contexts. Subject and topic will also influence learning styles selected by the user, drawing upon and adopting sensory routes as applicable. Learning approaches, how to proceed in most effectively addressing the specific learning need or task, will be determined by the choices of styles and skills that are a composite part of the behaviours that are held.

In this depiction of the relationship, learning behaviours (as will be described and apparent from the illustrations in subsequent chapters) are central to the concerns,

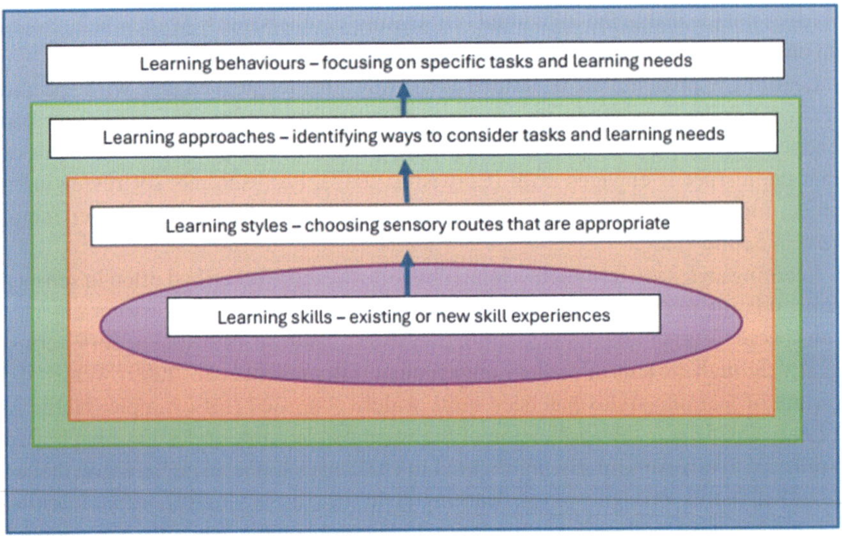

Fig. 1.2 A possible relationship between learning approaches, styles, skills and behaviours

thinking, needs and interests of the individual, chosen and developed by the individual to address specific tasks or actions, but accommodating features that the individual considers appropriate in terms of learning skills, learning styles and learning approaches for that specific learning task. For example, to learn some essential background details about a specific town in France, a learning behaviour would be to consult a known online search engine likely to provide accurate details, using digital skills to access the site through a mobile device, skimming and selecting appropriate text, listing key points in a bullet point format or as an image appropriate for reviewing, and accessing a selection of three other sets of details in other sites online to check accuracy as an appropriate review approach.

Across this text, learning behaviours will be considered in the way visualised in Fig. 1.2. It should also be recognised that a learning behaviour is not a singularity that an individual holds; learning behaviours are individual, but an individual can hold many elements within a learning behaviour, and the application of those elements can, for example, be dependent on the subject and focus of the context of the learning.

Research into learning approaches, learning styles and learning skills has recognised through categorisations and definitions that these three concepts (approaches, styles and skills) describe a range of variations and differences in the ways that they are demonstrated by different individuals. In terms of learning behaviours, a consideration of the involvement of all three of these concepts can apply, as they are involved in and influence an individual's learning behaviours. Considering the degree of variation that can arise from the different ways in which each of these three different categories are demonstrated when learning is undertaken by different individuals, then the level of variety that can be anticipated for learning behaviours is likely to be high. Hence the difficulty in seeking to find a 'one-size-fits-all' approach. In subsequent chapters, these variations will be explored as they relate to digital technologies, and to specific forms of digital technologies.

Chapter 2
Behaviours and Emerging Technologies: The Potential Impacts of Artificial Intelligence, Robotics and Virtual and Augmented Realities

Abstract Educational behaviours of all those involved in educational practice are being seen to be influenced and affected by emerging technologies. In the case of artificial intelligence (AI) and generative AI (GenAI), uses are affecting behaviours that involve more questioning approaches and concerns about privacy. Robotics are opening up avenues for enhancing some social behaviours. Virtual and augmented realities are enhancing behaviours where greater visualisation and width of perspectives are sought. Whilst there are existing reported effects of these emerging technologies on learning behaviours, it is also clear that they may also be affecting teachers, parents and guardians, and adviser and policy makers in their teaching, support and guidance behaviours.

Keywords Emerging digital technologies and education · Educational behaviours and emerging digital technologies · Generative artificial intelligence and educational behaviours · Robotics and educational behaviours · Virtual and augmented realities and educational behaviours

2.1 Emerging Technologies

That emerging technologies have the potential to support personalised learning has been reported already in the research literature (for example, Peng et al., 2019; Zhang et al., 2020). However, this is not a new claim, as will be discussed in the next chapter. But what is clear, is that emerging technologies are providing forms of interaction that had not been previously possible.

In this context and in this chapter, the influences of three major emerging digital technologies on educational behaviours will be discussed and considered: artificial intelligence (AI) and particularly generative AI (GenAI); robotics; and virtual and augmented realities. As these emerging digital technologies are likely to be developed further over the next 5 years at least, it is relevant to consider these from an emerging learning behaviours perspective.

D. Passey, *Shifting Educational Behaviours*,
https://doi.org/10.1007/978-3-032-18942-4_2

Given the fact that these digital technologies are emerging, it is also a fact that their uses in education have only fairly recently been explored, and that research into their uses, applications, and certainly outcomes, is currently limited.

2.2 AI and GenAI

Artificial intelligence (AI) uses in education have been accessible for educational applications and practices for quite a long time, certainly since the 1990s (Gill, 1995). AI systems rely upon built-in algorithms to produce feedback to the user. Until recently, this feedback has been normally text based, and many systems (for example, institutional data management systems), have relied upon data from the institution itself or from known sources. More recently, developed GenAI systems can be stimulated by audio input (for example, Siri[1] or Alexa[2]) and others can respond in audio form (both with speech and music), and yet others can create images. GenAI can be considered different from AI in that outputs can be stimulated through audio as well as textual formats and the systems can create text, images or sound that are responsive to the individual, and created rather than copied from a data source directly.

Responses and reactions from both learners and teachers to the idea of using GenAI for educational purposes are certainly varied (Wu et al., 2025). Some teachers and learners advocate use (they regard benefits for use in practice) (Belkina et al., 2025), some oppose it (they recognise ethical issues such as bias) (Farangi et al., 2024), and some believe that piloting uses and offering recommendations for the future are important (they recognise both advantages and challenges and wish to assess outcomes arising) (Chiu, 2024).

Uses of GenAI in education have only recently been highlighted (Kanbach et al., 2024), particularly since the launch of ChatGPT[3] in 2022. Whilst research in the field is ongoing and is growing, uses have not been based on fundamental prior research. There is clearly an ongoing need for research as GenAI systems continue to evolve, and this is especially needed when views about GenAI's potential benefits and challenges can be divided across educational populations. For example, health educators are often positive about the value of GenAI systems that have been produced to support the health services (The Lancet Regional Health-Europe, 2023), whilst law educators are less convinced about the value of GenAI systems when ethics and morals are taken into consideration (Balan, 2024).

Research articles and policy documents highlighting uses of GenAI (for example, The Open Innovation Team and Department for Education, 2024) show that these systems are both used and offer outputs that are age-independent, as uses are demonstrated across higher education (for example by Belkina et al., 2025), secondary

[1] https://www.apple.com/uk/siri/.

[2] https://alexa.amazon.co.uk/.

[3] https://chatgpt.com/.

education (for example by Wu & Zhang, 2025) and primary education (for example by Cheah et al., 2025). Uses are also considered to be potentially inclusive, but, by contrast, have opportunity to increase digital and social divides (Meletiadou, 2025), as outcomes indicate both potential benefits and challenges across the age spectrum with increased or decreased forms of accessibility. Examples of current research evidence show uses ranging from examples with teachers in primary and secondary schools (Kaplan-Rakowski et al., 2023), to administrators in universities (Luo, 2024) and to adult educators (Cacicio & Riggs, 2023), demonstrating age-independent GenAI uses.

GenAI was developed from earlier developments in the AI field (Hermann & Puntoni, 2024). But digital technology facilities that respond to human interactions are not new. Tutoring systems and integrated learning systems were available and developed for educational purposes from the 1970s (Guo et al., 2021). But it is the range of background data that a GenAI facility can draw upon, ways responses can be matched to requests (prompts) individuals make, and forms of responses that are possible, that make GenAI systems what they are (Passey et al., 2024). Often, a user may not know the data sources that a GenAI system is drawing on, let alone whether those data have been specifically selected and may lead to bias or provide specific responses that might be considered misrepresentative of a wider picture. For responses from key requests, it is also not necessarily possible for the user to know how valid or accurate or ethical they might be (Khosrowi et al., 2024).

From an educational perspective, these elements that make up a GenAI system are important. The data that are held and searched can determine levels of width, accuracy and bias; this can determine the quality of outcome that is generated. A match between the input request by a learner and the data that are sourced, captured and provided as an output can determine sensitivity, focus and interpretation of that output; this can determine for the user qualities such as its value, use or acceptability. Given this context, users need to be in a position where GenAI outcomes are judged with critical concern; accepting them at face value could mean that they are used even though they lack width, accuracy or non-bias, that they may not be sensitive to the user's needs or focus upon the topic at hand, or indeed that they may not provide a worthy interpretation. Users need to develop approaches that are critical of outcomes, and when recommending GenAI systems, there is a need for awareness of these three elements of any GenAI system.

To exacerbate the challenges for users, the range of GenAI systems available for education is undoubtedly increasing (WIPO, 2024). GenAI systems are being developed to support specific topics and subject areas, including reading, numeracy, career choices, mental health issues, and social challenges. At the same time, widely used software products and ranges, such as Microsoft Office[4] or Google,[5] are also integrating GenAI facilities, providing audio (speech and music generation), image (still and video generation) as well as textual responses, on request.

---

[4] https://www.microsoft.com/en-us/microsoft-365-copilot?msockid=2b77ea2bd6f969ec2cf4fc8bd7676857.

[5] https://gemini.google.com/?hl=en-GB.

2.3 Robotics

Robotics are concerned with the design, construction, and use of robots (machines), which can perform tasks that would traditionally have been undertaken by humans. Robots are already widely used in industries (Grau et al., 2021), including those in the automobile manufacturing industries and those where machines can undertake actions in hazardous environments, such as those in the nuclear energy industry. Robots are often engaged with repetitive or what might be regarded as simple tasks, but in more recent cases, more exacting tasks and environments have seen the emergence of robots and robotic devices, such as those used in surgery, for example (Reddy et al., 2023). AI is often associated with robotic devices, in that algorithms are used to undertake tasks that require delicate interactions, where the device can itself gain input from the outside environment and respond to this in a range of ways (Ribeiro et al., 2021).

Robotics uses in education are not new, but they have developed and are developing rapidly in some areas (Darmawansah et al., 2023). There has even been discussion about whether robots could in some ways replace human teachers (Orhani, 2023). Certainly, the use of robots in some educational institutions for certain activities has been seen to be highly successful, engaging young people positively (Fung et al., 2025); these examples are suggesting to some that opportunity might exist to develop this engagement further, beyond use within specific lessons or for specific topics.

2.4 Virtual and Augmented Reality

Virtual and augmented realities offer two distinct ways of bringing experiences to a learner or user. Augmented reality (AR) allows the physical world to be enhanced through the use of digital artefacts, images, videos, or experiences that are offered through computer-generated images (CGI) and three-dimensional (3D) models. Virtual reality (VR) offers a virtual experience that places the user in a generated and different world to that surrounding the user. For AR, the 'headsets' or 'glasses' allow the user to look through them to see their immediate environment and surroundings, but images are created that add to the environment. For VR, the headsets provide a new environment, so that the user does not see their immediate surroundings.

From an educational perspective, both of these forms of computer-created environments have been recognised to enhanced learning. For AR, for example, Chang et al. (2022) identified gains in learner responses, knowledge and skills, and performance through a meta-analysis of previous studies, with higher gains identified in terms of performance. Learning enhancements have also been reported from uses of VR, not only with learners in the school sector (Hu-Au & Lee, 2018), but also with adult learners in teacher training courses (Rodolico & Hirsu, 2023).

Uses of AR and VR have also been shown to support learning for students who have specific needs. For example, social skills of students with autism have been shown to be enhanced and supported by uses of VR (Yang et al., 2025), while students with moderate to severe disabilities have been supported through VR technologies in developing literacy, mobility and safety skills (Jeffs, 2009).

AR and VR have been recognised to support education and learning practices, and wide applications across subject areas have been reported. However, whilst the cost of the individual headsets and glasses is often a limiting factor, nevertheless, increasing uses and access in schools and colleges is reported (Al-Ansi et al., 2023).

2.5 AI, GenAI and Educational Behaviours

Different actors have had access to AI-supported systems for many years. In all cases, the actors have identified benefits from their use, which have also led to changes in learning, teaching or support behaviours.

Learners have gained access to AI-supported systems since the 1990s (Becker & Hativa, 1994). Integrated Learning Systems (ILSs), such as SuccessMaker[6] or Jostens ILS, provided content to learners in forms where learners needed to provide responses, perhaps through a question format. Even in those early cases, learners were provided with answers, often accompanied by supportive comments and opportunities to retry questions that they did not succeed in completing successfully, and they were provided with overall scores from their responses. Learners have continued to use these forms of system to the present day, and have identified two key benefits that have affected their learning behaviours: immediate feedback provides a positive incentive to continue to work with such a system; and overall totals of their responses allows them to compare their own scores with those of other learners, leading to competitive forms of learning behaviour that are emotionally different from those of competing with the teacher's answers in a classroom test environment, for example.

Teachers have also gained access to AI-supported systems over a similar time period. Data systems presenting collations and analyses were developed and used increasingly extensively from the 2000s. Indeed, some nations, England (Department for Education, 2024) and Australia (Australian Skills Quality Authority, n.d.), for example, have introduced requirements for schools to report specific data to a central authority, so that individual schools have needed to adopt and use data management systems that will allow them to do this. Some locally accessed systems that were provided within a single or group of schools, and, increasingly online systems, have also provided teachers with evidence about student outcomes, such as the Bromcom[7] management information system (MIS) (Bromcom, n.d.). Using these systems, teachers were, and still are, able to monitor group as well as individual performance, for specific topics, across whole subject areas, or across one or more years. Key benefits from uses of these systems that have affected teacher behaviours

[6] https://www.savvas.com/solutions/supplemental/successmaker-adaptive-personalized-learning.

[7] https://bromcom.com/.

are: access to monitoring facilities at times and in places that the teacher determines; and provision of access that does not depend on extensive testing.

Parents or guardians have had access to AI-supported systems more recently, since software used in schools has also become available and accessible in homes. Some teachers and schools enable software to be accessible at home for parents and guardians as well as for learners, so that parents and guardians can take an active part in supporting their children. Some parents regularly monitor their children's performance and support them if they have problems or to more generally provide reassurance (Cleveland et al., 2024). Parent and guardian behaviours for those using such systems has shifted, as they have found that they can more effectively support their children, emotionally and sometimes cognitively. However, there are examples where parents' and guardians' behaviours have been found to be negative (Gür & Türel, 2022).

Advisers and policy makers have had access to AI-supported systems for as long as teachers and schools have had access. Indeed, some countries have published results from these systems, sometimes to support improvement (for example, Education Scotland, n.d.) and sometimes to support parents and guardians choosing a school for their children (Bokhove et al., 2023). Policy maker behaviours have been seen to shift as a result of access to and uses of such systems, as achievements and outcomes can more easily be reported publicly, and those data can also be used to focus on specific challenges where support could be of help.

GenAI systems have more recently become accessible to learners, teachers, parents and guardians, advisers and policy makers. Learners can access such systems outside as well as inside schools, to fulfil a range of learning purposes. Text-generated systems such as ChatGPT can produce answers to questions, or even an essay when requested. Learners who have used such systems are often cautious about their uses, however (Stanford, 2025). Some learners do not wish to become dependent on such systems, and others find that the systems do not necessarily produce either accurate outcomes or those that they feel are as thorough as they would make if they did it themselves (Dehdary & Meschi, 2024). Learner behaviours are shifting in this respect, in that feedback or detail can be gained at times that students choose, and outcomes can be used as models that either provide an end-result or one that would be considered a draft.

Vignette 1 In one primary school, the children in one class are asked to use a GenAI system to create an image of the character in a story that they have written in a creative writing lesson. The children, using the GenAI system on a tablet, use keywords as prompts to create an image. When this is completed, the teacher asks them to incorporate the image into their written work. In another primary school, the children are asked to use GenAI to complete a well-known story by Dickens that they are studying. When the GenAI system has completed the story, the teacher asks them to read the ending, and to ask whether they feel it is 'good enough', whether they would make amendments or additions in any ways, and how they could improve it.

In the first school, children use the GenAI system to create an image more quickly than they might do otherwise. The practice could lead to behaviours where digital technologies are concerned with generating rapid outcomes. In the second school, children are asked to question the outcomes of the GenAI system. They are asked to be critical, and to consider how they would judge and improve the outcome. The practice could lead to behaviours where outcomes from digital technologies are considered critically.

Teachers are beginning to use GenAI systems to support their administrative and management needs. Indeed, there are reports that uses of these systems may save a teacher 25% of their time on a regular basis (Taggart & Roulston, 2025). Examples of use include asking a system to generate questions, to provide a summary, to identify sources, and to draft minutes or notes or documents. Teacher behaviours are shifting in that these sources provide a rapid form of drafting that shifts the way that final products may be generated. Models of outcomes allow teachers to assess whether drafts can be adopted or developed further.

Vignette 2 A teacher wishes to generate questions for an intermediate test with her class. She wants to explore the topic of metabolism, as a part of the biology curriculum covered during the previous school term. She is aware of the key terms and concepts that have been introduced to the students, so she uses these as prompts to create a series of 12 questions using a GenAI system. She highlights the type of questions that are needed, with some of these being multiple-choice, while others are devised as short-answer format questions. Given the age range of the class, the scope and topic of the test, the GenAI system generates the 12 questions as requested. The teacher reviews the questions, and she feels that there are only a few where some minor changes would improve the focus of the questions, so that a more specific answer might be created by the learners. Given the teacher's experience, she is able to quickly review the outcome and provide a test that she would feel would be comparable to that she would create without use of the GenAI system. Using the GenAI system, the teacher's behaviour has shifted from a focus on creation to a focus on critical review.

Parents or guardians are not being widely reported to be using GenAI systems currently for supporting their children's educational needs (FE Online, 2024). However, there are reports that some parents and guardians suggest that their children use GenAI systems to search for details or to answer questions that are posed of them (Polikoff et al., 2025). Some parents and guardians access GenAI systems for their own needs, but without exploring uses with their children. Parent and guardian behaviours relating to their children's education do not seem to be largely affected by GenAI systems at this time, but it is also true that schools are enabling children to undertake learning activities at home that they can share with their parents or guardians. This is an area where ongoing research may better inform about shifts that are occurring over time.

Vignette 3 The teacher wants the children to use an online system to monitor and record their reading activity, which they can access at home as well as in school. The teacher encourages the children to let their parents and guardians know that they can also see and use the system to monitor and record the reading that the children have completed. The teacher asks the children to alert their parents or guardians to the short announcement that the teacher has put onto the site to tell them about the activity. It asks parents and guardians to take an interest in the children's reading, and to help the children to record the pages of reading that they have completed when at home. The teacher stresses that the children should be encouraged to do the reading, rather than the parent reading out to them. In this way, the parent or guardian is asked to positively support their children. The parents and guardians are being encouraged to take a positive behavioural position in supporting, monitoring and recording. The results will be seen by the teacher, who can feed back to the parents or guardians.

Policy makers are beginning to recognise that GenAI systems provide them with potential benefits. Audio and video recorded meetings are being transcribed, summaries are being generated, and drafts are being produced using GenAI systems in some cases. Similar to the behaviours arising for teachers, policy makers are finding that the process of drafting is being reconsidered, and that final outcomes might be more quickly attained. Such practice, may, however, lead to a dependency on GenAI systems that creates a dependency on shorter time outcomes. This form of dependency arising from behavioural changes is already clear in other situations; for example, some individuals expect rapid time response from emails or from social media messages that are sent. More rapid feedback, expected response times and shorter outcome times can have a major impact on behaviours that can be negative as well positive. Whilst an individual may benefit from rapid feedback from a GenAI system, another individual may be under stress when expected to respond to emails or social media messages outside working hours.

Guidance for policy makers to consider educational policies on GenAI is emerging, both focused at national and local levels. For example, UNESCO (2023) created a set of guidance, stressing the "key steps for governmental agencies to regulate the use of GenAI tools including mandating the protection of data privacy and considering an age limit for their use" (p. 3). Similarly, Chiu (2023) offers recommendations at school and local policy levels.

Vignette 4 Following a key meeting of the education department, a policy strategist in the department wishes to draw out key features from the meeting that need to be shared and further elaborated on. Using a transcript from the meeting, the policy strategist uses a GenAI system to draw out the key points that have emerged, that are likely to be strategically relevant. From the bullet points that are generated by the GenAI system, the strategist is able to review these, chooses the bullet points that are listed as being those she feels are relevant, and makes small amendments that relate to her recall of certain points. The points raised are then shared with other members of the meeting for their further consideration, before the outcomes are shared more widely. The behavioural shift that has happened is to use the GenAI as a drafting instrument, that allows the policy maker to focus on review and refinement rather than initial drafting.

As is shown by research and practice examples, overall, behaviours arising from educational uses of AI-supported and GenAI systems can be positive, for learners, for teachers, for parents and guardians, and for advisers and policy makers. However, behaviours arising could also be negative; so, awareness of the impacts of the range of behaviours on individuals is important to know and to consider.

2.6 Robotics and Educational Behaviours

There have been two main ways in which robots have been used in education. The first way is the constructive creation of robots, which is concerned with coding, programming and its trialling. In this context, effects on programming success and transfer of learning have been reported, as have impacts on computational thinking (Yolcu & Demirer, 2023). The second way concerns the use of robots with audio input and output facility within learning environments to support subject or social learning. In this context, effects on subject learning including language learning have been reported (Banko et al., 2025), as have effects on social interactions and learning (İnan & Güldenoğlu, 2025).

Vignette 5 One student is having difficulty in remembering vocabulary when learning about outdoor activities in a French lesson. The student does want to try to remember more of the keywords, but rather than discuss this with the teacher, prefers to do this with a robot. The student knows that the robot will be very patient, that the robot will be prepared to repeat certain words or phrases many times, and she knows that the robot does not mind how long it takes to go through the list of words. The learner behaviour has shifted, where the choice of support is selected for comfort with forms of interaction or for social reasons (such as regarding the talking to a robot as an equal, not having a hierarchical status).

Whilst there has been discussion about the ways that robots might replace teachers in the future, there is also discussion and research that has explored how robots might support teachers by providing teaching assistant roles (Ružić & Balaban, 2023). The role of a robot as a tutor or tutee is generally recognised positively by teachers who deploy them in their classrooms, rather than them seeing robots as competitors to the roles that they themselves take (Chu et al., 2022).

Vignette 6 In a digital skills lesson, a teacher thought that one learner was not getting on very well with coding and programming on his own. She felt that he would benefit from working with another learner, where they could jointly explore how to code and program a robot that would need to move certain distances and turn certain angles to take a particular pre-selected route. Her choice of the two learners to work together was to enable sharing of expertise, but in ways that would build confidence and independence. After working on the task for two lessons, the learners managed to code and program the robot to take the path required. The teacher recognised how both learners had enjoyed the chance to work together, and how they felt they had achieved the outcome required by jointly working as a team. The teacher had consciously moved the learners to a teamwork situation, considering this as an alternative positive behavioural model.

Whilst few parents and guardians are likely to have access to robots at home at this time, nevertheless some parents have engaged in activities with robots that support their children's education. In some cases, this is concerned with social learning. For example, Passey et al. (2016) reported on the ways that building and programming Lego robots[8] had supported children's social interactions with their fathers and male guardians. On other occasions, interactions are concerned with subject or topic learning. For example, Ho et al. (2023) reported a study where parents were introduced to the ways that robots could prompt their children when learning mathematics.

Vignette 7 In one school, a teacher wanted to explore how a robot might support children's reading at home. The school provided parents with robots and discussed how the robot would encourage the child to read. The school discussed with the parents how they would respond to this in their homes, and what roles they would take. The parents observed 'at a distance' and

[8] https://www.lego.com/en-gb/categories/coding-for-kids.

found that the children responded positively to the robots, and that they read more than they had previously. On reflection, the parents recognised that their support behaviour had shifted from a persuasive role to a role concerned with observation, monitoring and encouragement.

Policy makers often are able to support educational practices through the policies they formulate and the financial support that they provide to enable those policies to be put into practice. The two ways in which robots can support educational outcomes are through coding and programming of robots, and uses of robots in subject lessons. Trültzsch-Wijnen et al. (2021) explored policies in three countries relating to coding and programming of robots, while policies that relate to uses of robots in classrooms for subject lesson purposes are not evident within the current research or policy literature.

Vignette 8 An adviser is aware of a number of schools that have invested in robots, used in classrooms to support social interactions including language development. He has asked a local university if it would be possible for them to explore how the robots are being used, and whether any challenges or issues as well as positive outcomes have been noted. Given the recent interest in robots in schools, but the uncertainty of how the robots might support learning, the adviser is concerned that any advice is based on understandings of the local uses and outcomes in classroom, moving to a more research-informed behavioural approach.

2.7 Virtual and Augmented Realities and Educational Behaviours

VR and AR have been used in different ways in educational contexts. As AR augments the real world with overlays, the educational uses are mainly concerned with exploring situations where additions or amendments to an environment allow discussion or practice to be considered or developed. For example, AR might be used to support navigation to a particular item or location. By contrast, VR offers a virtual environment, one that the learner may not have experienced before (for example, looking around a specific castle in another country), or one that the learner could not experience before (for example, experiencing a street in a city in the thirteenth century).

Across the research literature, uses of AR by learners have been reported widely. Chang et al. (2022), for example, reported uses in the training of nurses using simulated hospital environments, as well as in engineering, earth sciences, history, physics and language learning. However, research also points out, importantly, that the subject in which VR is used can have a major influence on applicability and outcomes, as can the ways that the VR is used.

Vignette 9 The lesson is concerned with ancient Egypt. Learners in the class have never experienced visits to Egypt to see a pyramid or a tomb. Using VR headsets, the learners are able to see what it is like inside a Pharoah's tomb, and to experience the environment by moving through it, in the way that the learners wish. Through this form of digital technology, learning behaviours concerned with experience can shift from one arising through the individual's imagination to one arising through visual stimulation (that might also be supported by an audio track, by music or text).

Research has found that appropriate and considered pedagogical practice with uses of VR can lead to more effective learner outcomes (Chang et al., 2022). It has been shown that teachers can influence the outcomes in terms of student engagement, knowledge retention, skill development, and inclusivity, for example (Leong et al., 2023).

Vignette 10 A teacher of religious education in a secondary school would like to enhance the learners' understanding about the interior workings of a church. He decides to use VR, and he asks the learners to work in pairs. One of the learners uses the VR headset to explore the interior of the church, while the other learner asks the VR user questions that the teacher has posed. What the learner with the VR headset says, is recorded by the other learner. When all the questions have been answered, the learners change roles, and the learner now with the VR headset sees if he can identify more or different detail from that observed by the first learner. At the end of the session, both learners have experienced the environment, they have needed to answer specific questions that relate to what they could observe, and they have created a set of outcomes that are supported by two views of the accessible details. Learning behaviours have been influenced by the VR, shifting learning from being text-based, perhaps imagined or remembered from previous experiences, to learning from being visually based, observation-based and supported by peer co-operation.

It is likely that many parents or guardians are neither aware of uses of VR in education, nor aware of experiencing uses of VR themselves. A few studies have explored parent and guardian interests in and responses to uses of VR in education. For example, Chiu and Zhu (2025) gathered evidence of responses when learners used VR to support mathematical task completion in a serious game environment. The study found that parents and guardians were supportive of uses where learners gained knowledge, technical skills, and understandings of different contexts or historic periods.

Vignette 11 A school is aware that it is seeing benefits of using VR with learners, but that their parents and guardians are not necessarily aware of these digital technologies or recognising the benefits that can arise for their children. The school arranges an open afternoon, where parents and guardians can come into the school to join their children, and see how the teachers are using VR, how their children are responding to these forms of activities, and to have chance to use the VR headsets themselves. Parent and guardian behaviours to learning are being influenced through this approach, moving from an understanding gained from imagination arising from what their children are telling them, to an understanding arising from first-hand use and experience.

Uses of VR in education have been of interest to those concerned with educational policy. For example, the Australian Government Department of Education commissioned a report on this topic (Southgate et al., 2018). The authors highlighted that:

> When using [immersive virtual reality] IVR for learning, teachers should consider how children at different developmental stages might respond to the content, modes of interaction between students and computer-generated characters in the virtual environment, and affordances of IVR technology… There is no way to predict if a child might become cybersick (a type of motion sickness) and so teachers should educate students on identifying symptoms for early opt-out during VR sessions, especially when using highly IVR (p. 5).

Vignette 12 A policy maker is concerned that schools should be informed about safe uses of VR technologies. She commissioned a report to gather data nationally, supported by any other research that had been undertaken in other countries, to identify the extents of difficulties such as cybersickness that children experience when they use VR, and what factors might indicate that such reactions could either be predicted, or identified, or avoided. The policy maker is concerned with using a research-based approach to support schools, teachers and children, in avoiding or handling issues that might arise when digital technologies are being considered for use.

Across the research literature, uses of AR by learners have been reported widely. Chang et al. (2022), for example, reported uses in language learning and social sciences where improved learner motivation and more positive attitudes to learning had resulted, concerned with abilities of the AR to support visualisation and immersion.

Vignette 13 A learner is exploring aspects of plant biology in the field. Although it is possible to gain an overview of the external features of the plant, the internal features and how they relate to those externally is less obvious. Using AR, the learner is able to 'see' the inner part of the plant, and can focus on the internal elements, zooming in on particular features and functional parts. As a result, the learner can visualise the internal elements and gain a deeper understanding of the forms and functions of the plant. From a behavioural perspective, the learner's behaviour is shifting from direct observation to related observation through supported visualisation.

Currently, the research reports that teachers face a range of challenges when seeking to use AR (Wyss & Bäuerlein, 2024). Alzahrani (2020), for example, indicated that lack of training and complexity of equipment were major factors that could lead to user resistance. However, teachers are using AR in a range of ways (Perifanou et al., 2022), including developments of virtual field trips and interactive textbooks.

Vignette 14 A teacher of chemistry wanted learners to explore the ways that molecules interacted in a particular reaction. Having set up a practical lesson where the interaction was demonstrated, the teacher provided access to AR so that the learners could 'see' the molecules in three dimensions, and they could also see how the molecules interacted to produce alternative chemical compounds. The teacher's behaviour had shifted from providing only a partial direct observation to a more in-depth observation offered at a number of different levels, supporting the association of abstraction with concrete viewing.

Studies that have explored parent and guardian views of using AR suggest that both positive and negative outcomes and indicators can emerge. For example, Cascales et al. (2013) reported from a controlled experimental study in a pre-school setting that uses of AR had enhanced motivation, knowledge, reading and writing, creativity and activity satisfaction. By contrast, Cheng (2017) found that for children 7–14 years of age, when parents used AR in reading a book with them, positive outcomes arose in terms of increased presence, drawing attention to detail, supporting motivation, extending the content, attaining a greater in-depth understanding and enhancing interaction, but negative effects arose leading to obstructions with reading, and diminishing imagination.

Vignette 15 A parent wants to support her child by increasing engagement with reading. She reads with the child most days, but notices that the child does not really engage and enjoy what is being covered in the stories. The parent has heard that having a smartphone where specific words or specific topics in the story can be explored in greater detail has had positive effects in some cases. She decides to adopt this approach, and when she notices that her child seems to be disengaging more, she uses the smartphone to explore words that might be difficult to understand or to explore topics where illustrations can help with understanding. She notices that over some days her child's engagement improves. She recognises that her behaviour is moving in terms of a shift of focus on what is being monitored—from ensuring reading is completed-to ensuring reductions in engagement are noted and positively supported where possible.

Whilst research has not explored the ways that educational advisers and policy makers consider AR uses in education, nevertheless some research identifies both the features that are likely to be important for these stakeholders and indicating implications (for example, Palada et al., 2024).

Vignette 16 A policy maker has heard that some schools in his district are using AR to support learning. Wanting to know whether this might be a technology that would be worth exploring for wider dissemination, he asks a local university if they would undertake a short study to find out the extent of uses across the entire school population in the district, how and how often the AR is being used, and what benefits are being seen after specific periods of time. Given that communication technologies can be used to gather the evidence required, this research can be carried out within a short timeframe. Based on the outcomes, the policy maker would like to decide what, if any, further action is needed. The policy maker recognises that in this case his behaviour is shifting in terms of moving from decisions based on previous knowledge to decisions based on future knowledge.

2.8 Summary of Identified Educational Behaviours

In this chapter, the focus has been on emerging digital technologies that have only recently been considered in supporting education, learning and teaching. From across the chapter, a number of identified behaviours has been recognised. These are summarised in Table 2.1.

These shifts in behaviours relating to educational practices show that emerging digital technologies can positively support those who manage learning as well as those who are engaged in direct learning. There is, however, a balance to be had—which will also be explored in further chapters—in terms of when and to what

Table 2.1 Behaviours associated with recently emerging digital technologies

Form of technology	Learner behaviours	Teacher behaviours	Parent and guardian behaviours	Adviser and policy maker behaviours
AI and GenAI	Rather than accepting outcomes, learners being critical of outcomes becomes a norm	Rather than using digital technologies to create an outcome, pedagogy focuses on how to be critical of generated outcomes	Rather than recording when something is completed, ways for supporting and monitoring are encouraged prior to recording	Rather than needing to spend time on drafting, the focus is now on reviewing and refinement
Robotics	From a position of more limited choice for learner support, choice of support can now include robots whose forms of interactions such as patience and neutrality of social responses are regarded as positive	From a focus on individual work and outcomes, choice of groupwork to enable teamwork and wider social interactions and understanding is now possible	Rather than trying to persuade children to engage, support has shifted to observing, monitoring and encouraging	Rather than relying more on previous existing knowledge, the focus is now more on research-informed approaches, as needed and as they arise
VR	From a reliance on observation, greater visual stimulation is now possible as a choice for learners	From a reliance on text-based and memorisation approaches, greater visually and observationally based approaches can incorporate peer collaboration	From a reliance on being told about certain experiences from memory, first-hand experiences can now be observed and discussed	From a reliance on ad hoc feedback, informed research-based approaches can now detail specific features and factors
AR	From having to rely on abilities to abstract outside unknown contexts, visualisation in context is now possible	From offering a limited range of direct observations, a wider range of related observations in contexts is now possible	From a focus on ensuring completion, parent and guardian focus can now be shifted to monitoring when and how to support engagement to greater extents prior to recording outcomes	Relying only on previous knowledge, plans and directions can now be informed more readily by short-term research feedback on specific details of interest

extent digital technologies are used to support the handling of learning. An important point that arises from this chapter is the way that digital technologies are seen to be supporting social interactions, collaboration, co-operation, groupwork and teamwork. Those qualities require sufficient time and opportunities for them to be developed and demonstrated—and the time and opportunities required are likely to go beyond screentime and onscreen engagement. The qualities require the development of interactions that are outside screentime and engage learners in other ways which will be considered further in subsequent chapters.

Chapter 3
An Historical Perspective: Educational, Learning and Teaching Behaviours Shifting Over Time

Abstract Considering an historical perspective provides an important background and context when considering shifts in educational, learning and teaching behaviours. As many digital technologies have emerged in the past and are still in present use, the forms of behaviours that can and have shifted should be considered in the current, contemporary and wider context. Digital technologies that have emerged in the past and that still affect behaviours in the present include desktop facilities and their access, physical computing devices, the Internet and information access, communication functionalities and access, and the uses of a variety of mobile devices.

Keyword Past digital technologies and current educational behaviours · Physical computing and educational behaviours · The Internet and educational behaviours · Mobile devices and educational behaviours

3.1 The 1980s

The 1980s saw many educational institutions in a range of countries gaining access to microcomputers for the first time (Tatnall & Davey, 2014). These microcomputers were usually cassette driven at that early stage (Andersen et al., 2014), but the integration of these early desktop devices into educational institutions and educational practice led to the wider integration of devices today. Devices at that time allowed individuals and groups to gain access to information technologies (IT), offering access mainly to numeric outputs, relatively simple graphical displays, and texts, for example.

D. Passey, *Shifting Educational Behaviours*,
https://doi.org/10.1007/978-3-032-18942-4_3

3.2 Physical Computing

Physical computing (i.e., the use of additional devices, perhaps gathering data or driven from the computer itself) was associated with some of the early microcomputer devices and has remained a focus of interest to the current time (Grillenberger, 2023), especially involving devices that provide access to external data, which might measure temperature, for example, or could provide light outlets (Ruipérez-Valiente et al., 2022). The linking of these devices led to later developments, such as those created by Lego,[1] and more recently the Micro:bit,[2] that have allowed a continuation of physical computing inside and outside classrooms (Mello et al., 2021).

3.3 The Internet

In the late 1990s and early 2000s, networking, both internally within institutions and externally across institutions, was a frequent focus of digital developments (Bluhm, 1986). Networking and the Internet provided means for communication, initially focused mainly on access to text (Wells & Lewis, 2006), but increasingly enabling images, videos and audio to be developed, shared and accessed (Arms, 2012).

3.4 Mobile Devices

The advent of mobile devices, whether laptop computers, tablets or mobile or smartphones, opened up wider communication technology opportunities (Calderón-Garrido et al., 2022). The fact that mobile devices could be carried by the individual supported access in wider ways, offering use both at times to suit the individual, but also in places to suit the individual (Moura & Carvalho, 2007).

However, it should be stressed that as communication technologies have continued to develop and be used, so access has been widened and has opened up issues and challenges (Gath et al., 2024). The fact that an individual can email or send a message via a mobile text at any time during the day can mean that this can put pressure on the individual receiving that message to respond promptly. So, whilst benefits are reported by some (Campbell et al., 2024), major issues and challenges are reported by others (Smale et al., 2021).

[1] https://www.lego.com/en-gb/categories/coding-for-kids.

[2] https://www.bbc.co.uk/teach/microbit/articles/zfjg8p3.

3.5 The 1980s and Educational, Learning and Teaching Behaviours

In the 1980s, computers were desktop machines, and an institution might then have had a single machine. The computer programs available were often used to demonstrate, so the learning behaviours accommodating this facility were perhaps mostly associated with viewing and general interest. Often group discussions resulted, and there was sometimes collaboration between peers in coding or using outputs arising when functionalities enabled this.

As the functionalities of computers have developed since that time, the forms of educational, learning and teaching behaviours that would have been seen at that time have now themselves shifted. In some cases, these educational, learning and teaching behaviours have been integrated into practices that are associated with current forms of digital technology. Examples are provided in sections and chapters that follow.

3.6 Physical Computing and Educational, Learning and Teaching Behaviours

Opportunities to develop physical computing for teaching and learning purposes arose around the same period. For example, sensors could be added to microcomputers, but these tended only to measure certain external factors such as temperature and light levels. Nevertheless, these sensor systems and links enabled physical computing to be undertaken by learners themselves. Some would say that physical computing, whilst aligned to more recent developments termed 'the Internet of Things', has tended to be neglected in school-based curricula and practices, with greater focus on the consumerism of company-created functionalities that can be accessed online taking a stronger lead. In terms of learning behaviours, sensors have enabled computers to be associated with physical action and activity that is often offscreen. In parallel, teaching behaviours have developed that have led to similar focuses on physical action and activity, bringing forward the potential for more kinaesthetic and offscreen forms of engagement.

There has been research about the ways that physical computing can be implemented in schools for learners of different ages. For example, Katterfeldt et al. (2018) explore this topic in the context of secondary age learners, while Kastner-Hauler et al. (2022) explore it in the context of primary age learners. Overall, the research indicates that physical computing can not only be applied across school sectors, but that it also offers specific features that support computational thinking and practices.

Vignette 1 A primary school learner has access to a Roamer turtle.[3] The turtle can be programmed so that it moves according to the instructions given by the learner. The learner wants the Turtle to move forward a particular distance, to then change direction by a certain angle, to move forward another specific distance, and then to stop. The learner programs the Turtle to do this, and notes whether the movements are those that were intended. When the turtle fails to change direction as intended, the learner needs to reprogram to try to amend this. The learner here uses a computer system that requires computational thinking and reflection. The activity does not involve screen use, and the learner recognises that using computers does not always require the use of a screen but requires behaviours that are concerned with logical thinking and reflection.

Research has also explored the ways that teachers use and consider physical computing with their learners. Kalelioglu and Sentence (2020), for example, discussed physical computing practice with secondary teachers, while Durk and Sentence (2025) explored this from primary teachers' perspectives. Some educational advisors (Passey, 2025a, 2025b, 2025c) argue that there is a need to increase the uses of physical computing in schools.

Vignette 2 The secondary school teacher is concerned that learners have sufficient opportunities to explore computing, computational thinking and uses of digital technologies, but is also concerned that levels of screen time are adequately considered. The teacher decides that activities where creation of a system to monitor and record nesting behaviour of birds can offer a balance, especially if learners are asked to work in groups to collectively develop a system that is time operated, that video records what is happening in a bird's nest for 2 hours each day, and is wirelessly networked. The teaching behaviour has shifted from ensuring that computing and computational thinking is implemented through individual screen-based activity in school, to one where learner wellbeing and developing learners' future wellbeing practices is considered as a priority.

There is limited research into parent and guardian involvement with and perspectives on physical computing with their children relating to school practice. Passey et al. (2016) explored this issue in the context of Lego activities that involved children working with their fathers and male guardians in programming Lego devices[4] to follow specific routes and pathways.

---

[3] https://valiant-technology.com/uk/pages/roamer_home641e.html?cat=1&1.

[4] https://www.lego.com/en-gb/categories/coding-for-kids.

Vignette 3 The guardian has been asked if they would be interested in working with their child in an after-school session where children within a class need to program a Lego device to travel along specific pathways. The male guardian is interested, and he agrees to take part. In the session, the child and the male guardian find that they are in competition with other pairs of children with their parents or guardians. The child and guardian pair are shown the track, and they are asked to program the Lego device so that it follows the pathway. After initially programming the device and trying it out on the course, they find they need to amend the program a number of times, and the guardian and the child discuss what the problems might be and what amendments they might need to make to the program. Eventually, they are successful, and although they are not the first pair to achieve the goal, they are delighted that they have managed to work out how to program the Lego device successfully. The guardian recognises that his behaviour has shifted, from observing what the child does and has done, to discussing the learning activity and offering suggestions that help their success.

At a policy level, there is very limited research that has explored how policy makers consider, advise or implement physical computing into educational practices. Even wide curriculum review papers (Kemp et al., 2024, for example), do not mention specifically the importance of physical computing, or uses of physical devices such as floor turtles or Beebots.[5]

Vignette 4 A policy maker feels that schools should become active in considering the issue of climate change. She decides that schools should have the capacity to monitor regularly the local climate, and how this might relate to the climate measures recorded in earlier years. She finds out whether the schools have sensors to be able to measure outside temperature, wind speed and direction, and sunlight levels. Where schools do not have these, she provides these through a central grant and also ensures that there are professional development personnel who can support the schools if they are uncertain about how to use the sensors with their computer systems to record and compare the measures. In this instance, the policy maker's behaviour concerns how physical computing can be applied to gain awareness of a specific environmental concern and need.

It is clear that physical computing leads to outcomes for learners that go beyond uses of software onscreen. Whilst physical computing was supported at earlier times when introducing computing practices into schools, the focus on physical computing

[5] https://uktechteam.co.uk/boost-your-stem-club-with-tts-bee-bot-and-blue-bot-programmable-robots-fun-engaging-and-curriculum-aligned/#:~:text=Welcome%20to%20the%20world%20of%20hands-on%20learning%20with,curiosity%20and%20fostering%20critical%20thinking%20in%20UK%20schools.

has not necessarily been retained at those initial levels. Yet learners should be prepared for a future where there are greater needs for understandings of physical computing and its practices. Current evidence suggests that ways need to be identified so that parents and guardians, advisers and policy makers can be involved to greater extents in supporting these practices.

3.7 The Internet and Educational, Learning and Teaching Behaviours

Whilst the Internet was introduced into schools from around the late 1990s to early 2000s, this facility has persisted and developed so that schools still have wide access to the Internet in the mid-2020s. The forms of shifts in educational, learning and teaching behaviours that occurred when the Internet was introduced have persisted to this day. However, the forms of resources that are accessible in the mid-2020s have developed markedly from those accessible in the early 2000s.

The Internet increasingly offers multimedia resources that enable exploration through different media and sensory pathways. Abdulrahaman et al. (2020) reviewed the literature in this context and showed that multimedia resources have provided wider access to resources that can support high quality education and have improved performance for learners, especially when considered from an inclusive perspective. Kveselava et al. (2024) explored multimedia uses by learners from the perspectives of practicality and learning improvements. Access, options and choices were highlighted in the research as important positive contributors from the points of view of learners. Learners are seen in some instances to be working to greater extents with multimedia formats.

> ***Vignette 5*** An 11-year-old learner knows that the Internet provides access to a lot of detail about the subject she has been asked to explore—the music of Bela Bartok. She searches and finds that there are different forms of detail that she could use—text, sound recordings, and images of musical notation. She knows that her teacher wants a summary document that is no more than one A4 page in length and is not a copy of a document that already exists. She decides that she will try to incorporate different media into the document, using text to link her view of the approach Bartok took, short audio-linked examples of his music, and a few images of what his musical notation looks like. The learner's behaviour has shifted from producing only text, to producing a multimedia outcome that can more effectively display what is needed from a subject perspective.

In terms of identifying useful sources from the Internet, in his early research, Ó Dochartaigh (2007) highlighted many issues that arise for those needing to search the

Internet. These issues have remained; successive generations have access to wider resources, but the challenges for effective searching remain. At a similarly earlier stage, Henry (2005) identified strategies to support effective searches, while Topal and Shargh (2023) offer ways for supporting students through teaching effective strategies. Teachers often identify sources that they then pass on to learners, but other teachers are concerned also with how the learners themselves have the information skills to know how to find and appraise sources.

Vignette 6 The teacher is concerned that learners can be bombarded with possible sites where information might be available on a particular topic. The teacher considers what might help the learners in his class, and he decides that two practices should be the focus of a lesson—search terms and site reviews. He asks the learners in the lesson to work in pairs and to decide on a topic in geography that they would like to explore using the Internet. He asks them to decide on ten search words or phrases that they feel would highlight information successfully. He asks the pairs to share their search words, and he discusses these with the class, highlighting where and why the learners and he feel that alternatives or amended words or phrases might be more effective. When the learners then search using these search words or phrases, he asks the pairs to consider why the first 20 sites that the search engine has offered might be legitimate or not in giving correct, unbiased details. He then asks the pairs to share their thoughts on these, and again he opens a discussion with the class, asking them to offer their ideas about whether and why they feel the sites are legitimate or not. The teacher, in this context, has shifted teaching behaviour to a focus on the features learners need, to consider effectiveness of publicly accessible information rather than their using accessible information without reviewing how this is done to ensure effectiveness.

As the Internet provides access to a very wide range of resources, and as some of these sources are unsuitable for children, children's online safety is an issue that concerns educators at all levels. That parents and guardians should be aware of the risks and know of ways to help protect their children is addressed through support at international, national and local levels. At the international level, the International Telecommunication Union Development Sector (2020) has produced guidelines for parents and guardians. Whilst the need for parents and guardians to gain support and guidance in an ongoing way is often described, it is also found that parental and guardian confidence in this respect is an important matter to also take into consideration (Kuldas et al., 2024).

Vignette 7 The parent is concerned that her children use the Internet safely, but that she does not appear to be creating an authoritarian environment. She feels that the school might be able to offer her some guidance. The school does have teachers who have explored different online resources that can offer guidance for children. The school suggests two resources that they have reviewed, and that they feel are age appropriate for the children. The parent discusses the issue with her children, and they agree to view and work through the online resources that were suggested. Afterwards, the children discuss online safety with their parents, and they agree to have an update discussion about once a month. The parents feel reassured, and they feel that they have shifted in their behaviour from one of concern to one of open discussion.

In terms of advice about uses of and access to resources, Internet usage and practices have been a focus of educational policy at different levels—local, national, and international. Research has sought to offer recommendations for policy in this context (Throuvala et al., 2021, for example), while policy formulation has been supported by international groups (Kampylis et al., 2017, for example). How advisers and policy makers can approach the formulation of policy has itself been a key question.

Vignette 8 The policy maker is concerned that learners in schools might gather information from the Internet that is just copied, rather than being carefully considered and reviewed as needed when used to complete activities inside and outside school. The policy maker discusses this issue with an online consultancy group of head teachers, and they feel that a policy statement would be a good way to raise awareness of this with schools widely. The policy maker drafts a policy statement, shares this with the consultancy group, and then posts this on the online portal that all school head teachers will access. In this context, the behaviour demonstrates that online discussion, online drafting and review, and online posting have become a behaviour that is used to consider and address issues that arise from concerns at a policy level.

Whilst the Internet and the access to resources have been found to offer advantages and benefits for learners, the range of resources has itself created concerns from the earliest stages of implementation in schools. Firewalls were put in place in many systems from early implementation stages, and software to ensure safety is now continuously developed to seek to protect not just the users but also the data held by the systems themselves.

3.8 Mobile Devices and Educational, Learning and Teaching Behaviours

The past development of communication access has been paralleled by the development of access devices. Whilst mobile devices in the form of laptops have been used in educational institutions since around the early 2000s, smaller and more powerful mobile devices in the form of smartphones have only been in use since the latter 2000s, and those with video recording capability some 10 years later. The advent and uses of mobile devices have often been associated with the concept of 'anywhere, anytime learning', and while there have been proponents of this form for practice, research (Du et al., 2019) cautions that learning across a range of different locations might not lead to the highest levels of educational outcomes possible. Indeed, Bernacki et al. (2020) argued that the lack of integration of mobile learning practices with existing psychological, motivational, social, metacognitive and educational theories of learning, limited the potential for supporting and implementing practice.

Reviews of research literature on mobile learning practices have highlighted both benefits and challenges (Calderón-Garrido et al., 2022, for example). Some reviews have specifically explored these practices from a learner perspective (Kadel et al., 2021; Kaur et al., 2022). Indeed, learners are seen to use mobile devices in a range of ways to support their learning.

Vignette 9 One learner knew that trying to remember all the details from a lesson would be difficult. She asked the teacher if it was possible to audio record the lesson, so that she could review details again later. The teacher asked if the recording was just for that purpose and if it would be deleted afterwards. Having gained reassurance about this, the teacher agreed to the recording. The learner was able to review the recording later, in a quieter environment, where she was able to pick up more detail than she remembered earlier. In this context, the learner is shifting learning behaviour from reliance on a single instance for learning to a reliance on reviewing learning to gain from reflection at later times.

The increased use of mobile devices by learners for learning purposes has not necessarily been paralleled by the same levels of increase by teachers for teaching purposes. Some research has noted that teachers may not in some contexts feel confident or comfortable with supporting learning through mobile teaching (Latifi & Kasumi, 2022). Other research (Chen & Tsai, 2021) has indicated that teachers can foster more student-centred learning when supporting mobile learning, while the need for teachers to consider other stakeholders has been highlighted also (Passey, 2010).

Vignette 10 A teacher wanted the field trip to offer all the children as much benefit as possible. The teacher knew that he would not be able to deal with all the queries that the children might raise during their time in the botanical garden. He asked them to make sure that they went around in pairs, but to take images of anything that they did not recognise or could not name. When they returned to the classroom, the teacher showed the children how they could use a search engine to match their images to a known source, to identify the plant or its features, and to gain more detail about it. The children then created a list of images and short descriptions, so that they could refer to these 'unknowns' at a later date. In this way, the teacher was conscious of moving the teaching behaviour from providing the teacher's immediate responses and knowledge to providing a route where the children could at a later time gain knowledge themselves from known sources.

Whilst some teachers have adopted the uses of mobile devices in their lessons to support specific activities, the support practices that parents and guardians might offer has not necessarily developed to the same extent. Many young people have mobile devices that they use at home, and many parents and guardians also use mobile devices. But the extent to which these devices are used for educational purposes clearly varies considerably from home to home. Research has explored parent and guardian views about their children's mobile learning. For example, Hsu et al. (2020) have explored this in a Taiwanese context, while Conry (2020) explored this in a special education context. Parental views appear to be dependent on their understanding of how mobile devices are used, when they are used, and for what purposes.

Vignette 11 A mother is concerned that her daughter is not supported at home by access to educational resources that the school provides as much as she would wish. The only access possible would be through her husband's laptop device, which is not normally available during the evenings or at weekends. The mother decides to ask the school if there is any way that they might help with her daughter's lack of access. The school says that her daughter can come to school early or stay late in order to use the computers in a common computer area. They also say that they can arrange for her daughter to have a loan laptop from the school, and that this can be provided without charge while the child attends the school. The mother is delighted with the school's support, and she discusses with her daughter how they will arrange at home for her to have access to the educational resources online. In this context, the mother's behaviour has shifted from viewing educational resources as being accessible only within the school to seeing them as being importantly needed and accessible at home as well as at school.

As well as research that has explored parent and guardian uses and views of uses of mobile devices, uses of mobile devices have also been researched from policy perspectives. At an international level, UNESCO (West & Vosloo, 2013) has produced guidelines on policy for education. In a much more specific context, Morris and Sarapin (2020) explored this topic in terms of university classes and policy effectiveness. In recent years, from about the year 2020, there have been increasing uncertainties about the ways that mobile devices are used when these are taken into schools by students. As a consequence, some national policies have sought to restrict uses for social purposes. In the Netherlands, for example, personal smartphones in classrooms have been banned across all schools from the 2024 school year and students have reported consequent benefits (Brummer & Achterberg, 2025). Nevertheless, mobile learning is still a major focus of interest in some countries, particularly where smartphones are the devices to which the majority of students have access. Advice and policy for schools can vary considerably from one context to another.

Vignette 12 A policy maker is concerned that schools are finding students are increasingly distracted in lessons using digital technologies. She feels there is a need to understand more detail about the contexts in which this is occurring. She gathers information from school head teachers and teachers about the forms of digital devices that are creating the distractions, what forms of uses are happening, and when and why this is occurring in lessons. As a result, she finds that distractions are occurring as students use their own smartphones within lessons for non-learning social purposes. She formulates policy guidelines for schools to enable them to consider different ways to tackle this issue, when teachers experience it. The shift in this context is concerned with distinguishing between uses of digital technologies that are used and focus on learning and those that are used for purely social purposes within a learning environment or context.

Some forms of digital technologies will inevitably be viewed in different ways over time, as they are developed, as uses become more recognised, and as new developments arise. From the perspective of current practice, there has been a continuation of uses from the past introduction of physical computing, Internet access, and mobile devices. However, what is currently being seen is that the balance and focus of these forms of digital technology is not the same as it was at the outset of their introduction. Whilst the educational benefits of these forms of digital technology are still recognised, educational behaviours have shifted with regard to uses.

3.9 Summary of Identified Educational Behaviours

In this chapter, the focus has been on an historical perspective of digital technologies. From across the chapter, a number of identified behaviours have been recognised. These are summarised in Table 3.1.

Table 3.1 Behaviours associated with an historical perspective of digital technologies

Form of technology	Learner behaviours	Teacher behaviours	Parent and guardian behaviours	Adviser and policy maker behaviours
Physical computing and educational, learning and teaching behaviours	There is a shift of understanding away from computational thinking always requiring onscreen activity and time, to recognising the importance in developing computational thinking using offscreen devices and collaborative activity	From implementing computational thinking as an independent, individual learner activity, there is a shift to activities where groupwork, learner interest and wellbeing, and developing future learner wellbeing practices are a priority	From observing what is being done by children at home, there is a shift to discussing and being involved in activities where suggestions in programming physical computing devices can be offered	From viewing the need to provide digital devices as the main focus, there is a shift in thinking about the ways that physical digital devices can address specific concerns and needs
The Internet and educational, learning and teaching behaviours	From creating learning outputs as texts, there is a shift in thinking about the possibilities of creating multimedia outputs to demonstrate learning outcomes more effectively	From reviewing details in accessible sources on the Internet, there is a shift towards the importance of initially reviewing how search words and phrases and reviewing source legitimacy can support questions and concerns about detail legitimacy	From concerns about online safety for children, there is a shift towards consulting schools and teachers to provide possible and effective ways forward to address this need	From a position where policy is developed by the individual, there is a shift towards more initial online discussion with practitioners, online drafting and practitioner review, before online posting of policy details

(continued)

Table 3.1 (continued)

Form of technology	Learner behaviours	Teacher behaviours	Parent and guardian behaviours	Adviser and policy maker behaviours
Mobile devices and educational, learning and teaching behaviours	From a reliance on memory of details in specific contexts, there is a shift towards mobile devices allowing more reflection and review of details at a later time	From teachers providing immediate responses and knowledge, there is a shift to them providing routes and ideas about digital resource functions that can allow children to gain knowledge themselves from known sources	From relying on personal support for digital devices at home, there is a shift towards asking schools whether support through onsite access, loans and external digital resource access is possible	From a position where student independence enables access to their own digital devices in schools, there is a shift towards policy which distinguishes between digital device access for learning purposes and that for purely social purposes

These shifts in behaviours show that digital technologies that have been in place and are regularly used in many learning environments can be managed in ways that can positively support all stakeholders. There is, with these digital technologies, however, a similar balance to be had—when, how and to what extent digital technologies are used to support the management and provision of learning. Different stakeholders may need to view the when, how and to what extent from different perspectives. But an important point in this context is that the management of learning through digital technologies involves social interactions, collaboration, co-operation, groupwork and teamwork, not just in the school, but beyond the school, enabling understanding and appropriate actions within the home and for policy. Those interactions require time and opportunity—but digital technologies have been shown to offer possible support in this respect also.

Chapter 4
Theoretical Perspectives: The Importance of Educational Change and Continuous Change Concepts, Challenging Critiques of Educational Theories, Including Behaviourism

Abstract Educational behaviours are also linked, in particular and different ways, to approaches that are described through a variety of learning theories. Learning theories have led to approaches to education that have determined particular forms of behaviour. Whilst learning theories have continued to emerge over the past decades, the integration of approaches and behaviours that are associated with all of these theories can be seen in current practice, even though one or more learning theories might be valued and endorsed more in specific settings. The ways that behaviourism, cognitivism, constructionism, social constructivism and connectivism are seen in educational behaviours currently suggests that digital technologies are influencing behaviours across this spectrum.

Keywords Learning theories and educational behaviours · Behaviourism and educational behaviours · Cognitivism and educational behaviours · Constructionism and educational behaviours · Social constructivism and educational behaviours · Connectivism and educational behaviours

4.1 Learning Theories

Learning as a concept can be defined quite easily, but there are difficulties in detailing what constitutes learning and how learning might occur. As a simple definition, learning is described by Barron et al. (2015) as behavioural change. This definition, of course, suggests that learning leads to a change that can be viewed externally. Yet from an educational perspective, cognitive change could be considered as an internal change that might or might not be able to be observed externally.

This consideration of learning being concerned with either internal or external change, or indeed the relationship between them, has led to research studies in this context that have been focused in different ways. The focus of Skinner (1938), for example, could be considered to have explored the external behavioural change arising from learning, whereas the focus of Piaget (1936) could be considered to have explored the internal changes potentially leading to external behavioural changes

D. Passey, *Shifting Educational Behaviours*,
https://doi.org/10.1007/978-3-032-18942-4_4

arising from learning. What is important to recognise is that researchers have taken specific contexts and focuses for their research. Skinner was aware of the fact that his work focused on animals rather than humans, and Piaget was aware of the fact that his work focused on observations of a small number of children. Does this mean that we cannot gain from considering a range of different research perspectives on learning? Whilst this would be one possible response, it is also possible to argue that if we consider different contexts and focuses, and understand how we might relate them, that perhaps we could gain a wider understanding of learning itself (Passey, 2013).

If different contexts and focuses are considered when reviewing past research literature on learning, then different perspectives on learning become clear. Whilst some research has focused on motivational aspects (Ryan & Deci, 2000, for example), others have focused on social aspects (Vygotsky, 1978, for example). Whilst research that derives theories about learning can show, for those subjects studied, how aspects, features and factors can affect learning, what they cannot easily show is how this relates to a specific individual, yet learning is known to be individualistic in some respects. Whilst it is possible to use theories that have been derived from research and wider considerations of contexts in which that research might apply, individual context is still important.

Learning is also not a singularity; a learning aspect such as memorisation of a string of numbers, for example, is quite different from a learning aspect such as creating the design outline for a new toy. Both of these aspects concern learning, but in quite different ways. When considering the individual nature of learning, we should recognise that individuals have interests; they have motivations that focus not necessarily on all matters, they may well see the value of depictions in specific media formats, and they may feel that they can cope better with language than with science. But this means that generalisations when considering learning is difficult and potentially problematic if the generalisation leads to a simple requirement that all adhere to a specific set of learning ‘rules’.

How we can use learning theories and research outcomes in these contexts does need to be considered carefully, therefore. In the context of digital technologies this is even more the case, as the effect of the digital technologies can be different with different individuals, and different individuals may choose rather different functions to support their interests, their motivations, their values of multimedia formats, and with what they feel they can cope best.

Adding to this complexity is the fact that in many cultures learning and teaching are considered as separate concepts. Whilst learning has been explored through a range of learning theories, there is much more limited research that has provided outcomes that could be regarded as teaching theory. A quick search via an online search engine will soon show that most references to teaching theories are, in fact, none other than learning theories. For this text, learning and teaching, learning theories and teaching theories, learner and teacher, are all considered separately. The reasoning for this is clear—decisions that need to be made about uses of digital technologies require different perspectives from learners and from teachers, for learning and for teaching.

This distinction forms the basis of the detail that is discussed and reported in this text.

4.2 Learning Theories and Learning and Teaching Behaviours

Some researchers (Wang, 2023, for example) have argued that a student-centred learning approach is fundamental to students for the longer term and that this approach takes the control from the teacher to the learner. It is also clear that descriptions of student-centred learning highlight how the student is responsible for actions and outcomes, some of which, of course, are likely to be exhibited as behaviours (Khatter et al., 2024). If this line of argument is accepted, then it could be inferred that teacher-centred learning approaches perhaps limit exhibits of shifts in learning behaviours, as similar behaviours might be expected to arise over time. Student-centred learning approaches, on the other hand, highlight the focus on and from the individual, and hence learning behaviours are seen as outcomes that can be assessed (perhaps observed, or recognised through assessing qualities of forms of media output) and are welcomed. Student-centred learning, therefore, is an important conceptual or theoretical position with regard to considering how learning theories relate to learning and teaching behaviours.

In the following sub-sections, a number of learning theories are introduced, together with discussions about their relationships to learning and teaching behaviours when using digital technologies. The learning theories considered are behaviourism, cognitivism, constructionism, constructivism, and connectivism.

4.3 Behaviourism

From a learning perspective, the application of the theory of behaviourism is widely discussed (Phillips, 2012) as well as being widely used in some contexts (Leeder, 2022) and contested in others. Whilst concerns about the application of behaviourism often arise from applying the concept of stimulus–response in learning, nevertheless, learning is often associated with stimulus–response behaviours. It could be argued that the stimulus for completing an examination paper is linked to the response identified by the value of a certificate being awarded. Similarly, positive encouragement in classrooms might be seen as a stimulus that can lead to a positive response to learning through remembering what is being covered.

4.4 Behaviourism and Learning and Teaching Behaviours

Whilst the application of the theory of behaviourism continues to be an aspect for discussion in education, it is also clear that the advent of uses of digital technologies has opened up the possibility for wider observation and identification of behaviours arising as a result of learning. That teachers are often stating that they are observing more as a result of the possibility to monitor to greater extents what is happening when students use digital technologies, this also implies that they are identifying features that might have been missed previously when digital technologies were not being used. Examples of learning behaviours that teachers are reporting from observations of learning include:

- Recognising the "oh! I get it!" moment.
- Observing pleasure when an activity or problem is completed.
- Identifying increased discussion about a task in hand.
- Seeing willingness to see the strengths and weaknesses of others working together.
- Observing dedication through the time given to solving a problem.
- Accepting that something is not correct and being willing to address it.
- Seeing how multimedia formats are created to summarise and describe points or outcomes.

These learning behaviours can be described in the context of behaviourism, and they offer additional and alternative ways for student outcomes to be 'measured', compared to using more traditional handwritten test or examination paper style formats.

In addition to learning behaviours being identified, similarly, there are examples of teaching behaviours that are reported, including:

- Allowing students to work together to address tasks or problems.
- Setting up possible competitive elements and activities, either competing with others in the class, or more widely.
- Giving students the opportunity to share and help others.
- Providing techniques that the students themselves use to explore a topic or to address a key point of interest.

In all of these examples, the practice can be described in the context of behaviourism. But at the same time, these teaching behaviours also align to a more learner-centred approach, where the teaching behaviour is enabling the learner to take more control over their learning and the learning outcome. The teaching behaviour enables the teacher to monitor more, to observe and help shape positively the behaviours of the learners.

4.5 Cognitivism

Cognitivism as a learning theory focuses on the internal processes of learning, and indeed, Piaget (1936) described the development of the internal processes of learning through four distinct stages, which he related to age ranges. However, it should be noted that Piaget's work was founded on a small number of children he observed, many of whom were his children, and they were clearly developing cognitively within a specific social context. The importance of that latter aspect, the social context, was considered later by other researchers, associated with learning theories described in later sections of this chapter.

4.6 Cognitivism and Learning and Teaching Behaviours

Cognitivism focuses on the internal processes of learning, and cognitive concerns and theory can clearly be considered and applied appropriately to learning and teaching practices (Yilmaz, 2011). Giannoukos (2024) describes the theory of cognitivism as a theory that concerns a range of internal processes, including perception, attention, memory, or problem-solving. The structure of mental processes has also been a focus for researchers in this field, relating observation to memory, reflecting on that which is already known, and forming schema that are retained for future reference (Meylani, 2024).

Learning behaviours that have been reported when digital technologies have been used include:

- Responding with perceptions and reactions about learning resources or provision.
- Using digital technologies as a source of details that no longer need to be memorised.
- Being able to focus more on higher level skills such as analysis or evaluation.
- Easily constructing simple forms of presentation such as tables or diagrams.
- Referring to details as and when needed.
- Reflecting on previously acquired and recorded details.
- Taking account of a wider range of sources and perspectives.
- Easily searching for topics of interest or need.

These learning behaviours can all be described in the context of cognitivism, offering students opportunities to build mental schema, that seek to enhance attention, sensory engagement, and problem-solving. However, uses of digital technologies have been seen to shift aspects of memorisation, which some researchers say has a potentially negative effect (Calinescu, 2024), while others offer a more nuanced view (Lodge & Harrison, 2019).

From a teaching perspective, forms of teaching behaviours that have been reported when digital technologies are used include:

- Offering choices of sources or resources.

- Providing material in multimedia formats.
- Enabling access to sources as and when needed.
- Offering rapid response to queries or questions that can be sourced online if needed.
- Providing resources that offer rapid responses and reflection.

These examples can all be described in the context of cognitivism. Teaching behaviours align to approaches that offer greater choice and offer greater options through multimedia. In this context, teaching behaviour is again enabling the learner to take more control over their learning and the learning outcomes. Teaching behaviour enables the teacher to align more with cognitive concerns that help learners to build mental schemas.

4.7 Constructionism

It is generally recognised that the concepts and theory of constructionism can be related fairly easily to uses of digital technologies in education. In this context, the theory was particularly developed by Papert and Harel (1991), who recognised the importance of handling and making objects in activities that would lead to learning. Constructionism focuses on making rather than using; it emphasises the importance of acting as a 'producer' rather than as a 'consumer'. In this sense, the theory is concerned that learners are active in construction rather than just in use of digital technologies.

4.8 Constructionism and Learning and Teaching Behaviours

Constructionism focuses on practice within learning, which concerns the forms of learning activities that learners experience. Research has explored the forms of learning activities that can be developed to ensure a relevant focus on construction for learners (for example, Csizmadia et al., 2019). In the contemporary context, construction would involve the use of physical computing elements such as Micro:bit[1] or Raspberry Pi[2] processors, as well as networking of sensors and video cameras, with appropriate coding and programming.

In terms of learning behaviours related to constructionism, some examples reported when digital technologies have been used include:

- Coding on-screen to program physical devices.
- Networking sensors and additional devices to address specific needs.

[1] https://microbit.org/.

[2] https://www.raspberrypi.org/.

- Coding physical devices to perform specific actions.
- Developing apps that can be used by specific audiences.
- Creating on-screen environments that mirror real environments and allow changes and additions to be viewed.

These learning behaviours all relate to the concepts and theory of constructionism, offering learners opportunities to handle and make, to build and review outcomes. These forms of activities seek to enhance understanding, sensory engagement, motivation, links to the external world and future employment, and problem-solving. Uses of digital technologies in this context have been seen to shift aspects of engagement, especially when the construction is linked to later use and involvement with others, for example, when learners create their own games (Kafai & Burke, 2015).

From a teaching perspective, forms of teaching behaviours that have been reported in this context include:

- Enabling students to build their own computers.
- Forming groups that will code and pilot an external physical device.
- Asking students to develop a system that will allow new additions to be added and trialled.
- Developing an app or a game that others will use at a later time.

These examples all relate to the concepts and theory of constructionism. Teaching behaviours align to approaches that offer involvement in creating and making, sometimes with wider use that goes beyond the classroom itself. In this context, teaching behaviours are again enabling the student to take more control over their learning and the learning outcomes, as well as offering insights into practices adopted in future employment. Teaching behaviours that enable the teacher to align with constructionist concerns help learners to develop social as well as practical skills.

4.9 Social Constructivism

Social constructivism as a theory applied to learning focuses on the importance of social interactions, on direct student involvement, on discussion, and on ways to support knowledge exchange. Using a social constructivist approach, described often as being based on the initial work of Vygotsky (1978), speaking and listening, and sharing between peers as well as between teachers and students, should be central to the activities that teachers and students are engaged with. From the research work of Berger and Luckmann (1966), social constructivism argues that learning should be an active process, and that each individual develops a world view that is based on not just the knowledge that they come into contact with, but additionally that influences of interactions with others are crucial in this respect.

4.10 Social Constructivism and Learning and Teaching Behaviours

Research has explored the theory of social constructivism and its applications to teaching and learning fairly extensively. For example, Zajda (2023) describes how social constructivism might be used to support learning outcomes, while Trent et al. (1998) explore this from a special education perspective, and Ahmadvand and Khoshchehreh (2023) view this through a teaching lens.

In terms of learning behaviours, some examples reported when digital technologies have been used taking a social constructivist approach include:

- Working in pairs to code a light sequence for a Micro:bit[3] processor.
- Sharing a video created for homework that is then discussed with the class.
- From group discussion, developing search words to gather evidence about a language topic on the Internet.
- Working out roles in a team to create an online presentation about their town.

These learning behaviours relate to the theory of social constructivism, offering students opportunities to work with others, to share and build understanding and knowledge. These activities seek to enhance social interaction that will support learning at an individual level through working with others. Uses of digital technologies in this context have been recognised to positively influence aspects of social interaction and engagement.

From a teaching perspective, forms of teaching behaviours that have been reported in this context include:

- Asking pupils in pairs to solve a coding problem.
- Engaging parents and guardians with their children to work on an online activity that will be shared with the class.
- Encouraging groups of students to prepare a presentation of their week's work to share in a year assembly.
- Asking class assistants to engage and gather details about their preferences from students who are not able to communicate easily.

These examples relate to the theory of social constructivism. Teaching behaviours concern approaches that offer social involvement, but at the same time have learning direction and purpose. These social learning activities may involve others that are outside the immediate classroom. In this context, teaching behaviours enable students to take more control over their learning and the learning outcomes through social engagement. Teaching behaviours that accommodate social constructivist concerns can help students to apply knowledge and skills, and to solve problems with others.

[3] https://microbit.org/.

4.11 Connectivism

Connectivism is a theory that has been developed and discussed within the digital era, and it certainly aligns with the affordances that digital technologies can provide for the learner and for the teacher. Following the research of Siemens (2004) and Downes (2022), connectivism focuses on the ways that digital technologies can support connections, between learners, between learners and teachers, between learners and others, and between learners and digital devices. The concepts in connectivism align with the practices that are often engaged in online learning, and with remote learning.

4.12 Connectivism and Learning and Teaching Behaviours

Research has shown that connectivism applies in many learning situations. However, critiques have been raised about this theory (for example, Dennis, 2024). The theory's strong implied applicability to digital technologies such as massive open online courses (MOOCs) has also been examined (Ozturk, 2015). Learning benefits arising from practices that apply a connectivist approach have also been reported (for example, Downes, 2019).

In terms of learning behaviours, some examples reported when digital technologies have been used taking a connectivist approach include:

- Sharing a document online with a peer to create a joint report.
- Using eye movements to select preferences for reading resources.
- Emailing a teacher with a question for the next week's homework.
- Selecting university websites to consider applications for courses.

These learning behaviours relate to the theory of connectivism, offering students opportunities to work with others online, to share and build understanding and knowledge through online means. These activities seek to enhance social interaction through online means, both at an individual level and through working with wider groups online. Uses of digital technologies in this context have been recognised to influence aspects of social interaction and engagement.

From a teaching perspective, forms of teaching behaviours that have been reported in this context include:

- Enabling students to ask questions online through a virtual learning environment (VLE) portal during a specified time period on certain days.
- Creating a collage of ideas created and shared online by students responding to a question about politics.
- Creating a quiz on the topic of gravity that students can take online and gain immediate responses and scores.
- Suggesting that a school class can communicate online with another class in another country, so that they can practice using the language of both countries.

These examples all relate to the theory of connectivism. Teaching behaviours in this context concern approaches where there is online interaction, but at the same time they have distinctly detailed learning aims and objectives. Such online learning activities can involve others outside the communities that they know, but in this context, teaching behaviours enable learners to develop their learning through online means, perhaps involving them in situations where they need to develop appropriate online social interactions. Teaching behaviours with connectivist practices can be developed and used to help learners gain knowledge and skills, and to work with others.

4.13 A Summary of Learning Theories Related to Learning and Teaching Behaviours

Across this chapter, examples of activities that relate to learning theories and the forms of learning and teaching behaviours that are involved in applying those have been offered. In summary, Table 4.1 provides an overview of these examples.

4.14 Choices of Learning Theories Related to Learning and Teaching Behaviours

Some research takes the position of seeking to show that the learning outcomes from one learning theory applied in practice outweigh those of another learning theory applied in practice. However, from the summarised behaviours shown in Table 4.1, a question that should be asked is whether, on the basis of the examples provided across applications that align with five different learning theories, any one of them is felt to be either better than another or whether any of them should not be considered. On the basis of observed practice, the author can say that all of these examples have been observed in one situation or another, and all of them have been recognised by teachers and learners to be worthwhile and to lead to positive outcomes. The implication is, perhaps, that practice that aligns with theory (whichever it might be) can be fruitful and worthwhile. Choice, therefore, is a matter of context, purpose and desired outcomes for learners—there is perhaps an overriding teaching theory that could apply here—a teaching theory of 'fitness for learning purpose'.

Table 4.1 Behaviours associated with learning theories

Learning theory	Learner behaviours	Teacher behaviours
Behaviourism	• Recognising the "oh! I get it!" moment • Observing pleasure when an activity or problem is completed • Increasing discussion about the task in hand • Being willing to see the strengths and weaknesses of others working together • Dedicating time to solving a problem • Accepting that something is not correct and being willing to address it • Seeing how multimedia formats can be created to summarise and describe points or outcomes	• Allowing students to work together to address tasks or problems • Setting up possible competitive elements and activities, either competing with others in the class, or more widely • Giving students the opportunity to share and help others • Providing techniques that the students themselves use to explore a topic or to address a key point of interest
Cognitivism	• Responding with perceptions and reactions about learning resources or provision • Using digital technologies as a source of details that no longer need to be memorised • Being able to focus more on higher level skills such as analysis or evaluation • Easily constructing simple forms of presentation such as tables or diagrams • Referring to details as and when needed • Reflecting on previously acquired and recorded details • Taking account of a wider range of sources and perspectives • Easily searching for topics of interest or need	• Offering choices of sources or resources • Providing material in multimedia formats • Enabling access to sources as and when needed • Offering access to rapid responses to queries or questions that can be sourced online if needed • Providing resources that offer rapid responses and reflection

(continued)

Table 4.1 (continued)

Learning theory	Learner behaviours	Teacher behaviours
Constructionism	• Coding on-screen to program physical devices • Networking sensors and additional devices to address specific needs • Coding physical devices to perform specific actions • Developing apps that can be used by specific audiences • Creating on-screen environments that mirror real environments and allow changes and additions to be viewed	• Enabling students to build their own computers • Forming groups that will code and pilot an external physical device • Asking students to develop an interactive system that will allow new additions to be added and trialled • Developing an app or a game that others will use at a later time
Social constructivism	• Working in pairs to code a light sequence for a Micro:bit processor • Sharing a video created for homework that is then discussed with the class • In a group, developing search words to gather evidence about a language topic on the Internet • Working out roles in a team to create an online presentation about their town	• Asking pupils in pairs to solve a coding problem • Engaging parents and guardians with their children to work on an online activity that will be shared with the class • Encouraging groups of learners to prepare a presentation of their week's work to share in a year assembly with invited parents • Asking class assistants to engage and gather details about preferences from students who are not able to verbally communicate easily
Connectivism	• Sharing a document online with a peer to create a joint report • Using eye movements to select preferences for reading resources • Emailing a teacher with a question for the next week's homework • Selecting university websites to consider applications for courses	• Enabling students to ask questions online through a virtual learning environment (VLE) portal during a specified time period on certain days • Creating a collage of ideas created and shared online by students responding to a question about politics • Creating a quiz on the topic of gravity that students can take online and from which they can gain immediate responses and scores • Suggesting that the class can communicate online with another class in another country, so that they can each practice using the language of the other country

4.15 Future Learning Theories

Whilst this chapter has explored educational behaviours that relate to a number of learning theories, a question that is worth asking is whether the future will see a shift in learning theory, or whether new learning theories will arise. Learning theories have arisen, at least to some extent, as a consequence of social practice that aligns with particular time periods. As digital technologies continue to emerge, and as social practice and society shift over time, it is very likely that learning theories will emerge to accommodate these features.

What can be seen from the evidence and argument provided in this chapter and elsewhere in this text is a widening of the roles of different actors concerned with education and its support. Learners can take the opportunity to use digital technologies outside schools to learn from interactions with online resources; teachers can gather evidence from a wider range of sources beyond the school; parents and guardians can support their children through home access to devices and resources online; advisers and policy makers can suggest ways that learning can be accommodated outside the school environments. This widening of learning settings questions the ways that terms such as formal, non-formal and informal learning have been applied in the past and to date (Council of Europe, 2025). This text argues that these boundaries are being blurred; that understanding how learning behaviours can support effective learning across these boundaries is more important than distinguishing the setting in which learning may be occurring. Implications and future directions in this context are explored more in Chap. 11.

Chapter 5
Learning and Learner Behaviours: Shifting Technologies and Shifting Possibilities

Abstract Computers began to be introduced into schools in the 1980s. At that time, microcomputers were run from, generally, either punch-card or cassette tape systems. Using these systems, it was possible to either use the computer as a demonstration tool, or to use it as a device for programming. Since that time, digital technologies have developed and have diversified very widely, both in terms of hardware and software. Some learning and learner behaviours have not necessarily shifted, however, as the behaviours adopted to gain most effective outcomes from the early devices still persist. In this chapter, learning and learner behaviours that have become adopted to gain from devices that have been present and have been developed since the 1980s are explored.

Keywords Learning and learner behaviours · Desktops and learner behaviours · Subject topics and learner behaviours · Information technology and learner behaviours · The Internet and learner behaviours · Communications technologies and learner behaviours · Interactive whiteboards and learner behaviours · Specific software and learner behaviours

5.1 Desktops and Learning Behaviours

The presence and uses of desktop computers have persisted since the 1980s, albeit the desktop devices being developed further in a wide range of ways. Often, the power of the desktop is concerned with visibility; in essence, the monitor provides access to the power and facilities behind the screen. By 2015, the Organisation for Economic Cooperation and Development (OECD) (2015) had already identified that a digital divide was apparent—between those who had access to a desktop and those who did not. The concern for this digital divide was at least twofold: that those without access could not gain from the uses and facilities available; and those without access could not gain from an understanding of its potential and future. Whilst research has explored the potential that digital devices can bring to learners and their learning, the overall findings can be seen to be contradictory or uncertain from an educational

D. Passey, *Shifting Educational Behaviours*,
https://doi.org/10.1007/978-3-032-18942-4_5

outcome perspective, but the salient message that arises from a view across the literature is that the way the digital device is used makes the difference between achievement levels (Simões et al., 2022).

Some schools and geographic regions have enabled digital devices to be accessible for each learner. However, some research studies have found that this level of access can lead to reduced rather than enhanced achievement in some cases and where certain outcomes are measured (Mora et al., 2018). Other studies have found that when computers are used in ways that enable understanding and solving of problems, that this facilitates achievement for the learners that goes beyond outcomes where an approach concerns learners only seeking to find correct answers (Radović et al., 2019).

Vignette 1 A learner accesses his mathematics homework on a home desktop machine. He uses this device as it allows a wide visual display, enabling him to insert notes and answers without difficulty. The mathematics homework set by the teacher is a set of algebra problems, and the teacher has set questions so that each learner in the class receives different questions but they are aligned with the same levels of problems that need to be solved. The learner answers the questions, and he finds that some of these are incorrect. When in the class the following day, the teacher has accessed the results, and she identifies those questions that received fewest correct answers so that she can discuss these with the class. When she has done this, she asks the learners to try other questions that she has set, and if they do not answer correctly, to find someone who has done this successfully and to discuss it with them. The learning behaviour is shifting from finding a correct answer to finding out ways to solve a problem correctly.

Research has highlighted that effectiveness of uses of computer desktops in schools by learners is not only related to learner and learning behaviours, but also to teaching effectiveness (for example, Monserate, 2018). Research has pointed in this context to the importance of professional development (Ghavifekr, & Rosdy, 2015).

Vignette 2 The teacher is keen that learners share their homework and discuss how they would each make improvements. The teacher uses a computer suite so that desktop machines enable easy access and allow learners to note and make changes easily on screen. The learners work in pairs, one learner showing their homework about the causes of social uprisings. The other learner reads and then comments on the work, pointing out where there are differences with her own homework, and balancing a review of those points that show positive differences as well as negative differences. The other learner then reviews the other homework and applies the same sort of approach. When they have finished, they need to construct a list of key points that they would use next time they do a homework of this type. The teaching behaviour has shifted from marking individual work to enable the sharing of work between peers and gaining highlights from their own work for use on subsequent occasions.

As is the case for research about shifting teacher practices using digital technologies, the ways that parents and guardians can support their children through uses of digital technologies at home is also not a new research area. Hollingworth et al. (2011), for example, reported that parents and guardians who use digital technologies in the workplace can have experiences that can support their children in ways that parents and guardians who do not have this background would not be able to apply in home situations. Uses of digital technologies by parents and guardians in their workplaces has increased since 2011, and the ways that these changes have affected forms of communication and support are more recently reported in the research (for example, See et al., 2020).

Vignette 3 Working in an office in a professional services capacity, a guardian is aware of the ways that digital technologies are used to support communication. At home, with a desktop computer accessible, the guardian makes sure that communication is set up between the child and the teachers, as required by the school. The guardian questions the child about every other day to ensure that the child is communicating and keeping records as needed, but this practice is also ensuring that the guardian knows what is happening in terms of learning needs and the focus of study, as well as ensuring that the child is safe in the communications that are happening. The guardian recognises that using the desktop device is shifting behaviour towards a closer monitoring of communication that can support positive links and safety.

With the advent of digital devices that are more mobile, the role of desktop devices has tended to be researched to a lesser extent. However, the benefits of desktop devices are still apparent; they provide a large screen view, enabling discussion with others, and ease of editing and viewing. Whilst educational policies have been adopted to support access to more mobile devices, the importance of desktop access has sometimes been less considered.

Vignette 4 At a school policy level, the senior leadership team recognise that most of the families whose children attend the school have access to smartphones and mobile devices, but their children have less access to larger screen facilities that support easier visualisation, discussion, and editing. The school decides that children should have access to these larger desktop facilities, so they offer access for the children at times before school lessons start and after school lesson times, so that children can use desktop facilities to support their educational work. The school policy group recognises that their behaviour in this context is moving to closer monitoring of communication that supports positive links, promoting opportunities for access in a safe environment.

The role of desktop devices is sometimes now considered less when more mobile devices have become accessible to learners, teachers, parents and guardians, and advisers and policy makers. However, the specific functionalities that desktops offer is an important aspect for consideration. In some cases, the linking of mobile devices to large screen monitors, external keyboards and an external mouse have helped to address this.

5.2 Subject Influences and Learning Behaviours

Research has explored how digital technologies have been used to support learning in different subject areas. One outcome of that research shows that different subject areas can use different forms of digital technologies that apply to what Shulman (2005) described as 'signature pedagogies' (that is, specific practices that apply to specific subjects, for example, the use of experimental activities in chemistry, or the use of lists for learning vocabulary in language learning). Clearly, when digital technologies are applied to support learning, these distinctive practices can call for quite different forms of digital facilities. In this context, research has reported how digital technologies have been applied to specific subject needs. For example, Shadiev and Wang (2022) explored digital technologies that supported language learning, while Toktamysov et al. (2023) explored this in the context of the learning of history.

Vignette 5 To help with learning a list of vocabulary for an upcoming test in a German lesson, the learner decides to use an app where the teacher has uploaded the words in English and in German. The learner is presented with either the English or the German words and needs to enter the correct translation into the app. The app checks the response and moves the learner to the next item, dependent on whether the answer is correct or incorrect. For words that are only slightly incorrectly spelt, the app provides an opportunity for the word to be corrected. After 30 minutes of use, the learner is satisfied that sufficient words have been translated successfully, but the learner tries again after an hour, and then again the next morning to make sure that the words are committed to memory. The learning behaviour is shifting here from short-term memorising (which can lead to short-term retention) to longer-term reviewing, reflection and memorising (which can lead to longer-term retention).

In terms of specific subjects or topics, research has reported on the ways that digital technologies can be applied to the teaching of specific subjects and topics. For example, Walan (2020) reported on case studies of science teaching using digital technologies in secondary schools, Momani et al. (2023) reported on science teaching uses from a wide literature review, while Liu and Zhu (2025) reported how artificial intelligence may be used to support the teaching of art.

Vignette 6 A teacher of English wants the students in the class to explore how speakers use different forms of language—to persuade, to argue, and to inform. She wants the students to listen to some well-known politicians and to identify what key words and phrases are being used when speaking to the audience to persuade, to inform or to argue for a stated position. She has identified a number of online video excerpts, and she asks the students initially to listen to the speeches. After a brief discussion about their views on the topic, she then asks the students to use the video facility to transcribe the audio into text, to download it, and then in small groups of three or four learners, to highlight those words or phrases that they feel show persuasion (in blue), informing (in yellow), and arguing for a position (in orange). The teacher then shares the group outcomes. The teaching behaviour in this context is shifting from identifying and remembering ideas, words and phrases through notetaking to highlighting ideas, words and phrases through discussion and highlighting of text transcription.

As well as exploring teaching approaches, research has also studied how parents and guardians have supported their children with specific subject learning. For example, Dominke and Steffensky (2025) undertook a literature review of studies about how parents and guardians supported their children in the field of science, while Picton et al. (2024) reviewed parent and guardian ways to do this in the context of early years' literacy.

Vignette 7 The parents wanted to support their children in learning mathematics, but they did not feel they had the background in the subject to be able to help. They contacted the school, and the subject teacher was able to send them a link to some online resources that the teacher had put together. This included a video about the current mathematics topic (created by the children as well as the teacher), some ideas of the sorts of questions and tasks that the children might be asked to complete, and some notes on suggested ways to support their children (who were of different ages and in different classes). The parents recognised that their behaviour had shifted from accepting that support was not possible except for generally reassuring their children, to seeking and gaining support through digital means that allowed them to engage about specific learning topics with their children.

From a wider policy perspective, most country government ministries or departments of education publish documents that relate to specific subject areas and topics. These might be in the form of national curriculum documents, or these could be in the form of guidelines or advice. In South Africa, for example, there is a Curriculum and Assessment Policy Statement (CAPS) that is written for parents, students and teachers (CAPS 123, 2025). In Wales, a curriculum is defined in subject and topic areas (Hwb, n.d.), whilst in Estonia, a full national curriculum is offered (Republic of Estonia Ministry of Education and Research, 2022). These documents are accessible to all educational stakeholders, whether they be learners, teachers, parents and guardians, or advisers and policy makers themselves.

Vignette 8 From a policy perspective, the difficulty that the group of policy makers faced concerned how to suggest approaches to schools that they might take to the teaching of digital technologies. Rather than requiring schools to create individual lessons focusing on digital technology education specifically, the decision was taken to enable schools to integrate digital technologies in any subject lessons as appropriate, offering ways to support the long-term interests of users—both in terms of understanding and being able to develop techniques concerned with coding, programming and computational thinking, but also developing techniques concerned with safe and effective ways to use digital technologies across and within any subject areas. From a policy perspective, behaviour was seen to shift from ensuring coverage in specific lessons within a curriculum to ensuring long-term interests and potential for further development, adaptability and employment through wide integration and application.

Digital technologies can now support and be integrated into the learning and teaching of any subject within a school curriculum. The width of support and integration has continued to increase and widen. Learners, teachers, parents and guardians, and advisers and policy makers are shifting in their behaviours to take advantage of this increased width and diversity.

5.3 Information Technology and Learning Behaviours

Information technology functionalities have provided possible applications for education from fairly early times. However, through these facilities, communication itself was not a feasible option. The digital information technologies allowed access to information, with forms of searching of information also occurring at fairly early stages, from 1990, with Google becoming accessible from around 2000 (Seymour et al., 2011). Images have also become more accessible but were supported on the web from around the early 1990s (Ferraz et al., 2025).

Since the Internet has provided opportunities for information searching and gathering, aspects of learning have been concerned with the strategies that students could adopt in order to most effectively address the questions they wished to answer (Mao et al., 2022). As well as developing strategies for effective text-based searches, aspects of learning have also required effective strategies to be developed for image-based searches (Tsai & Wu, 2021).

Vignette 9 A student wants to find the answer to a question—what factors affected the downfall of the Roman period in Britain? The student knows that the Internet is likely to provide some possible answers, but the choice of keywords to search and the choice of legitimate sources is known to be crucial to gaining useful information. The student uses the keywords 'Roman Britain' and 'downfall', and a range of sources are rapidly found. The student is not sure which sources might be best, so decides to select article from magazines that are published by known publishers and also to use a key phrase 'research article' as well. This last key phrase draws out a number of academic sources and known publications that are peer reviewed. The student uses five different sources from this range, draws out the reasons from those, and surprisingly finds that the sources say that downfall was not as rapid as might have been anticipated.

In the context of information access, the teaching of information literacy has become an important part of educational curricula. Whilst the role of teachers in this respect is often considered, it is also important to recognise that other key roles within educational institutions play a major part in the development of strategies and techniques that can develop across age ranges. Laretive (2019), for example, highlighted the role of the teacher librarian, while Samson and Millet (2003) explored the role of teaching assistants.

Vignette 10 A teacher wanted her children to know more about how to effectively search for information online. She contacted a local university library, and one of the librarians agreed to go into the school to offer a session for the children on how to do successful searches. The librarian discussed the access that the children would have during the session, and she suggested that the children should work in pairs, so that they could discuss the processes they would use and their responses to the searches. The librarian also asked what subject topic the teacher would like her to focus on, and she was then able to do a search herself in preparation for the session. In the session, the librarian highlighted the idea of key words and phrases, the search engine to use, and how to identify sources that would be considered independent rather than biased. She also explored with the children how to select sources by carefully reading titles and abstracts, and then the importance of understanding the context of the sources so that information could be appropriately framed. The teacher recognised that she was moving in her behaviour from knowing sources to suggest to her learners, to understanding the processes that would enable her learners to identify useful sources themselves.

Whilst teachers have sought ways to develop successful information literacy practices for their learners, in parallel, parents and guardians have increasingly relied upon digital technologies to support their engagement with schools and with their children's learning. The value of details provided through forms of information technology has been evident in this context. For example, Cleveland et al. (2024) identified from their survey of parents and guardians how details about homework and study assignments was regularly accessed. Uses of information technology to monitor children's study progress by parents and guardians was similarly noted in the literature review completed by See et al. (2020).

Vignette 11 A guardian is concerned that her child may not be completing all of the home assignments that the teachers are requesting. Before discussing this with her child, she decides to check with the child's teachers whether there is an online way for her to see what assignments are being set. Given the details from the teachers, she is able to go online and check the assignments set for any one day or week. After monitoring these for a week, she is then able to discuss with her child how assignment completion is progressing. The guardian recognises that her behaviour is shifting from having to confront her child with potentially challenging questions about homework completion, to having chance to monitor the situation before involving her child in direct discussion.

While positive impacts of information technology have been identified for parents and guardians, it is recognised that access to information technology has had both positive and negative effects on policy maker practices. For example, Myeong and Choi (2010) from their study in Korea demonstrated that policy makers were more able to consider alternative contingencies, to search for examples of parallel practices, to consider goal setting and alternative options more widely, but that costs, technical issues, ethical sharing and organisational differences could have negative effects on individuals and institutions.

Vignette 12 The policy maker was exploring ways to develop a policy about Internet access for schools. Whilst details and considerations had been provided by members of the internal department, a wider view was felt by the policy maker to be of potential value. Knowing some colleagues in other institutions and countries, he emailed to find if any sources could be made accessible to provide him with some alternative perspectives. A number of his contacts sent copies of published documents that he could review. Having viewed these, he was then able to identify the key highlights that needed to be considered by schools in his area. The policy maker recognised that his practices were shifting from using largely local advice about practices, to approaches that enabled wider national and international options, similarities and differences to be considered.

Information technologies have provided easier access to online resources for all educational stakeholders. However, whilst there are clearly advantages and benefits from this level of access, issues and challenges have also arisen. The development of information literacy to support all online users has been an important concern and focus, often involving individuals and groups across the entire educational system.

5.4 The Internet, Communications Technologies, Networking and Learning Behaviours

Following information technology facilities becoming available to the educational sector, digital technology developments focused increasingly on networking that in turn led to communication opportunities that went far beyond the sharing of text and images. Subramanian (2018) charts developments in this field and argues that networking and communications technologies have had both positive and negative impacts on forms and qualities of communications between individuals. The use of mobile technologies for communication purposes, for example, is highlighted as happening in places and at times that would previously have been considered not possible or unacceptable.

Whilst social uses of mobile technologies have been highlighted as a major issue in some educational contexts, learners have also recognised that communication through uses of digital technologies can enhance their learning. Palines et al. (2025), for example, highlighted the benefits for learners when using communications technologies to support research practices.

Vignette 13 Learners in a class are being asked to explore the patterns of activity of bees gathering pollen and pollinating flowers. The learners are asked to study the patterns according to the time of day, and whether factors such as temperature, wind speed and direction, and levels of daylight appear to have any influences, either positive or negative. The learners are keen to do this study in their school garden area, but they have no experience of undertaking studies of this sort. The teacher arranges an online discussion session with a local university academic, who specialises in studying insect behaviours. The learners are asked to think of the questions that they would want to ask the academic during the session. They created a list of 10 questions, and following the session, they were asked how they felt about the advice they were given. The learners were positive—they felt they knew better how and when to take readings, and what factors to consider. The learners recognised that they had shifted from relying on information from their teachers and from online sources, to thinking about the questions to ask, gathering advice from an expert online through direct communication.

In this example, the behaviours of both learners and teachers have been seen to potentially shift. In parallel, the functionalities of communication technologies have supported the development of online learning. Teacher perceptions of online learning and uses of communications technologies are mixed; some teachers see advantages, while others see disadvantages. Chui et al. (2025), for example, identified the importance of both wider school support and digital technology competence and confidence if online learning is to be used successfully by teachers within classrooms.

Vignette 14 A teacher feels that the learners in his class could benefit from engagement with another class in another school. Having established initial contact with a teacher from another school, the teachers use Google Meet to establish a shared lesson. The learners are able to see each other as well as the teachers, and the teachers share the activities across the lesson, engaging both the learners in their onsite class as well as learners in the online class. The teachers share outcomes and ask learners to briefly present to their class and the online class. The teachers value working through this shared class environment. They recognise that their focus is shifting from one where the classroom is their focus of interaction, to a shared classroom where they are working and sharing with another teacher and another class.

Through communications technologies, teachers have often widened their links beyond the school walls. As many parents and guardians now have access to forms of communication technologies, some use these forms of access to widen their links beyond the home, to support their contact and engagement with schools and teachers. Others use these communication technologies to support their children's learning at home. Kurum Tiryakioğlu (2024) studied the ways that parents enabled home learning, and the author found that many parents shift their social practices to accommodate the needs of their children's online access and learning needs.

Vignette 15 A parent wishes to make arrangements to meet with his child's teachers to discuss progress. The parent uses the online booking system that the school provides, and he finds a time and day when both he and the teachers can meet. The system accepts the booking and sends the parent an invitation to an online meeting. The parent connects with the school at the appropriate time on the day arranged, and he is able to discuss progress in different subjects with a number of the subject teachers. The parent values the fact that the meeting does not require him to physically attend, and that the meeting can be made at a time and on a day that does not conflict with his work. The parent recognises that there is a shift from the challenges of physical attendance to the ease of online attendance that suits all parties.

Whilst some parents and guardians have taken advantage of increased communication facilities to support their children, others have identified issues with online rather than face-to-face communication. From a policy perspective, the roles of communication technologies that are discussed and considered possible for education are similarly mixed. Whilst online learning became a common practice in many jurisdictions during the Covid-19 pandemic (Passey, 2021), it is also recognised that many jurisdictions have not followed through in developing online practice but have reverted to previous practices (Butler et al., 2024).

Vignette 16 A policy maker explores the evidence about learner outcomes arising from online and remote learning that had previously occurred in his jurisdiction. The evidence indicated that more disadvantages were identified than advantages. As a consequence, the decision needed to be taken that previous forms of school-based practice needed to be reintroduced. However, the policy maker did not want to stop schools from using online or remote learning practices if these were felt to be of benefit to learners, particularly in specific cases where individual learners were seen to benefit from this form of support. The policy maker recognised that he was shifting in his approach, from one of accepting the evidence relating to the majority, to one where individual circumstances leading to benefits could be considered as viable options or exceptions to a general approach.

Whilst communications technologies have undoubtedly potentially shifted the levels and ways that individuals across the educational sectors can make contact and engage, there are also recognised balances to be had. For example, some teachers have reported that they can become overloaded with messages through social media or emails from parents. In this context, schools have often introduced policies to ensure a balance that supports the teachers' wellbeing. Communication technologies have also enabled wider involvement of individuals in education; for example, there has been an increase in online tutor engagement (Data Insights Market, 2025), as well as an increase in sharing practices across jurisdictions.

5.5 Interactive Whiteboards and Learning Behaviours

Interactive whiteboards, developed initially for business practice, were also developed and applied for educational uses. At the time of their development, a focus on developing teaching practices that was considered more socially constructivist, supported the notion that interactive whiteboards could be of value in schools and education institutions (Higgins, 2010).

Learner perspectives about uses of interactive whiteboards have been researched, and Digregorio and Lojeski (2009), for example, noted that learner outcomes and benefits were associated with external influences such as teacher practices and confidence. Whilst some teachers have used interactive whiteboards as digital projectors, other teachers have developed more collaborative practices to involve their learners to greater extents.

Vignette 17 A teacher wanted to enhance the discussion about a topic in an English lesson. The topic concerned 'the American dream'. The teacher used the interactive whiteboard to show a short video about 'the American dream', and she then asked the learners in pairs to write down key features of what had contributed to views of 'the American dream'. The learners were then asked to send their key features to her using the email facility on their tablets. When the teacher received these, she presented them on the interactive whiteboard and asked the learners whether they agreed with each one, and whether they would suggest amendments or additional points. At the end of the lesson, the teacher was able to send the completed list of key features to each of the learners. The learners recognised that their forms of discussion and collaboration had shifted from them working in a pair and focusing on notes on their desks, to having open discussions about widely visible details with others across the class.

Just as learners have reported benefits of uses of interactive whiteboards on their subject or topic learning, teachers across age groups and subject areas have also used interactive whiteboards to support their teaching and have reported on benefits arising; for example, Nur Fitria (2024) described uses for the teaching of English and outcomes arising. Teachers of different age groups of children and of different subject disciplines have explored different facilities that can be provided through the interactive whiteboard medium.

Vignette 18 A teacher wanted to explore the topic of gravity, but she did not want the lesson to be mainly lecture based. The teacher decided to start the lesson by showing a short video that explained gravity and some of the history of research into the topic. After this, the teacher wanted the students to think about how they would measure the effect of gravity on an object moving through the air. She gathered ideas from the students and recorded key points on the interactive whiteboard, using her laptop to generate the texts. Once an experimental outline was created, she told the class that they would undertake an experiment during the next lesson. At the end of the current lesson, she wanted to find out how much of the key points in the lesson they could recall. She set up an online quiz and asked them to respond to the questions on their tablets. As they responded, the responses were shown on the collated table on the interactive whiteboard, but they were shown anonymously. At the end of the lesson, the students could see how they had done, and whether their answers were correct or not. The teacher recognised that her teaching approach was shifting from an individual lecture style to a more varied style using different multimedia resources that involved different forms of input and output.

Whilst many teachers have experienced or know of interactive whiteboards, it is likely that only some parents and guardians have experienced uses of interactive whiteboards within the contexts of their employment. They may have experienced uses during training sessions, for example. While many parents are not likely to have interactive whiteboards at home, parents and guardians may well be aware of schools that use interactive whiteboards, either from details relayed by their children or through school visits.

Vignette 19 A parent knows that the nursery school regularly sends images to parents, via an online app, to show them what their children are doing within the classrooms. The parent sees the activities that children are involved in and sees the forms of digital technologies that are used in the class areas. One of these is an interactive whiteboard, which the children work on in small groups. In one activity, they are moving pictures of animals around so that the animals are grouped in particular ways. The parent recognises that the activities are shifting from those that he experienced as a child at that stage in education, from imagining how to group items together to seeing and being able to physically move the items.

Overall, there is currently limited research that investigates how parents and guardians might perceive of or know about uses of interactive whiteboards. From a wider policy perspective, research on uses of interactive whiteboards has often highlighted policy considerations rather than taking a perspective from a policy standpoint. Saville et al. (2014), for example, highlighted the need for professional development and training, and the need to consider how uses develop across longer periods of time rather than only across a short time period of perhaps a few months.

Vignette 20 A policy maker has seen the use of interactive whiteboards in another jurisdiction, but he is not convinced that all teachers would be able to very quickly use the digital technology effectively. He identifies five pilot schools and teachers who would like to explore the use of an interactive whiteboard, and he provides the digital technologies for them to use these in their classrooms. He gains an external evaluation of the progress of use over a year-long period. On the basis of the findings, he asks the teachers whether they would be willing to support professional development of other colleagues in their schools and in other schools. He sets out a three-year plan to continue to implement across a wider range of classrooms. The policy maker recognises that he has shifted from a position of just providing the digital technology to a position of piloting uses to enable wider implementation through professional development.

Whilst interactive whiteboards have been in classrooms in some jurisdictions for some time, the benefits of uses of interactive whiteboards are still not widely recognised. Some jurisdictions have opted to use projectors and screens linked to teacher laptops or classroom desktops. Cost implications have sometimes led to choices that are feasible within particular contexts.

5.6 Specific Software and Learning Behaviours

Software to support specific subject and topic areas has been developed continuously over many decades. Agbo et al. (2024), from their literature review of software used in school practices, identified how educational software for some learners and teachers had offered benefits, while for others there were challenges and issues. This review and the research that informed it highlights the point that choice and individual approach can make a difference; whilst accommodating variation in education can be a challenge, it is important to achieve if benefits are to be seen at the widest possible levels.

Research into specific educational software used in school practices has been widely undertaken, over a period of decades. In a review by Farooqi et al. (2024), previous studies have shown that educational software has supported, in specific instances, cognition, behaviour, emotional development, subject outcomes in mathematics, science, and literacy, and has supported autonomous learning and motivation.

But in this review, there were issues identified also, concerned with the design of the software, the ways that uses were implemented and with access.

Vignette 21 A teacher recognises that she has a class that is difficult to motivate. The subject she teaches is mathematics, and the learners find it difficult to engage for any length of time with mathematics, even though the teacher has tried a variety of ways to devise activities. She is introduced to a new educational software that is based on a questioning approach, where learners need to answer questions online. Their answers are shown in a table displayed on the interactive whiteboard at the front of the class, so that individual learners can see how well they are competing with other learners in the class. The learners report that they not only enjoy this form of activity, but they are happy to compete and try to do as well as they can. The learners recognise that they are moving from seeing tasks as items that just need to be completed, to items where they enjoy trying to complete correct answers and compete positively with others.

As well as research into learners' uses of subject software, research into uses of educational software has also been undertaken from teachers' perspectives. In the case of teaching reading and writing in primary schools, for example, Şahin and Özenç (2021) demonstrated that primary teachers were identifying parallel benefits to those identified by students in Farooqi et al.'s (2024) study.

Vignette 22 A teacher wanted to help learners undertake experiments where it would be possible to vary the conditions without needing to take the time to do this on every occasion in the laboratory. Using educational software, the teacher was able to select an experiment so that the learners could work in pairs, using a tablet, and could vary the temperature and pressure that was applied in a series of experiments that then related the results in a table. The teacher recognised that her approach was shifting from one where the single experiment was fundamentally important, to one where the results that arose when conditions were changed across a series of experiments was fundamentally important.

Beyond classrooms and learners' and teachers' uses of subject software, more research has been undertaken about parental perspectives of digital technology and educational software uses at home as a whole, rather than about specific educational software packages. A review by Levido et al. (2025) indicated tensions that can exist; whilst parents could see benefits, they were also concerned about amounts of screen time that their children spent online, both from an educational and social perspective.

Vignette 23 At home, the child has been asked to complete an online quiz, as a means to recall and reinforce the topic that was covered in a lesson earlier in the day. The child tells his parent about the topic, and that the teacher has asked him and others in the class to complete an online quiz. The parent is pleased that the child is discussing what has happened today in school, but is a bit concerned about the amount of online time that might be involved. The parent monitors the activity at a distance, and when half an hour has passed, just checks how his child is progressing. He is pleased to hear that the quiz has been completed, and that the child is just checking answers before submitting them. The parent recognises that his approach has shifted from limited involvement with the child's homework, to more direct concern and monitoring.

At a wider policy level, policy makers have tended to take different stances with regard to purchase of educational software. In some cases, such as in England, for example, the decision is felt to be best placed with the individual school. In this case, school funding enables schools to purchase the educational software that is felt to support school needs appropriate to its context. By contract, in Northern Ireland, for example, the decision is taken to centrally procure educational software as a part of the overall managed service provision (Passey, 2025a, 2025b, 2025c). Whilst schools in Northern Ireland have the option of purchasing additional educational software, a wide variety is provided, including options for learning environments such as Google Classroom or Microsoft 365. As the purchasing power for the number of schools is high, the cost of educational software is negotiated to lower the price to gain additional benefit.

Vignette 24 The policy maker is concerned that appropriate educational software is provided for the area's schools. Having discussed the possibilities with a range of advisers in this field, the policy maker is then in a position to make a decision about the levels of purchase required, and to negotiate the costs with the providers. Where possible, support for schools is also requested as a part of the purchase, so that professional development is offered for teachers as required, both onsite and online. The policy maker recognises that there is a shift from considering purchase of educational software as a facility for provision, to one where the purchase needs to be supported by social practice including ways to support professional development.

Educational subject software has been developed widely over many decades. The range of educational software available is now very wide. Whilst choice is becoming an increasing challenge in some respects, there are educational behaviours concerned with practices of using and supporting subject software that persist from early implementation to current times.

5.7 A Summary of Shifting Educational Behaviours Influencing Learning

In this chapter, the focus has been on how developing digital technologies that are known to positively influence learning have led to shifts in educational behaviours. From across the chapter, a number of identified behaviours have been recognised. These are summarised in Table 5.1.

These shifts in behaviours show that digital technologies that have developed over time and used in learning environments are affecting the ways that engagement and support are considered by all stakeholders. An important point in this context, already stated in the previous chapter and supported by the shifts shown in this chapter, is that the management of learning through digital technologies needs to consider and accommodate important social interactions, collaboration, and teamwork, not only in

Table 5.1 Behaviours associated with a learning perspective of digital technologies

Form of technology	Learner behaviours	Teacher behaviours	Parent and guardian behaviours	Adviser and policy maker behaviours
Desktops and learning behaviours	There is a shift from finding a correct answer to finding out ways to solve a problem correctly	There is a shift from marking individual work to sharing work between peers and gaining highlights from their own work for use on subsequent occasions	There is a shift to closer monitoring of communication that can support positive online links and safety	There is a shift to closer monitoring of communication that supports positive online links, promoting opportunities for access in a safe environment
Subject influences and learning behaviours	There is a shift from short-term memorising to longer-term reviewing, reflection and memorising	There is a shift from activities identifying and remembering ideas, words and phrases through notetaking exercises to highlighting ideas, words and phrases through discussion and highlighting of text transcription	There is a shift from accepting that support was not possible except for generally reassuring their children, to seeking and gaining support through digital means that allows them to engage about specific learning topics with their children	There is a shift from ensuring coverage in specific lessons within a curriculum to ensuring long-term interests and potential for further development, adaptability and employment through wide integration and application

(continued)

Table 5.1 (continued)

Form of technology	Learner behaviours	Teacher behaviours	Parent and guardian behaviours	Adviser and policy maker behaviours
Information technology and learning behaviours	There is a shift from using sources that the teacher suggests to understanding the principles of information literacy	There is a shift from knowing sources to suggest to learners, to understanding processes that will enable learners to identify useful sources themselves	There is a shift from having to confront children with potentially challenging questions, to having chance to monitor situations with online information before involving children in direct discussion	There is a shift from using largely local advice when devising policy to practices that enable wider national and international options, similarities and differences to be considered
The Internet, communications technologies, networking and learning behaviours	There is a shift from relying on information from teachers and from online sources, to thinking about questions to ask that gather advice from experts online through direct communication	There is a shift from teaching approaches where the classroom is the focus of interaction, to working with both an onsite and online shared classroom where activities are undertaken with another teacher and another class	There is a shift from the challenges of physically attending school meetings to the ease of online attendance that suits all parties	There is a shift from developing policy through accepting evidence relating to the majority, to one accepting that individual circumstances leading to benefits can be considered as viable options or exceptions to a general approach
Interactive whiteboards and learning behaviours	There is a shift from working in a pair and focusing on notes on desks, to having open discussions about widely visible details with others across the class	There is a shift from an individual lecture style to a more varied style using different multimedia resources that involve different forms of input and output	It is recognised by parents and guardians that learning activities are shifting, for example, seeing items and being able to physically move them on a desktop screen	There is a shift from a view of needing to just provide the digital technology to piloting uses that can be developed later into wider implementation linked to professional development

(continued)

Table 5.1 (continued)

Form of technology	Learner behaviours	Teacher behaviours	Parent and guardian behaviours	Adviser and policy maker behaviours
Specific software and learning behaviours	There is a shift from seeing tasks as items that just need to be completed, to items where enjoyment and engagement lead to completion of correct answers, comparing results and competing positively with others	There is a shift from one where a single physical activity is fundamentally important, to one where a series of online activities can produce a range of results when conditions are changed	There is a shift from more limited involvement with a child's homework, to more direct concern and monitoring	There is a shift from considering purchase of educational software as a facility for provision, to one where the purchase needs to be supported by social practice including ways to support professional development

the school, but beyond the school. The uses of digital technologies are in this sense supporting what are sometimes regarded as important soft skills—collaboration, cooperation, groupwork, teamwork and communication.

Chapter 6
Teaching and Teacher Behaviours: Developing Technologies and Accommodating Inquisitiveness

Abstract When considering shifting behaviours across the educational landscape, a number of common key features emerge. The importance and need for professional development is one of these; but within that category, the importance of individuals needing to find ways to accommodate upcoming changes when the digital technologies themselves develop, is clear. Some commentators have considered the need for those involved in education to be able to adapt, but within adaptation, a key factor that is observed is the need for inquisitiveness (Lee & Passey, 2019). It is clear that when individuals, whether learners, teachers, parents and guardians, or advisers and policy makers, take an inquisitive approach to uses of digital technologies to support education, that practices emerge allowing individuals to find ways that they can adopt these for their benefits and the benefits of others. Teachers, parents and guardians, and advisers and policy makers all have a part to play in developing inquisitiveness for learners. In this chapter, the concept of inquisitiveness (Watson, 2016), linked to approaches to lifelong professional development (Van den Broeck et al., 2024), will be explored. Main digital technologies will be considered in this context, both from an historic and contemporary perspective.

Keywords Teaching and teacher behaviours · Desktops and teacher behaviours · Subject topics and teacher behaviours · Information technology and teacher behaviours · The Internet and teacher behaviours · Communications technologies and teacher behaviours · Interactive whiteboards and teacher behaviours · Specific software and teacher behaviours

6.1 Desktops and Inquisitive Behaviours

Desktop machines are often associated with earlier uses of digital technologies. However, they still persist in use, often when a large screen is of benefit to the user and when computer education is the subject of teaching and learning. In some respects, individuals perhaps, still associate the desktop machine with 'a black box',

D. Passey, *Shifting Educational Behaviours*,
https://doi.org/10.1007/978-3-032-18942-4_6

but they do not always consider what is 'in the black box' or what advantages it would have to know this.

Since the 2020s, two concepts have been discussed more widely that highlight the benefits and needs of individuals recognising more about 'the black box'. The first of these is computational thinking. Benefits of developing computational thinking practices from early ages throughout educational sectors have been identified (for example, by Montuori et al., 2024), aiding problem-solving, planning and working memory. The second concept is moving from accepting using digital technologies as a 'consumer' to considering developing them as a 'producer' (see, for example, Auerbach, 2021).

From a desktop perspective, learners from nursery and kindergarten ages upwards can be introduced to activities that support inquisitiveness, linked to the development of computational thinking and digital production. Uses of desktops, however, are more common for higher primary or secondary aged learners, when desktops are used more for activities that are concerned with coding, programming and the development of computer education. The location and numbers of desktops in many schools have changed across the previous few decades, and learners undertaking digital activities now tend to experience access to and uses of desktops in specific lessons within a computer suite, with perhaps additionally only one or a few desktops in class areas or shared areas.

From a teacher perspective, teacher attitudes towards using digital technologies including desktops are still known to vary, within a school, or across a region. Novković Cvetković et al. (2022), for example, identified differences in perceptions across teachers in Serbia. How schools can accommodate this range of differences varies, but in some schools, principals and a lead teacher take responsibility for integrating inquisitiveness as a part of ongoing development of practices (Passey, 2025b), while in other schools, all teachers who use digital technologies enable a balance of plugged and unplugged digital activities across a learner's experience.

While parents and guardians may well have increased access to digital devices, these are not necessarily desktops, and encouraging their children to be inquisitive about computational thinking and production is likely to be supported more from school and through policy encouragement. Liu (2023) demonstrated variations across parental attitudes in the context of online learning, which supports the notion that parents and guardians may be encouraging a consumer approach to a greater extent than a producing approach.

From a policy maker perspective, it is not at all clear that the importance of inquisitiveness is yet being considered as a major concern for educational and social policy. Some national policies have focused much more on the acquisition of subject knowledge, rather than the acquisition of approaches to knowledge that focuses forward. Policies that have been concerned with access to desktops in schools, however, have shifted over the years, from suggesting the creation of desktop rooms, suites or laboratories, to implementation of desktops that are more spread out across a school, integrated into classrooms more, with fewer computer suites that are more dedicated to specific examination and digital qualification subjects (see, for example, Passey, 2025c).

Given the shifts in how desktops are located in educational institutions, the encouragement of inquisitiveness about what is 'in the black box' and what this can mean for 'producing digital outcomes to support specific needs', is likely to require a focus on inquisitiveness through other forms of digital devices that learners of younger ages initially encounter. Applying this encouragement for inquisitiveness to later practices and devices will then be important if that factor is to be adopted at later stages of education and into adult life.

6.2 Subject Influences and Inquisitive Behaviours

It is certainly true that digital devices can be used to support subject learning widely. Applications of uses of digital technologies in different subject areas and for different subject topic areas differ (Anderson et al., 2011; Evans, 2009; Finney & Burnard, 2010; Oldnow & Knights, 2011), with some being recorded in specific case studies (for example, Passey, 2025b, 2025c). However, as the focus of attention may be on the subject rather than the application of the digital technologies to that subject, then how the focus of inquisitiveness about the digital technologies can be ensured is also of importance and concern.

Learner inquisitiveness is a focus that is encouraged in many classrooms and in many schools. Learners may be encouraged to consider how the uses of digital devices are supporting their learning. Learners might also be encouraged to think about how the use of the digital technologies could be adapted to enhance their support of learning. If the adaptation of the digital technologies involves the learner in making changes, not only to the ways that the digital devices are being used, but also to the functionalities of the digital devices in those situations, then inquisitiveness is being encouraged that can develop producing approaches rather than consumer approaches.

From a teacher perspective, if inquisitiveness is to be developed about the digital technologies, then it is the questions that learners are asked that matters. Asking learners to consider how the digital technologies are supporting their subject and topic learning, followed by asking how the digital techniques could be used or applied differently to further enhance their learning, allows learners to take forward this form of inquisitive model whenever they are using digital technologies in other contexts and in the future. That teachers are concerned about learning that applies to the future rather than just to the present is paramount in this respect.

Parents and guardians are in a position to support the development of inquisitiveness. Parents and guardians can support their children in thinking forward, to consider how their learning might be applied to future social, societal and employment contexts. Parents and guardians can support their children to aspire, and a part of that future aspiration is a concern for inquisitiveness. Whilst parents and guardians are likely to be users of digital technologies, these uses may well be consumer forms of uses rather than production forms of uses. When children are undertaking learning activities at home, in whatever subject areas, parents and guardians should seek to encourage inquisitiveness, even if the parent and guardian's past experiences of that subject in their education have not necessarily been positive. The relationship between parent and guardian attitudes to the subject of mathematics, for example, is known to affect their children's engagement and outcomes in that subject in school (Mohr-Schroeder et al., 2017). As parents and guardians have known differences in attitudes towards digital technologies, then this is also likely to affect the development of features including inquisitiveness.

Advisers and policy makers have important roles to play in this field. Policy can influence what parents and guardians think and do, as well as what teachers think and do. Often, policy that can support positive attitudes for teachers is separately concerned at national levels from policy that can influence parents and guardians. There have been national policy approaches taken to seek to address this issue. For example, in the UK, the engagement of parents with schools has been a focus of concern for some decades (see the Department for Children, Schools and Families, 2009). In this case, a single government department focused on education from a family perspective. In jurisdictions where this community perspective does not exist, clear links and strategies are recommended to be made across and between the representative government departments to enable the forms of linkage and communication that are recognised as developing and being relevant to digital technology support and education.

6.3 Information Technology and Inquisitive Behaviours

When information technology facilities became accessible to schools, inquisitiveness about the resources becoming available was often raised in schools, both by learners and by teachers. The advent of the Internet allowed access to textual material initially followed by access to still imagery. At that time, during the late 1980s and early 1990s, investment was often made in education to develop not only the access to these resources, but also investment to develop resources that would be of wider use. As computers became accessible in schools, learners became aware of the ways that computers at that time operated. In some schools and in some localities, the endeavour became increasingly focused on applying the uses of the digital technologies to subject areas. Managing a balance between subject applications and uses, and understanding digital technology functionalities and being able to develop or amend these through adaptation, coding or programming, varied widely across and between jurisdictions.

Learners during the late 1980s and early 1990s were often encouraged to understand how to code and program in order to address specific needs to problems (Papert, 1980). Programming languages such as Basic, Fortran, Cobol and Pascal were introduced into some schools, often on a trial or school club basis. Learners often self-selected to program at that time, while this was also the case for teachers. However, these earlier practices did not always continue or persist for either teachers or for learners.

When information technology became accessible in schools, some teachers used the facilities for demonstration purposes, some used them to support programming, and some adapted and developed the facilities for use within their school. Whilst professional development of teachers became a priority for many countries and areas during the 1990s, few teachers had taken specific qualifications that would enable them to have expertise in either uses of digital technologies or the development of digital technologies to address specific needs. This situation has shifted to some extent, but still the numbers of teachers with specific qualifications is low (see, for example, in the England context, Office for Standards in Education, 2022). Inquisitiveness with regard to digital technologies at that time and subsequently has not necessarily been a focus that has been applied generally or persistently for all learners and all teachers.

At that earlier time, few parents had access to digital technologies at home. Television, radios and cassette recorders were still widely used, and the uptake of home computing was in its infancy. By Dutton et al. (1983), reported that "Personal computers are being acquired by increasingly larger percentages of the public" (p. 5). However, it appears that few families explored options of how to adapt and develop facilities through programming. Hence, the notions of inquisitiveness were restricted often to inquisitiveness about the forms of resources that could be accessed, rather than thinking about the potential that the devices might have for addressing specific problems.

From a policy perspective, the issue of how to address the balance between educational policy that addresses uses of digital technologies to support education at any age and for any subject or topic area, compared to the creation of digital technology devices and facilities through adaptation, programming and coding, has often been raised. With individuals often taking particular stances on this, and supporting either the one option or the other, policies have often been defined in a more polarised way, supporting either the one or the other. More recently (Wing, 2006), the concept of computational thinking has brought forward the need to consider a producer perspective rather than only a consumer perspective for digital technologies being at the centre of the learning focus. With policies that accommodate both approaches, inquisitiveness can be supported that focus on what the digital technologies can provide as well as what they are capable of going on to develop and provide in terms of specific problem-solving.

6.4 The Internet and Networking and Inquisitive Behaviours

Networking and Internet access, coupled with increasing access to multimedia resources over time, led to increased inquisitiveness for many. However, the provision of resources has also led to greater consumer approaches in many instances (Lee, 2023), rather than leading to producer approaches. Instances of levels of access that have led to addiction (Milková et al., 2022; Sawant & Naik, 2022) have highlighted that the consumer approach is evident. Evidence also shows that levels of usage and addiction are not restricted to certain countries. Indeed, some researchers have indicated that neuropsychological changes have been happening on a wide scale (for example, de Barros, 2024), although caution is also raised by researchers that longer-term studies need to be undertaken to fully understand whether or to what extent the changes happen. On a positive note, the researchers also indicate that access has been developed that has increased communication of different sorts, and how this has added time and place opportunities for many (Ulum, 2022).

It is known that learners are using the communication aspects of digital technologies to support enquiries online (Niraula, 2023). Inquisitiveness in this respect is coupled often with two other features—self-directed learning and collaboration. Inquisitiveness is something that is taken forward by the individual, to meet specific needs and interest at different times. Similarly, inquisitiveness and its findings can lead to collaboration, as individuals often share their findings with others, or share the techniques that they have used with others (Johnson et al., 2025).

Teachers play important roles in developing inquisitiveness. This might arise from encouraging enquiry into online resources (Haleem et al., 2022), or it might arise from encouraging learners to build devices using sensors (González Crespo & Burgos, 2019). In both cases, teaching is encouraging and maintaining inquisitiveness. The balance between these two forms of activities is also important—the one is concerned with longer screen time uses while the other involves less screen time. Fostering this balance can also help to offer a model that can lead to balanced levels of use, reducing the possibilities of screen addiction.

Parents and guardians also have important roles to play in terms of supporting the management of forms of communication technologies with their children. Whilst communication technologies can open up many opportunities to develop educational access and outcomes, it is also clear that over-use of communications technologies can arise (Harverson et al., 2025). In some cases, education itself appears to be blamed for the issue. However, it is also clear that learners spend more time at home than they do at school, and practices that happen at home also need to be considered in this respect. Similarly, access to unsuitable social media sites is much more likely to be happening out of school or at home than it is in school, as monitoring can regularly occur in school environments. Responsibility for handling the use of time outside school falls within the realm of parents and guardians, but some governments have taken wide-ranging steps to ban children's access to social media (Goodyear et al., 2024). In terms of supporting the managing of time outside school, some parents might consider online homework to be detrimental, but the benefits that can arise are also clear. Managing the balance at home between onscreen and offscreen time is clearly important and may well be influential in terms of modelling longer-term practice.

As indicated in the previous paragraph, policy is tending to take specific routes with regard to access of at least some forms of communication technologies by young people, that would apply to schools as well as to wider home and social use. Research has started to emerge to offer ways that policy might consider the current situation, where both negative and positive influences arise from Internet access (Byrne & Burton, 2017). With regard to policies in schools, the banning of digital devices has tended to focus on smartphones rather than other devices, with other devices still offering schools the possibilities of developing digital practices in classrooms. However, research is not uniformly agreed that such bans are appropriate for the long-term development of learners (Böttger & Zierer, 2024).

Overall, communication technologies, devices accessing online sites and resources, and the influence of different online sites and resources are areas of focus that are being considered from educational perspectives and areas of focus that are developing as the digital technologies themselves develop. From an educational perspective, it appears to be important that there is adequate distinction considered and made between social communication technologies such as social media and educational technology software, where the benefits of the one and the disadvantages of the other are not confused.

6.5 Interactive Whiteboards and Inquisitive Behaviours

As discussed in the previous chapter, interactive whiteboards have allowed both learner and teacher to gain access to wider multimedia resources, enabling pedagogic approaches to be widened so that collaboration is opened up to wider groups of learners. Through these two features, inquisitiveness could be enhanced for learners—either inquisitiveness about the resources shown on an interactive whiteboard, or inquisitiveness about the ideas shared within a wider learner group. In lessons where interactive whiteboards are used, learners can be aware of and recognise enhanced peer engagement, discussion and collaboration that can result (Mendez-Reguera & Lopez, 2021) and that this can heighten their inquisitiveness about what others both think and say.

From a teacher's perspective, inquisitiveness is a feature that can be supported when interactive whiteboards are used to show resources that engage the learners, where learners feel that they are gaining in terms of their understanding and their abilities to share with others in the class. In this case, the teacher's roles include managing the sequence and forms of activities and the ways that learners are responding, ensuring that voices can be heard so that all feel a part of the sharing and collaboration (Bidaki & Mobasheri, 2013).

Parents and guardians may well have seen interactive whiteboards and some of their uses in schools, especially where parents are either involved in collecting their younger-aged children from school or when they visit classrooms as part of a parental meeting with teachers. Parents and guardians might also be aware of how teachers use the interactive whiteboards from their children's descriptions of activities or when they save items and share them with parents and guardians at home. In this context, inquisitiveness can be maintained through forms of engagement and encouragement.

From a policy maker perspective, the focus has tended to be more on provision of interactive whiteboards and procurement of services of professional development.

However, professional development sessions that are focused on the technology rather than the pedagogy, and which do not provide follow-up sessions to enable sharing and amendment of pedagogical practices, tend to lead to limited uses and outcomes. This has been shown in a number of contexts, in South Africa (Mokoena et al., 2022) and in Saudi Arabia (Al Halaibi, 2021), for example, while some research has indicated ways that have led to successful development of outcomes through enhanced dialogic practices (Hennessy et al., 2017). These studies highlight the importance of developing inquisitiveness in teachers when they are implementing emerging digital technologies.

6.6 Mobile Devices and Inquisitive Behaviours

Mobile devices have enhanced the potential for inquisitiveness across the educational spectrum. However, the distinction between uses of mobile devices for social purposes and educational purposes has sometimes become blurred in certain ways, which has led to some issues.

For learners, mobile devices have enabled a range of practices to emerge that support inquisitiveness. That a learner can use a mobile device with Internet access to search for details when and as needed, can capture audio or images of events and items of interest, and can communicate with individuals at times to suit circumstances, all support inquisitiveness. However, enabling access to mobile devices with Internet capability has been of concern when learners are then able to access inappropriate sites such as those identified on social media.

Managing the uses of mobile devices in schools is crucial if learners are to gain from their uses, and if teachers are satisfied that privacy and safety are adequately accommodated. Early studies into mobile device uses by teachers and learners (Passey, 2010) identified a range of key ways that such devices could support practices that would enhance inquisitiveness. Some later studies have highlighted the roles of specific mobile applications (apps) when teachers and learners use mobile devices (Mouza & Barrett-Greenly, 2015). Going beyond learning uses that involve access to mobile apps, some schools have supported inquisitiveness by encouraging learners to develop their own apps (Passey, 2025c).

In this context, the important roles of parents and guardians and policy makers have been clear even from research undertaken and reported at earlier times. Parents and guardians have a dual role to play when it comes to mobile devices, in that they are the individuals who can see both the social uses and the educational uses of those devices. Monitoring in these situations may be important in order to recognise the extent of uses for each purpose, but parents and guardians may well need strategies to enable them to support their children with educational uses. In a time when digital technologies are becoming more ubiquitous, and when education is recognising that uses of digital technologies can offer benefits for teaching and learning, it can be argued that parents and guardians need to be a part of the wider systemic environment in which education is placed.

From a policy maker perspective, the balance between supporting learning benefit and ensuring safety and privacy can be a balance that is difficult to achieve. Where mobile devices are owned and managed by a school or an educational institution or area, it is possible for those devices to be set up in ways that prevent access to inappropriate sites and resources. However, costs associated with this can be higher than enabling learners to bring in their own mobile devices into schools. Some schools now insist that learners deposit their personal mobiles in secure areas so that they are not accessible during certain times in schools, and that they can only be accessed when teachers are able to manage specific uses in classroom activities.

6.7 Specific Software and Inquisitive Behaviours

Specific software is often seen to support inquisitiveness, both through inquisitiveness about the content, but also inquisitiveness that is engaged when producing or amending software or apps. In terms of the former, specific software with multimedia facilities often engages learners, and the forms of multimedia lead to learners being inquisitive about the content and approaches taken to topics or details. Sharing insights about specific software can itself lead to wider engagement by learners, as they can be inquisitive about what the software offers, as described by other peers. In this context, peer sharing can often offer an important influence on older learners, who may not respond in the same ways to teachers or parents or guardians. Certainly, it is recognised that the 'significant others' (Hatteberg, 2020) may change across a learner's lifetime, and influence may not arise from the same sources across all ages.

A teacher can be a 'significant other', and this is especially true for learners of certain ages and for learners in certain cultural contexts. In terms of specific software and inquisitiveness, teachers can clearly play a major part in suggesting appropriate software or apps and supporting access to software or apps that can encourage inquisitiveness. The choice of apps that support reading or writing, for example, can lead to engagement that then can foster inquisitiveness. However, teachers also recognise that software or apps that can engage one learner may not engage another; understanding the features that support how individuals engage is important in this context.

In terms of individual interests, parents and guardians often know about the specific features that will encourage and support engagement by their children. Encouraging inquisitiveness may, therefore, rely on a sharing of details about factors that can positively support individual engagement. Sharing is being seen to happen in this way in some schools. The boundary between the school and the home can become more blurred through uses of digital technologies, and the importance of communication between teachers and parents and guardians to support a more personalised approach is clear.

Policy makers also can influence inquisitiveness through their support for uses of specific software. Some school and national policies lead to the provision of specific ranges of software that all schools can access. It is important, therefore, that policy makers who need to take decisions about these choices can be appropriately informed about the features that are most likely to support engagement and inquisitiveness, that would come as factors supporting important learning outcomes (Rajabalee et al., 2019).

6.8 Summary of Teaching and Inquisitive Behaviours

In this chapter, the focus has been on behaviours that relate to inquisitiveness, particularly those where teaching is often leading this focus. From across the chapter, a number of behaviours that are shifting have been described and observed in this context. A summary of these shifting behaviours is offered in Table 6.1.

These shifts in behaviours align with educational approaches that are based on questioning and the encouragement of questioning. Whether that questioning arises socially when an individual seeks ideas from others, or whether it arises physically when an individual seeks to address a digital problem, or whether that questioning arises cognitively when an individual seeks to address an interest, nevertheless, questioning is the basis of an inquisitive approach. Whilst there might be a shift in terms of how that inquisitiveness is positively influenced across the age span, nevertheless, maintaining up-to-date practices depends on a willingness to be inquisitive.

Table 6.1 Behaviours associated with teaching and inquisitiveness perspectives of digital technologies

Form of technology	Teaching behaviours	Inquisitiveness behaviours
Desktops and teaching and inquisitiveness behaviours	Shifting to balancing the range of onscreen and offscreen activities	Shifting to activities that require producing rather than consuming approaches
Subject influences and teaching and inquisitiveness behaviours	Shifting to a regular reviewing of how digital technologies can be applied to each subject and topic area	Shifting to enquiring from learners about how the digital technologies are supporting their learning and what else could be done to enhance this
Information technology and teaching and inquisitiveness behaviours	Shifting to an approach that encourages individual and shared exploration of resources	Shifting inquiry from the teacher alone to a wider range of resources including those from digital sources
The Internet, communications technologies, networking and teaching and inquisitiveness behaviours	Shifting to activities that encourage inquisitiveness through enquiry of online resources and the building of digital devices and functions	Shifting to forms of inquisitiveness that encompasses self-directed learning and collaboration
Interactive whiteboards and teaching and inquisitiveness behaviours	Shifting to activities that support inquisitiveness about the resources that are seen and about ideas shared with the wider learner group	Shifting to ways of working both with digital devices and with others, centrally positioning inquisitiveness

(continued)

Table 6.1 (continued)

Form of technology	Teaching behaviours	Inquisitiveness behaviours
Mobile devices and teaching and inquisitiveness behaviours	Shifting to activities that encourage inquisitiveness through multimedia formats	Shifting to a mindset that focuses on problem-solving, creating digital facilities and collaborating with others
Specific software and teaching and inquisitiveness behaviours	Shifting to the selection of software and apps that align with features that will support inquisitiveness of individuals and the group	Shifting to maintaining a sharing focus, that can support the inquisitiveness of others

Chapter 7
Support and Home Behaviours: Encouragement, Awareness and Wider Engagement

Abstract In terms of education, home may not be separate from schools if the settings where education occurs are considered to be important. Digital technologies have increasingly blurred the boundaries between home and school. In some countries and cultural contexts, parents and guardians take a very positive interest and commitment in creating involvement with schools. In other countries and cultural contexts, parents and guardians find that they are increasingly needing to maintain links with schools. In yet other countries and contexts, parents and guardians increasingly hold schools and teachers to account for their children's education. Harris and Goodall (2007) drew an important distinction between parental and guardian involvement and engagement with schools, based fundamentally on the way that parents and guardians view their roles in the education of their children. With involvement, parents and guardians are more remote from mechanisms to support educational processes, whereas with engagement, parents and guardians use mechanisms to support educational processes.

Keywords Desktops and support and home behaviours · Subject topics and support and home behaviours · Information technology and support and home behaviours · The Internet and support and home behaviours · Communications technologies and support and home behaviours · Interactive whiteboards and support and home behaviours · Specific software and support and home behaviours

7.1 Desktops and Support and Home Behaviours

Desktop computers have tended to be superseded in some educational and home contexts, but nevertheless screen size is a crucial concern when it comes to educational practice. Writing on a small screen on a smartphone, for example, is not easy, and the screen does not easily allow for editing and amendment. Developing writing, reading and the creation of imagery such as tables and graphs, or imagery with detail, is often accomplished more easily with access to a large screen. Indeed,

D. Passey, *Shifting Educational Behaviours*,
https://doi.org/10.1007/978-3-032-18942-4_7

research studies have shown that screen size can have both a physical and positive educational effect (see, for example, Pakdee & Sengsoon, 2021).

Learners often now have access to a mobile or smartphone device, but their access to a larger screen size is not necessarily common or uniform. Research has shown that screen size can have effects on abilities to search for information or detail (for example, Raptis et al., 2013). Research advises that learners should be encouraged to consider what educational task they are performing, and what screen size would be most appropriate to undertake it most effectively.

Teachers now often have access to a laptop, both at home and in school. Laptops can vary in size, and this can have effects on their abilities to plan effectively for lessons and activities. Indeed, Caballero-Julia et al. (2024) highlighted that inappropriate screen size from a young age can present health and wellbeing risks. To seek to address this concern, some institutions now provide large monitors for those using laptops or mobile devices. Indeed, in some schools, learners are able to access larger screen facilities in the school before or after school lesson times.

Parents and guardians should be aware of the importance of screen size when their children are using digital devices for educational purposes. Specific educational purposes and activities may require a larger screen to allow features to be moved around, amended or deleted. Whatever the subject or topic, it is likely that a larger screen size will be needed to enable certain activities to be undertaken and for detail to be easily seen.

Policy makers have become aware of the importance of digital access at home. During the Covid-19 pandemic period, for example, some regions and governments supported schools in allowing learners who had limited access at home to take devices home, or they were provided through a loan arrangement that sometimes became more permanent. Ng et al. (2023) describe the approaches taken in Singapore at that time, for example.

7.2 Subject Contributions and Support and Home Behaviours

With regard to home and support behaviours, educational subjects and topics can have significant influences, in a number of ways. Li et al. (2019), from a study in China, concluded that: "Our results show that educational expectations, tutoring, and homework supervision have the largest impact on student academic performance" (p. 139). Given these results, clearly expectations can be influenced by experience and perception of subject choices, and while tutoring by parents or guardians can be supported by those who have specific subject knowledge, homework is likely to be monitored most easily by those with subject interest and perhaps levels of expertise.

In both the school and home environments, learners may well have and exhibit specific subject interests rather than a wider interest in education across the board. This being the case, learners may well engage with some subject areas but not with others, and parents and guardians may recognise these interests and respond to them in a variety of ways.

In terms of engaging with subjects and topics in home environments as well as at school, Balalle (2024) researched engagement outcomes through a literature review and concluded that learners can gain interest through gamification approaches. Certainly, teachers have reported that this approach can support engagement of learners in subject areas that they would not tend to engage with when other approaches have been used. However, in this context, teachers have reported that increasing numbers of learners are experiencing issues that can affect their levels of educational engagement. For example, Lipson et al. (2022) provided evidence across the 2013–2021 period showing the increase in mental health issues for learners in schools in the United States of America (USA). This is clearly an issue that is likely to be recognised in homes as well as in schools.

Parents and guardians may be in a position to support their children with general support at home, providing reassurance and encouragement. They may also be able to support with specific subject areas of interest or expertise or ideas of subjects that could lead to successive employment in the future. They may be less likely to be able to support with mental health issues. In these situations, knowing about the contacts that are possible that teachers in schools would share, may be vitally important. The importance of and ways for parents and guardians being able to work with schools to support approaches that can address behavioural issues is highlighted in the research literature (Butler et al., 2022; Shucksmith et al., 2010).

Whilst educational policy often offers ways to support individuals who can benefit from access to and uses of assistive technologies, there is less focus currently seen in policy documentation on the digital technology support that would enable more focused support to address disengagement and mental health issues through digital engagement approaches. Nevertheless, access to some digital apps has been trialled (Hugh-Jones et al., 2022) and some schools are actively involved in exploring different options.

7.3 Information Technology and Support and Home Behaviours

Access to information technology-enabled devices undoubtedly shifted behaviours for many people, across the age range, from the time that they were introduced and available in schools and homes. Even prior to Internet access, facilities such as video and audio recording cassettes and Compact Disc-Read Only Memory (CD-ROM) items enabled wider populations to gain from increasingly detailed resources from expanded contexts outside of their initial ranges of understanding, through audio and video, as well as text and still image formats. In this respect, early research highlighted the potential impacts of earlier forms of digital technologies on learning—CD-ROMs, for example (Hammond, 1995).

These earlier forms of digital technologies were used in schools, in some cases extensively. Perzylo (2006), for example, highlighted how uses of CD-ROMs in schools enabled learners to "engage more of their senses in the learning process as well as to develop their information searching skills and strategies" (p. 191). Similarly, learners have long had access to audio cassette recordings to support learning of subjects such languages, although these have more recently been superseded by podcasts (Rosell-Aguilar, 2015). Some learners have also gained access to these forms of resources within their homes.

Other early forms of digital technology were used in schools but not in homes. Teachers often used the range of early information technology-enabled devices to support subject and topic learning. In some cases, this was done on an individual learner basis, where a single learner had access to a device for a specific period of time; for example, this was commonly the case with uses of language laboratories (Mohammed, 2017). In other cases, teachers used access to these forms of devices with pairs or small groups of learners, ensuring that discussion about the topic was possible, and also presenting them with questions to answer once they had gained from interaction with the resources (from reading, viewing, or listening, for example).

Parents and guardians would also have likely accessed these earlier forms of digital technology devices, but more likely for social and entertainment purposes. Indeed, at that time, the development of 'edutainment' had already been in process for some years, having been initiated in 1975 (Aksakal, 2015). Some parents and guardians provided access for their children to these forms of resources, including provision for some where payment for access was required. In other cases, resource access was still largely through radio and television (Giraldo et al., 2022).

Advisers and policy makers have continued to grapple with local challenges that can determine access to information technology-enabled resources, but focusing on school rather than home settings. As these original resources did not require Internet access, but were known to be beneficial in supporting learning, these resources were often considered as an interim provision whilst movement to Internet-enabled access was developed.

7.4 The Internet and Networking and Support and Home Behaviours

Since the advent of local- and wide-area networking, access to online resources for many people has increased dramatically. This has affected potential access within homes as well as in schools. This has also meant that access to resources for educational purposes has paralleled access for social and entertainment purposes. For learners, this creates a potential situation where a balance across these access purposes is perhaps more challenging to achieve. Whilst online access for employment purposes also needs to be balanced with that for social purposes for many people, younger learners may not have the same choice with regard to how they balance access (and hence, onscreen) time. Younger learners may need to access resources onscreen as required by teachers, at home as well as in school, and the shifting home situations that many parents and guardians are finding (Yaffe et al., 2024), when they are often coping with employment needs at home, is sometimes meaning that children are directed to use onscreen time for entertainment purposes increasingly.

The pattern of access across homes and schools by learners is certainly not uniform. Puspita and Rohedi (2018), for example, from a sample of vocational high students in Indonesia, found that access for educational purposes varied across the sample widely, without a particularly strong mode arising. As Ghoshal and Upadhyay (2023) concluded, "By harnessing the positive aspects of the internet while being mindful of its potential pitfalls, students can fully maximise its impact on their studies and academic success" (p. 41). Ensuring a balance of onscreen time is clearly a behavioural need that learners have to accommodate, particularly in home settings where monitoring of onscreen time might be happening to a lesser extent.

Teachers have a crucial role to play in supporting learners with help in balancing their onscreen time. From early years, learners should ideally be exposed to the variety of activities that provide that balance across the curriculum and across the school day and year (Passey, 2025b). These practices need to persist into later years when learners are in secondary or high schools (Passey, 2025c). If teachers and schools can also support and guide parents and guardians in this respect, then important models could be developed before the next generation of digital technologies provides both enhanced onscreen and consumer-provided opportunities.

Research shows that parents' and guardians' perceptions about levels of appropriate onscreen time for their children is not uniform (Chong et al., 2023). The researchers in this case also identified some of the wider strategies that parents and guardians use to manage onscreen time. In other cases, it is known that guidance from schools and teachers can be of value in supporting parents and guardians, as they often need to be aware of the ways that schools and teachers manage this balance, so that they can either model it in this way themselves, or consider the levels that this might suggest they seek to achieve in their home situations.

Advisers and policy makers are also concerned with levels of onscreen time, not only of learners, but also in their own cases. The issue of long durations of onscreen time arose during the Covid-19 pandemic, when learners were often faced with the need to spend more onscreen time than had been needed previously (Zahedi et al., 2021). However, the issue of prolonged onscreen times and its effects on wellbeing have persisted, and some governments and education departments have taken action to seek to manage this in particular ways, through banning of personal devices in schools, for example (House of Commons Education Committee, 2024).

7.5 Interactive Whiteboards and Support and Home Behaviours

Whilst uses of interactive whiteboards require onscreen engagement, the form of these devices is such that they offer a large screen view that can be seen from a distance across a classroom. Whilst there are key advantages to uses of this format for learning, as discussed in earlier chapters, the system nevertheless provides a screen, and it could be argued that this adds to the onscreen time that learners might experience. In practice, however, teachers do not usually use this facility for the entirety of a lesson. Across a lesson, a number of activities would normally be planned, some using and some not using the interactive whiteboard facilities.

Lesson planning and learner support for uses of interactive whiteboards within lessons would normally be managed by teachers in classrooms. Behaviours that have been enhanced by the use of interactive whiteboards include ease of visibility of resources and details by a whole class, discussions that a whole class can take part in, collaboration in working with others at the interactive whiteboard, and sharing ideas and creating responses into images or tables. Overall, the support behaviours are enabling learners to focus outwards from their desks and books rather than always focusing inwards.

In classrooms with interactive whiteboards, and considering the range of positive outcomes stated in the previous paragraph, teachers have used interactive whiteboards in a range of ways that influence both support in school and home behaviours. Support behaviours that have been influenced include enhancing the variety of resources that learners can access, enhancing visibility of resources and details, creating activities that allow learners to interact directly with others at the interactive whiteboard, and sharing ideas and outcomes that can be discussed with the whole class or with groups within the class. In terms of home behaviours, as screens can be saved, teachers have used this facility in order to send details of lesson activities and individual children's interactions when using these facilities to parents and guardians, sometimes showing work that learners have completed, and sometimes showing details of work that should be completed at home.

With likely restricted access to an interactive whiteboard at home, parents and guardians have largely been involved in seeing them and their uses when teachers send them saved screens from lessons. Parents and guardians may then be aware of the sorts of activities that their children are undertaking in lessons, or they become aware of the work that teachers wish the children to complete at home. Sometimes, parents and guardians are asked if images of activities or learning outcomes generated at home can be sent to them, so that they can share these with the wider class via the interactive whiteboard. This latter approach has tended to be used more during the time of the Covid-19 pandemic, when activities at home were often recorded and shared with teachers and other learners.

Home access to interactive whiteboards is not known to have been a focus of educational policy. The interactive whiteboard facility is designed for large rooms that cater for group work and group discussion. For schools, the provision of interactive whiteboards has often resulted from a policy decision at a local, regional or national level. The cost of interactive whiteboards has decreased over the years, and there can be a considerable lifespan of an interactive whiteboard, so long as the system is able to accept software updates. More recently, the processing unit of interactive whiteboards has been uncoupled from the visual display board, so that updated processors can replace earlier processors that do not have the same levels of functionality. At a policy level, this has been recognised in helping to consider and plan replacement patterns.

7.6 Mobile Devices and Support and Home Behaviours

Considering devices that are not designed for large room display purposes, it can be argued that the development and uses of mobile devices have shifted educational behaviours in major ways. The concept of mobile learning, or m-learning, was introduced in the early 2000s (Traxler, 2009), and benefits arising for learners and teachers have since continued to be identified (for example, by Garzón et al., 2024).

Whilst access in school environments has become an issue for some schools and jurisdictions, due to learners sometimes accessing social media and other sites during lessons or even on occasions using the devices in ways that have led to bullying, learners themselves have often reported the benefits that they have gained from mobile device use, whether a laptop, tablet or smartphone. In some local areas and regions, mobile devices, generally in the form of smartphones, are the only accessible hardware devices that enable learners to gain from online access. In Japan, for example, smartphones are widely used by learners, who have reported ease of use and learning benefits arising, for example, when learning English vocabulary (Thornton & Houser, 2005). Learners also report that mobile devices allow them to take and continue their learning beyond the school, in home and external settings.

From the teachers' perspectives, Passey (2010) identified a number of ways that activities can support positive learning behaviours: "Review and reflect" (capturing audio, imagery, and video during and outside lessons, then reflecting on what had been covered, key elements learned, and how ideas might be taken further outside the classroom); "Think forward" (accessing future topics via the Internet and capturing relevant thoughts or ideas to contribute in class or through online discussions); "Listen to my explanations" (recording audio to complete homework assignments followed by teachers marking these verbal explanations); "Snap and show" (capturing downloaded imagery made accessible to parents so that they can see and discuss events that have happened in school); "This is what I've done and how I've done it" (creating presentations of how mobile technologies have been used to tackle particular activities, recorded and made accessible on appropriate websites for teachers and parents to see); and "Tell me how I could improve this" (sharing their work in multimedia formats with peers, mentors, teachers, or trusted adults to seek evaluative feedback, assessments of their work, and ideas for improvement).

If the mobile device is home-owned, then it is possible that parents and guardians will see details that their children have gathered on the device. Sharing of details becomes easier in this respect, although children will need to know about ways that details should be filed and stored, so that access to them is possible at a later time. Parents and guardians may well be able to support this form of important management behaviour.

Policy makers may well experience challenges with regard to guidelines about mobile device uses in schools. In part, these challenges can arise as a consequence of external levels of mobile device uses and the forms of uses that happen, including those in the home. Whilst smartphones have been banned in certain schools and jurisdictions, other schools and jurisdictions have supported the uses of mobile devices. Sometimes, these devices have been school-owned, whilst in other cases they have been home-owned. However, the banning of personal smartphone devices should not be confused with the uses of mobile devices in schools to support learning. There is a difference between social uses that interfere with learning, and educational uses that benefit learning. This distinction is an important one that may need to be, and in some cases is, managed locally (in schools and classrooms) and in policy and its guidelines.

7.7 Specific Software and Support and Home Behaviours

Whilst specific software can support a range of subject and topic areas, it is clear that the range of software applied to education is now becoming wider, so that learners with more specific needs can also benefit from their use. For example, Kirkpatrick et al. (2022) reviewed research that showed how software had been used to address behavioural challenges, while Loveys and Butler (2023) reviewed research that showed how software had been used to support independent learning of those with visual impairment. The access to and the uses of these forms of software can apply equally in home and school settings.

There are wide examples of how digital technologies can support students with specific needs (Passey, 2013). Rizk and Hillier (2022), from their study of digital uses in schools in Canada, including uses of robotics, interactive whiteboards and iPads, reported that: "digital technologies can play a major role in boosting engagement through support and greater access to classroom content and learning processes" (p.n.p.). Research has also shown how digital technologies can support learning where learners have specific needs. For example, Rehman et al. (2024) studied the benefits and challenges of implementing digital technologies to support learners with hearing impairment in schools in Pakistan. Research has also focused on those emerging software packages and devices that can support specific needs. From research into the emerging digital technology of artificial intelligence (AI), it is clear that the potential to enhance engagement in a range of instances has already been recognised. For example, Lavric et al. (2024) explored possibilities in this context for those with visual impairment.

These emerging forms of digital technologies are likely to be accessible within home settings as well as within school settings. In the case of AI technologies, to understand the potential for AI-driven assistive technologies to support teachers in classroom practice, researchers (Kooli & Chakraoui, 2025) recommend that appropriate professional development is put in place. In this context, Şahin et al. (2024) explored the factors that supported or hindered teachers in implementing assistive technologies in classroom practices, highlighting the importance of social influence (from parents and guardians, other teachers and professionals, as well as from policy), enjoyment (of seeing the end outcomes and results for learners) and innovativeness (aligning with the feature of inquisitiveness discussed in an earlier chapter).

Parents and guardians with children who have specific needs may receive guidance from schools about ways that digital technologies might support their children, or they may gain this guidance from external professionals. Apps et al. (2024) showed in their study that parents and guardians that they sampled had generally positive views about uses of digital technologies in engaging with rehabilitation services in the United Kingdom (UK), as long as in-person communication was also supported. However, Palmqvist and Danielsson (2020), in their study in Sweden, indicated that parents and guardians needed more support about how to set up activities and uses of assistive technologies that could enhance cognitive outcomes that could match their children's needs.

From a policy perspective, there are key challenges in creating useable and effective policy guidelines about uses of specific software in schools and homes, given that the scope and variation that needs to be considered is high. Fernández-Batanero et al. (2022) highlighted the need for policy to consider three key factors—teacher professional development, adequate information, and accessibility to the devices and software. Research has indicated that, from a policy perspective, uses of assistive technologies to support specific needs can lead to more inclusive practice (Jacob et al., 2024). But other research highlights the challenges and indicates the need for policy to engage with the ways that involve parents and guardians and not just teachers and leaders in schools (Alharbi, 2016).

7.8 Summary of Support and Home Behaviours

In this chapter, the focus has been on support and home behaviours that relate to learners, teachers, parents and guardians, and advisers and policy makers. These behaviours have been considered through the lens of a number of forms of digital technologies that are likely to be encountered in educational practice or in home environments (sometimes occasionally, as is the case of interactive whiteboards, and sometimes perhaps commonly, as is the case of mobile devices). From across the chapter, a number of behaviours that are shifting have been described and observed in this context. A summary of these shifting behaviours is offered in Table 7.1.

These shifts in behaviours align with educational approaches that are concerned with ongoing professional development and ongoing sharing across those who are

Table 7.1 Behaviours associated with digital technologies that relate to support and home situations

Form of technology	Support behaviours	Home behaviours
Desktops and support and home behaviours	Consideration is given to how access to appropriate screen size that relates to activities that are being undertaken might be accommodated	Parents and guardians are aware of how the school might support their children if activities require a screen size that they cannot necessarily provide at home
Subject influences and support and home behaviours	There is awareness of digital technologies that can support engagement with subject and topics that are not regarded by learners as interesting	There is awareness of school and external contacts available if children are in need of specific mental health or behavioural support
Information technology and support and home behaviours	Access to digital technologies that do not necessarily require Internet access are considered where possible for learning support as appropriate	Where Internet access is not possible, access to resources through offline means is considered where possible
The Internet, communications technologies, networking and support and home behaviours	How to develop practice that creates a balance between onscreen and offscreen time and activities is accommodated	There is guidance from schools or policy on how to create onscreen and offscreen time balance at home to match educational needs
Interactive whiteboards and support and home behaviours	Activities in settings where interactive whiteboards are used enable learners to focus outwards from their desks and books	Home situations can view saved details from interactive whiteboard sessions and activities to enhance engagement at home
Mobile devices and support and home behaviours	Access to and uses of mobile devices for educational purposes is separated from access and uses of mobile devices for social purposes	Guidance about monitoring mobile device uses and supporting management of recorded details for educational purposes is accommodated where possible
Specific software and support and home behaviours	Specific needs of learners are matched to the ways that digital technologies can support learning and cognitive functioning	Awareness of forms of digital technologies that can support specific learning needs and how these can be matched to the individual are made known to parents and guardians

involved with and support educational endeavour. Digital technologies are developing that allow greater support for the individual, but to enable this to happen across schools and in homes, this requires more sharing and understanding, across the range of those who are involved. In this context, systemic approaches need to consider the challenges that are present and likely to arise, as well as the benefits. Whilst there might be a shift in terms of how digital technologies can support the individual, nevertheless, addressing issues such as high levels of onscreen time, lack of access to appropriate devices, and safety when online, all need to be considered by all those involved (learners, teachers, parents and guardians, and advisers and policy makers).

Chapter 8
Peer and Online Behaviours: Time, Place and the Psychologies of Reliance and Independence

Abstract Digital technologies now enable, given that access is possible, ease of online communication. These forms of communication, whether via text, via forums, audio or video conferencing, can be used across a wide age range for a variety of purposes. An element of online behaviours that has shifted as a consequence of these facilities is the level of peer interactions in educational contexts. Peers are seen to be communicating and discussing points concerned with learning and learning tasks, to be sharing documents and drafts, and to be engaged with both of these activities simultaneously. Communication facilities now enable synchronous as well as asynchronous interactions, and there is a reported shift in the level of each of these instances, both inside and outside the school.

Keywords Peer and online behaviours · Desktops and peer and online behaviours · Subject topics and peer and online behaviours · Information technology and peer and online behaviours · The Internet and peer and online behaviours · Communications technologies and peer and online behaviours · Interactive whiteboards and peer and online behaviours · Specific software and peer and online behaviours

8.1 Desktops and Peer and Online Behaviours

Desktops or devices with larger screens have traditionally been used as a means to support online conference-style communication, especially when more than two people are involved in an online call or meeting. These forms of video communication increased dramatically during the Covid-19 pandemic, and in some schools and educational institutions, the levels since that time have remained higher than they had been prior to the pandemic.

The benefits of online learning have been widely researched, but the benefits of online peer learning have been researched to a lesser extent. Dao et al. (2024) gathered evidence from teachers in Vietnam about their perceptions of the benefits for their

D. Passey, *Shifting Educational Behaviours*,
https://doi.org/10.1007/978-3-032-18942-4_8

learners when engaged in the learning of English. A notable finding was the positive benefit arising from peer interactions. An et al. (2022) gathered evidence from learners during the Covid-19 pandemic, and they found that attitudes towards peer interaction could influence learners' motivations to engage in online learning, and that it could also influence their critical thinking abilities, as well as problem-solving and self-efficacy. This suggested that the online learning medium was supporting features of independent and self-regulated learning.

Moving towards a more learner-independent and self-regulated approach can require a shift in terms of teaching practice. He et al. (2025) found from a study in China that learner perceptions of teacher support influenced their interactions in the online environment, particularly regarding their views of their autonomy, their competence, interaction and engagement. Clearly, the approach that teachers take in the online environment can affect how learners feel they can engage, and to what extent they can establish peer networks. Indeed, research in the USA (Black et al., 2025) indicated that peer networks were important, as "peer social network selection and influence effects impact individual and group academic functioning and achievement outcomes across age groups in adolescence" and "structural effects and network position may be of special importance, particularly for low-achieving youth" (p. 1).

For parents and guardians, there are important messages to consider with regard to peer communication and networking. Whilst onscreen time is an important factor to consider, so too are the positive effects of peer networking that allow children to engage with others. Lao (2025), from a pioneering study in China, found that parent–child relationships of a peer were able to influence a child's cognitive and emotional state. There are factors that can affect peer relationships and learning outcomes, therefore, in online environments that happen in homes as well as in face-to-face environments.

How policy makers handle and consider peer interactions in online environments for learning can vary widely. In some jurisdictions and schools, peer interactions are not positively supported, whilst in others they are. The influence that teachers can have on peer interactions is clear from the literature (Chen et al., 2020). In view of this, it would be recommended that policy considers how to advise teachers about how they might manage peer interactions online most effectively (Ong & Quek, 2023).

8.2 Subject Contributions and Peer and Online Behaviours

Peer interactions have often been a focus with regard to certain subjects and topics for learning. Peers have often discussed subjects that either interest them, or subjects where one peer might help another. Indeed, peer help has sometimes been regarded as going beyond what should happen, as 'cheating' is sometimes felt to occur when one peer only 'copies' from another. On the other hand, Garcia (2016) explored how a learner in an elementary school in the USA gained with and without peer support and indicated that benefits did arise.

Peer learning in schools is often associated with collaborative activities, where learners work in groups to develop specific outcomes. Schulz et al. (2025), for example, described collaborative activities in primary school settings where young learners developed a video recording output. In this context, learners were involved in peer learning through "exchanging organisational tips, informing each other, or sharing different points of view" (p.n.p.).

In some schools, teachers have supported peer learning focused on using digital technologies, by involving and developing practices for those that have been termed 'digital leaders' or 'digital advocates'. In some schools, digital leaders have supported their peers, both in the same class (of the same age range) and in other classes, perhaps with younger learners (Passey, 2025b), whilst in other schools, digital leaders have supported teachers as well as learners (Passey, 2014). In the former cases, digital leaders have been seen to support other learners both in terms of uses of digital technologies as well as in the coding of programs (such as creating outputs that address a specific need or problem).

Research that explores how children at home use digital technologies to engage with other children outside their homes tends to arise from studies that explore wider pictures of digital use, rather than focusing specifically on this study area. It is known that children have used telephones in the past to discuss aspects of subject or topic learning with other children, and certainly now this is likely to be happening more through smartphone and video-conferencing facilities. Whilst some teachers are concerned about the amount of peer support that might lead to inaccurate outcomes of activities, where the influence of a peer is clear, there is opportunity for studies to explore this to a greater extent in a digital context.

From an adviser and policy perspective, research on peer learning shows educational benefits, often highlighting ways that peer-learning activities lead to important skills that are likely to support learners in the future. For example, collaborative practice leading to questioning and discussion, abilities for listening and sharing, and generating ideas that can shape outcomes. How these are built into educational practice is likely to be based largely on classroom and home perceptions of the benefits and challenges that can arise, focusing perhaps on those associated with implementation.

8.3 Information Technology and Peer and Online Behaviours

Information technology resources were often accessed in schools at the times they were introduced through activities involving pairs or small groups of learners. This form of grouping was initially set up to address limited hardware facilities, as well as to encourage discussion, sharing and checking of details and outcomes. To some extent, these forms of practice have persisted, even in cases where hardware access is not limited to the same extent.

However, information technology resources have also been accessed by individual learners, and some teachers and schools would suggest that this practice has its benefits. Indeed, Rodrigues et al. (1999), in their study about uses of CD-ROMs to support science learning in schools, found that pair and group access had not been implemented, while individual access was reported widely. However, successful group work practices have developed further across schools in many jurisdictions since that time.

Teachers have often been involved in professional development opportunities when information technology has been introduced into schools. Many researchers continue to argue for the need for continued professional development as digital technologies continue to develop and emerge (for example, Gondwe, 2021). Specific forms of digital technology have been used and studied, where peer interaction has both been supported and where it has tended not to be used. Audio books are a form of information technology that has persisted in educational use for some decades, and its positive use by teachers has been documented across a long time period (Walter, 2023). However, peer use has been reported less commonly.

Parents and guardians have used television as a form of information technology to support their children's understanding and learning, often with a number of children viewing at the same time. Kostyrka-Allchorne et al. (2017) reviewed the literature about uses of television at home with younger children and concluded that: "watching high-quality educational content during preschool years improves children's basic academic skills and predicts subsequent positive academic performance. Conversely, television viewing in infancy is disruptive to play; it reduces the quality and quantity of child-parent interactions and is associated with inattentive/hyperactive behaviours, lower executive functions, and language delay, at least in the short-term" (p. 19).

Educational policies and guidelines have shifted with regard to approaches and concerns about peer learning related to information technology. At times, individual access has been recommended, whereas at other times, group working has been recommended. Sometimes, this has been related to the forms of information technology, and certainly the modes of activity recommended have been different in many cases. For example, for audio books, listening is the major mode of interaction, whilst for video cassettes, the major mode has been watching and listening. In both of these cases, peer interactions have been reported that have supported understanding and sharing.

8.4 The Internet, Networking and Peer and Online Behaviours

The advent of communication technologies has supported multimedia formats to greater extents, which includes a number of active modes of interaction. Speaking as well as listening, creating as well as watching, for example, are now all possible using forms of communication technologies. These different forms clearly affect both peer and online behaviours.

Learners have taken advantage of both the multimedia and communications aspect of Internet-supported resources. For enhancing speaking and listening skills of learners of English as a Foreign Language (EFL), for example, Tran et al. (2024) reported on an "innovative practice where conversational interaction is fostered through an online talk project in which EFL learners from Vietnam have weekly conversations with volunteer English speakers from other countries via video-conferencing platforms" (p. 1). Communication technologies enable peer learning to happen online.

Considering active modes of interaction, in some schools, teachers are able to take advantage of areas called Makerspaces: "a collaborative and hands-on learning environment where individuals come together to create, experiment, and innovate using various tools and materials" (Amayou et al., 2025). These researchers have shown that collaborative groupwork can be undertaken in Makerspaces, through project-based learning, but that there are also significant challenges for teachers in implementing these forms of practice successfully. A part of those challenges concerns how to effectively manage group work interactions.

In a home context, parents and guardians may well be aware of peer interactions, both face-to-face and online, during their children's time in schools. Parents and guardians may be aware of the social advantages and outcomes arising from managed peer interactions, such as reports from teachers about the communication development of their young children. In many instances, however, parental involvement may decrease as their children become older, and the value of peer learning may not be so obvious to them.

In terms of advice and policy, Tang et al. (2022) from their study of online behaviours offer recommendations for policy: "strategies and constructive recommendations for educators to develop a new online learning pedagogy, construct sustainable online peer learning, and effectively manage students' online learning" (p. 12449). Whilst the development of educational independence is important, this needs to be balanced with the development of peer learning behaviours that can lead to positive outcomes in terms of communication, cooperation, collaboration and teamwork.

8.5 Interactive Whiteboards and Peer and Online Behaviours

Interactive whiteboards have enabled a shifting of classroom activities and classroom behaviours. This has affected learners and teachers to the greatest extents, but parents and guardians may have been affected also. These shifts have related both to how peers can collaborate and also how online behaviours can be organised to gain the most from the facilities that are accessible.

For learners, interactive whiteboards have enhanced a range of opportunities that expand possibilities for collaborative activity. Collaborative writing using interactive whiteboards, for example, has been shown to have positive effects on writing performance and co-regulation (Teng, 2021). Whilst there is potential for peer collaboration in mathematics learning using interactive whiteboards, De Vita et al. (2014) argue that this is not necessarily prevalent and that professional development is needed to support teachers in developing this practice to a greater extent.

Low incidences of uses of interactive whiteboards in the teaching of other subject areas have also been identified. Asare et al. (2023), for example, identified low levels of uses in physical education, whilst they argue that the potential for peer learning through this medium is high. In the Australian context, Murcia and Sheffield (2010) found that the teaching of science using interactive whiteboards could enhance the way that learners discussed science.

Many parents and guardians have had less direct experience with interactive whiteboards than their children. However, in terms of online behaviours, parents and guardians may well have received messages from teachers that either show details of activities undertaken in an interactive whiteboard (and using other classroom facilities) during the day, or details of tasks to be completed at home. In the case of younger children, captured screen images of work completed by children may well be shared with parents and guardians. At older ages, parents and guardians are more likely to receive details of tasks to be completed by learners at home. In the former case, the shift in behaviours is from being told about what children were doing during the day, to being shown what they were doing. In the latter case, the shift is from a paper-based record of tasks to be completed at home to an electronic form of record that can be reviewed easily.

Access to interactive whiteboards tended to be a focus of concern for advisers and policy makers at an earlier time period. Early uses and implementation of interactive whiteboards were also a focus of interest for researchers, some exploring policy issues and recommendations (Moss & Jewitt, 2010, for example). At this current time, advisers and policy makers are perhaps more concerned with the rationale for replacement or maintenance of these systems.

8.6 Mobile Devices and Peer and Online Behaviours

Mobile devices, whether laptops, tablets or smartphones, for example, have enabled wider and more regular peer communication, as well as opportunities to learn in contexts that are more time and place independent than they were prior to these devices being available. As described in previous chapters, mobile devices have allowed learners to open discussions with other learners and teachers outside of formal classroom lessons, and they have enabled learners to capture details that can be reviewed at later times and in places that are remote from the classroom.

Mobile device uses have influenced both peer and online behaviours of learners. For example, peers in classrooms can often see results from others when they respond on a mobile device, as the results can then be displayed by the teacher on a classroom interactive whiteboard. Similarly, learners can use the online environment to gather details to complete tasks, the device enabling individual online access in ways not feasible previously.

For teachers, mobile device uses in classrooms have often posed challenges in terms of adopting different forms of pedagogy and activities. Some of these relate to enabling peer interaction and collaboration. In this context, Burke et al. (2025), for example, in their study, identified that where learners were benefiting, teachers had coupled innovatory practices with digital pedagogies. Teachers who create successful new activities may well be considering their background understanding of what forms of activities would be likely to impinge on more effective learner outcomes.

Parents and guardians may well use mobile devices frequently, albeit for different purposes from their children. However, Rose et al. (2022), in a study that compared children's views about mobile device uses and policies in schools with their parents or guardians, found that they "held shared views of the importance of having phones to keep in contact alongside an awareness of the risks" (p. 1418). Undoubtedly, outside school, peers can use smartphones and mobile devices to quickly contact a peer if they wish to ask a question about a specific learning activity.

From a policy perspective, one issue that has been raised is that if mobile devices are felt to be of value in schools, then who should provide them and under what conditions should they be used. From a study in schools in Germany, researchers (Laumann et al., 2024) concluded that: "organizational, economic, and ecological aspects appear to be the main factors in deciding about the mobile device access concept" (p. 9463). Whilst mobile devices can support learning practices, different forms of peer learning, others not involving the uses of mobile devices, clearly need to be considered and to be balanced across the systemic educational environment.

8.7 Specific Software and Peer and Online Behaviours

Uses of specific software can also create a shift in both peer and online behaviours. For example, software located by one learner can be shared with peers, and this sharing might occur through a learner sharing an online link rather than sending a message online to provide only a name or indirect contact details.

In the context of peer learning, groups or teams of learners can be involved in creative digital producer activity. For example, some schools support learners in working together in teams, either in a face-to-face group or in an online group, in creating and coding an online game (Hughes-Roberts et al., 2023). This form of activity has been developed also for groups of learners who tend to be disengaged with other forms of learning in schools. Through this form of activity, both engagement and peer collaboration have been found to be enhanced.

Teachers are also involved in peer learning. Teachers now use online environments for professional development and for sharing examples of their classroom practices. Specific software to support these forms of collaborative and peer collaboration have been developed in some cases, while in others software such as Google Meet[1] or Zoom[2] have been used. de Jong et al. (2022), in their study of teacher collaboration online, found that there were three main categories of collaboration—sharing, experimenting, and designing. Teachers have been seen to be involved in all three of these categories when they work together online. Software that supports peer interactions of teachers, both within and across schools, has been considered by many jurisdictions when they are looking to implement virtual learning environments, such as those supported by Google Meet or by Microsoft Teams.[3]

In home contexts, parents and guardians can be guided by schools and teachers about the sorts of software that might be most suitable for their children. In some cases, schools provide access to software that their children can use both in school and at home. But in other cases, parents and guardians may try to select software themselves that they feel would be suitable. Brito and Dias (2020) gathered evidence from parents and guardians across Portugal and found that selection was often for quiz and puzzle formats, not based on the views of the children or the media formats that they would have felt most appropriate or of interest. By contrast, Montazami et al. (2022) found that, in North America, parents and guardians tended to select apps that would be considered educationally useful.

When considering software for schools, it is possible that advisers and policy makers are concerned principally with the potential that the software has to support educational outcomes. Those educational outcomes might not initially be thought of in terms of peer support or collaborative endeavour, yet these are skills that are identified as being desirable (or even crucial) for likely future society and employment scenarios. Consideration of peer online behaviours is likely to be, in the contemporary context, concerned with aspects of online safety and protection. Whilst still wishing to support peer interactions, jurisdictions may utilise protected networks or may implement specific software to ensure limited access to software and websites that are likely to be of any potential harm for learners.

8.8 Summary of Peer and Online Behaviours

In this chapter, the focus has been on peer and online behaviours that relate to learners, teachers, parents and guardians, and advisers and policy makers. These behaviours have been considered through the lens of the forms of digital technologies that have and are used in educational practice or, in some cases, in home environments. Across the chapter, behaviours that are shifting have been described and observed. A summary of these shifting behaviours is offered in Table 8.1.

---

[1] https://edu.google.co.uk/intl/ALL_us/workspace-for-education/products/meet/.

[2] https://www.zoom.com/.

[3] https://www.microsoft.com/en-gb/microsoft-teams/free?msockid=2b77ea2bd6f969ec2cf4fc8bd7676857.

Table 8.1 Behaviours associated with digital technologies that relate to peer and online contexts

Form of technology	Peer behaviours	Online behaviours
Desktops and peer and online behaviours	When working in groups, learners are aware of the screen sizes needed to carry out activities successfully	Online behaviours to support educational practices are considered in terms of the context of the location, space, screen size, environmental comfort, and whether and how peripheral digital technologies might be needed and available
Subject influences and peer and online behaviours	In terms of subjects or topics of less interest, learners are seen to engage with and gain from gamification formats that might involve competing with peers or with peers creating video recordings	For supporting ongoing uses of the online environment, peer support and support from digital leaders and advocates is increasing in schools
Information technology and peer and online behaviours	Continued engagement with digital resources such as audio books is reported	Online behaviours that support listening and viewing are still appropriate and of value to learners, especially those of younger ages
The Internet, communications technologies, networking and peer and online behaviours	Peer interactions are increasingly taking advantage of both multimedia and online communication via video conferencing	Makerspaces are enabling collaborative learning practices that are leading to long-term skills appropriate for society and employment
Interactive whiteboards and peer and online behaviours	Uses of large digital screens can enable an outward focus and wider discussion, rather than a narrow focus and limited discussion	Online facilities enable details from activities to be saved and shared with others beyond a classroom, including parents and guardians
Mobile devices and peer and online behaviours	Peer interaction is being encouraged through shared responses from individual mobile devices being shown on a large central screen	Online behaviour can be distinguished between mobile device uses for educational purposes and mobile device uses for social purposes
Specific software and peer and online behaviours	Peer learning and sharing through appropriate uses of digital facilities is being increasingly used by teachers for professional development purposes	Parents and guardians value advice and guidance from schools and teachers or from policy about the selection of software that might be most appropriate for their children to engage with other peers

These shifts in behaviours align with educational approaches that are concerned with peer learning, ongoing professional development and ongoing concerns about ensuring safety and protection for all online. Digital technologies are developing that allow greater support for the individual, but this focus can be balanced through the provision of appropriate peer interactions, across the age range. Although there are challenges as well as benefits, evidence indicates that peer learning that leads to important future skill outcomes such as enhanced communication, cooperation, collaboration and teamwork abilities, should be carefully considered and managed, and online access should accommodate provision that ensures safety and protection for all concerned.

Chapter 9
Policy and Guidance Behaviours: Long-Term Focus and Commitment, But with Continuous Curriculum, Practice and Assessment Review

Abstract In previous chapters, policy and guidance has been considered, but in the context of other features and factors. In this chapter, policy and guidance will be the main focus, especially considering how past experience and evidence might support future practice and endeavour. It has been said that education and policy concerned with education has neither taken sufficient notice of the past nor taken sufficient focus on the future, but current reports suggest that the potential impact of digital technologies on education is shifting the focus. Policy in this chapter will be considered from a systemic perspective, but, having said that, policy may still arise from national, regional, local or school levels, or indeed a mixture of these where governance is devolved. Policy might be offered in the form of specific legal requirements created as a regulated curriculum, or it might be in the form of guidelines that support practice. Guidelines and guidance are often derived from policy statements, but conversely policy can be created from guidelines and guidance. In this context, and in this chapter and text, policy is considered as a generally documented source that lays down statements of aims and requirements that should be fulfilled, which might perhaps be of a statutory nature. Guidelines or guidance, on the other hand, are considered as a set of suggestions or recommendations that might not need to be fulfilled as a requirement but seek to support specific actions or practices.

Keywords Policy and guidance behaviours · Desktops and policy and guidance behaviours · Subject topics and policy and guidance behaviours · Information technology and policy and guidance behaviours · The internet and policy and guidance behaviours · Communications technologies and policy and guidance behaviours · Interactive whiteboards and policy and guidance behaviours · Specific software and policy and guidance behaviours

D. Passey, *Shifting Educational Behaviours*,
https://doi.org/10.1007/978-3-032-18942-4_9

9.1 Desktops and Policy and Guidance Behaviours

In 2025, the Organisation for Economic and Co-operative Development (OECD) published a report that included a summary of approaches to digital procurement from their survey of 37 jurisdictions. In this report, for digital devices that would have included desktops, of 30 reporting jurisdictions, 16 stated that they provided schools or their regional or local authorities with procurement advice, 12 reported that they pre-authorised purchase eligibility, 12 reported that they stated criteria (most commonly security, sustainability, equitability of access, and interoperability) that needed to be met for devices purchased, and in 17 cases they reported that the central authorities of the jurisdictions negotiated directly with suppliers, in order to ensure economies of scale or administrative efficiency. In terms of funding sources, the report stated that, for 37 responding jurisdictions, local or regional authorities in 23 cases had a level of responsibility for procurement, whilst in 15 cases central authorities had responsibility. In 19 cases, responsibility was shared between levels of administration. Where schools were responsible for procurement, in 18 cases funds were earmarked for this purpose, and in 15 cases funds were non-earmarked from the central or local or regional authorities. In 6 cases, schools procured devices from funds that they had raised. This report shows the variety of approaches that jurisdictions take to digital procurement.

Learners are usually not in a position to determine or support the choices made about the range of digital technologies that are provided in schools or educational institutions (except where schools ask learners to 'bring their own devices'. In terms of desktops in schools, the number and location of such devices might be limited, for a range of different reasons.

Teachers in schools often consider location and numbers of desktops on the basis of learning purposes and teacher access. Fewer desktops in classrooms often align with increases in teacher laptop and mobile device access. However, for teachers of computing or ICT or IT, desktops tend to remain in computer suites or laboratories. In England, Ofsted (2004) advised that: "Where ICT suites are complemented by clusters of desktop machines, ICT rooms in other subject areas and sets of laptops, teachers are more likely to be able to use ICT as part of their teaching" (p. 12). Some schools find that this is still the case.

For learners who need to study using a desktop at home, research in the Philippines has investigated the most appropriate ergonomic setup to support wellbeing as well as use (Cadiz & Guerrero, 2021). The authors found that the learners' duration of study, the area of study, chair design and table design all influenced discomfort and wellbeing. This being the case, parents and guardians would be likely to benefit from being aware of the most appropriate ergonomic design to support their children if they are using a desktop (or a monitor linked from a more portable device) in the home.

In England, policy guidelines were published by the Department for Education (2022), stating that schools should ensure that desktops meet educational needs and support the digital technology strategy, that they are safe and secure, meet or exceed minimum requirements, and are energy efficient and can be disposed of sustainably. However, how these forms of details or advice relating to use are known to parents and guardians, for example, is not stated. It is clear that some schools do provide advice and guidance for parents and guardians, sometimes of their own volition and at other times arising from parental requests.

9.2 Subject Contributions and Policy and Guidance Behaviours

As noted in the previous sub-section, subjects influence policies that may be considered at classroom, school, regional and national levels. Forms of devices, forms of access, and forms of interaction, may all be considered within documentation that is developed at those different policy levels. For example, in some schools, some subjects consider the uses of Apple technology (with a MacOS operating system) to be most appropriate, whereas other subjects consider personal computer (PC) technology (with a Windows operating system) to be best suited to purpose. In some schools, uses by teachers with iPads (MacOS), for example, seems to be at odds with learners using PC (Windows) machines.

Learners might find in some schools that they are moving between using MacOS operating systems for subjects such as art and design, whereas for languages or mathematics they are using Windows operating systems. Observations in schools where these are in place does not indicate that learners have difficulties in moving from one to the other. In these instances, schools and teachers ensure as far as possible that the software used will enable files to be opened and accessed in either operating system.

Subject teachers are more likely to have opportunities to select appropriate software rather than necessarily hardware and pre-loaded software. However, in some jurisdictions, the opportunity for choice of both is not possible, while in others it is possible. This depends to some extent on the source of funding available, whether the funding is wholly or partly provided by the school or whether it is more centrally provided by regional or national government or agencies.

Parents and guardians, as discussed in previous sections and sub-sections, may have links to specific subject areas through their interests or employment. This being the case, they may well have devices and resources that are linked to those subjects. In other cases, where parents and guardians do not have these links, schools and teachers may be in a position to provide some forms of guidance and advice, about the forms of hardware as well as forms of software that might be used in schools and beyond in employment situations.

Hasnain and Rafi (2019) studied differences between the main three operating system—MacOS, Windows and Linux. They concluded that the key factors in making decisions from a policy perspective were "convenience, capability, security, interface, recovery, booting time and cost" (p. 11), and they found from their survey that:

> Most people choose Windows when they are a novice as they find Windows easy to work with. As people grow adept and want to go deeper and interact with the machine, they choose Linux. Usually, a programmer feels comfortable with Linux because they can customize their operating system to fit their needs and run their programs while minimizing the cost. On the other hand, photographers, graphic designers, and video editors choose Macintosh OS because it gives them better graphical processing power due to the power of the Central Processing Unit (CPU) and Graphical Processing Unit (GPU), coupled with complementary applications (p. 13).

These forms of details might be the basis for decision-making criteria that inform at a policy level. But from a subject point of view, this list may need to be considered from a support perspective, how devices can support an individual subject rather than supporting a whole system or institution as a whole.

9.3 Information Technology and Policy and Guidance Behaviours

Implementing uses of information technology in educational institutions requires a consideration of devices that go beyond a desktop, mobile device, networking, and software. Peripheral devices are crucially important, both from the point of view of ensuring adequate use of the digital technology facilities that are accessible but also ensuring abilities to gain from producer-style activities (for example, setting up a video capturing system identifying fauna within a remote area over a specific period of time). Examples of peripherals that are used in school education are digital cameras, digital camcorders, gamepads, headphones, joysticks, printers, plotters, scanners, sensors, speakers, and webcams.

Learners can use digital peripherals in order to either gather data or to create digital systems. Sensor and response systems are one example of these. Zhang et al. (2024) have usefully categorised sensors into environmental and biometric sensors. In the environmental sensor category, they list thermal, acoustic, infrared radio, carbon dioxide, photosensitive, and infrared camera sensors. Learners may well experience using these sensors in subject lessons such as science and geography. In many cases, the provision of these sensors is likely to be determined by classroom or school policy, where funds are locally provided. However, in some cases, local or regional authorities might support these forms of policy provision.

Teacher uses of sensors have been researched across the age range. Silva et al. (2024), for example, have shown how sensors have been used in primary schools in Portugal. Uses of sensors that enable learners to gather first-hand data are seen to lead to a greater awareness of environment conditions, both physically and cognitively.

Parents and guardians are becoming more aware of the ways that the Internet of Things (IoT) is gathering data and determining actions. For example, electricity and gas meters now send data about consumption wirelessly, not just on a monthly, but if needed, on a minute-by-minute basis. Whilst the use of sensors may be of value, this can also highlight issues concerning privacy and safety. For example, data that shows that electricity or water consumption is zero for periods of time could be used for illegitimate purposes rather than for good. Parents and guardians, with their children, need to be aware of the issues as well as the benefits that these forms of peripherals can create. Individual children and schools have been seen to both be involved and to help in this respect. Research has shown that there is a wide lack of awareness about uses of sensors with IoT systems, such as that found in a study by Levin et al. (2021) that explored parents' responses to systems where "motion data, physiological activity, and samples of audio and video data can be logged by mobile and wearable sensors" (p.n.p.). As Koohang et al. (2022) stated from their research: "IoT awareness can positively influence users' knowledge of IoT privacy and security. The users' knowledge of IoT privacy and security can positively influence users' IoT trust and subsequently, the users' IoT trust can positively influence continued intention to use IoT" (p. 1).

Policy guidelines about uses of sensors or the IoT are likely to be integrated into wider policy documents about the broader range of educational technologies. In terms of considering the ethical aspects of implementing IoT in educational practices, this topic has been explored by Kurni and Srinivasa (2025), who offer recommendations for policy at different levels.

9.4 The Internet and Networking and Policy and Guidance Behaviours

Considering the discussion about the uses of sensors with IoT systems in the previous section, it is clear that this form of activity clearly relies on the Internet and underpinning networking systems. Given the benefits that the Internet can provide, there have been international calls for universal Internet connectivity. For example, the OECD (n.d.) state that: "Ensuring universal access to digital hardware (such as laptops), software (like learning platforms), and high-quality broadband is essential for fostering equity and inclusion in education" (p.n.p.).

Learners can be subject to intermittent Internet access, regardless of location, but for a range of reasons. In some locations, interrupted Internet access is much more frequent than it is in others. Whilst provision of broadband on a frequent basis is often explored as a first option, other researchers suggest that other alternatives are possible. For example, Rangarajan (2020) suggests that: "By riding on the existing satellite channels for TV distribution, it is possible to push centrally controlled, curated content as well as teacher resources on a lesson-by-lesson basis into a compact receiver-server at all the desired locations. Teachers and students can then access the received information on their own devices from a local hotspot" (p. 14).

Teachers in some localities may experience poor Internet connectivity. A study in the Philippines gathered evidence from teachers during the Covid-19 pandemic (Agayon et al., 2022). Challenges faced by the teachers included power disruption, Internet connection disruption, and health risks. The authors found that teachers used coping strategies to address these problems, including: "The teachers secure a place where the internet connection is fast and stable… teachers always do their best to connect to the internet to download learning resources as well as to connect with their students. [They] go long distances merely to teach and find an internet signal for their online lessons" (p. 71).

Parents and guardians faced similar challenges during the Covid-19 pandemic. A study gathering evidence from parents and guardians in Peru (Chara et al., 2023) found that the parents and guardians: "sought help from specialists and family members to obtain technological and didactic support that would allow sustaining the parent-school dyad in the transition to online learning from home" (p. 359). These studies reinforce the recommendation for wider application of those behaviours that can offer support through involved and direct communication between parents and guardians with teachers in schools.

From a policy perspective, education is evolving and developing more features that enable wider systemic approaches. For education to function as effectively as possible, the ways that boundaries can be breached will be important. Policy makers, advisers, teachers, parents and guardians, and learners, all need to be involved if they are to develop efficient and effective models of communication and practice that meet local contextual needs and inform and increase awareness for all participants.

9.5 Interactive Whiteboards and Policy and Guidance Behaviours

The need for policy guidance in the form of professional development when interactive whiteboards are deployed in classrooms has been recognised within the research literature for many years. DeSantis (2013) suggested approaches to address this need, which also relates to the contemporary context as digital technologies are developing rapidly, and as they are being integrated into educational practice.

Learners may have experienced uses of interactive whiteboards in classrooms when they were first introduced, many from around 1990–2010. When first introduced, learners would probably have experienced these as a form of 'blackboard', or as a presentation device. The presentation facilities increasingly allowed images and video to be accessed as well as text, and for sharing to be facilitated to a greater extent. What is now more common, and often supported by policy documentation, is that learners have access to additional devices in classrooms, often in the form of tablets or smartphones. These additional devices allow learners to respond to questions and for their answers to be displayed, either anonymously or named, on the screen that is visible to the class. This has meant that individual responses can be generated, but outcomes are widely visible to the entire class at the same time.

From a teacher's perspective, the shift in facilities and uses with other devices has meant that different activities can be created and different pedagogies can be deployed. Professional development, therefore, has continued to be a need supported by policy, even though this digital technology has been in place for many years. Guidance on uses and applications certainly needs to be updated as new approaches are taken to new facilities becoming available. Research literature across the years has highlighted how professional development has been a continuous recommended focus. For example, Hennessy and London (2013) bring out the visualisation and dialogic potential of the medium, while Mourin Moral and de Marcos Ortega (2014) highlight the potential for uses of individual learner response systems with interactive whiteboards. In the contemporary context, these response systems have been replaced often by tablets or smartphones.

Parents and guardians have probably not been involved directly in the policy and guidance shifts that may have been associated with emerging pedagogic uses of interactive whiteboards. However, details from their children and screen shots from teachers might well have given them the idea that uses were developing over time.

From a policy perspective, developing guidance about uses of interactive whiteboards may well have been a focus at either school, regional, or national levels. Indeed, Al Halaibi (2021) demonstrated the importance of national and local policy if digital technologies such as interactive whiteboards are to be used and implemented successfully in classrooms.

9.6 Mobile Devices and Policy and Guidance Behaviours

The term 'mobile devices' can cover a range of different digital devices, which can include tablets, iPhones, smartphones, and laptops. Mobile devices in schools have tended to be accessible through two different routes—devices belonging to parents or guardians that are brought into school for school uses, and devices belonging to the school that are provided often through class sets. The first approach is often referred to as 'bring your own devices' (BYOD), whilst the second approach is generally referred to as a device pool. In either case, the provision and use are often covered within policy documentation that is created at school, regional or national levels.

Laumann et al. (2024) studied both approaches in school contexts, and found that there was no learning outcome difference that they could identify between the two groups; individual learners in the pool group tended to appreciate this approach if learners had concerns about the ability of their own devices to support the interactions required and whether they would not then have the same outcome access as others, and whether they might encounter technological difficulties with their own smartphones. In terms of the two forms of provision, schools have found different ways to support the funding of these, and as the authors say, it tends to be factors such as personal costs that can determine the extent to which either approach might be successful or be implemented.

Guidance for teachers developing practices of using mobile devices with learners in classrooms has been widely recommended and different approaches have been researched (Passey & Zozimo, 2016). Motene (2022), from a study in South Africa, concluded that: "continued technical and pedagogical support and having an ICT champion in the school contributed to the successful implementation of mobile devices for teaching and learning. Building and sustaining communities of practice for teachers to share ideas and support one another is also crucial" (p. vii).

Parents and guardians in many locations are likely to own or to have access to forms of mobile devices that they use for work or social purposes or both. During the Covid-19 pandemic, parents and guardians may well have been asked by schools to allow their children to use these devices to access learning resources. For example, this request occurred in India (Balakrishnan & Charania, 2023; Porkundil, 2023) where parents and guardians sought to address the challenges they faced, particularly in terms of what they regarded as their low levels of digital competence. These studies have highlighted the fact that uses of a mobile device for social purposes does not necessarily provide the digital skills required for using mobile devices for educational purposes. Guidance for parents and guardians is therefore likely to be needed if effective learning practice is to be gained by their children using their or similar mobile devices in the home.

As mobile devices are reported to be widely used by parents and guardians, teachers and learners, then policy or guidance for all groups would be advisable if education is to gain most effectively from uses for learning. As Papadakis and Kalogiannakis (2017) found from their research, whilst there are many apps that are available for mobile devices, parents or guardians do not necessarily know what criteria are important for selecting those most appropriate for their children's needs.

9.7 Specific Software and Policy and Guidance Behaviours

Whether software or apps, the range of these resources that are now available to support education and learning is wide and the number is high. Guidance and policy relating to these resources, to their access and to their selection is likely to be of value to all those involved in or supporting educational practice. Pearson et al. (2021) proposed and discussed some criteria for these forms of selection.

Learners may well be asked to use specific apps and software in lessons and activities. How these are chosen and selected can be important. As Meyer et al. (2021) found, from their review of the most used apps by young learners, that free apps tend to include many distracting elements, including advertisements. Those used in schools often do not have these distractions, and school, local and regional authorities or national government departments may well be involved in procurement of apps that are judged by advisers to be of specific educational application or value.

Teachers may be involved in choosing apps for use within specific classroom activities. Montazami et al. (2022b) indicated that criteria used by educators to select apps included considerations of the forms of scaffolding provided, feedback offered, curriculum match, development team affiliation to the subject or topic, and approaches to learning theory. Outhwaite and Van Herwegen (2023) highlighted, in this context, the need for consideration of how different learners can access an app and its features. Involvement of teachers and learners in development of choice is clearly an important consideration.

Research suggests that parents and guardians do not often gain guidance about selecting apps that their children might use. Whilst some schools do offer this form of advice, others do not. Dias and Brito (2021), from their comparative study of children, parents and industry stakeholders, found that parents tended to value apps that offered safe access as well as learning potential, that children tended to select on the basis of entertainment value, while stakeholders tended to identify with positive user experiences.

For policy makers and advisers, offering guidance for each group, given the increasing access that society has to a widening software and app population, appears to be increasingly important and likely to be welcomed. Some jurisdictions do identify software that is known to be valued by teachers and educators (see, for example, Passey, 2025a). Kay (2018) provided a framework that could support the development of guidance and policy in this respect, highlighting the need for those selecting apps to consider indications of learning value, content quality, identification of learning goals, how usable the apps is found to be, levels of engagement identified, how learners are challenged, how and when feedback is provided, and whether collaboration is an important feature.

9.8 Summary of Policy and Guidance Behaviours

In this chapter, the focus has been on policy and guidance behaviours that relate to learners, teachers, parents and guardians, and policy makers. These behaviours support the recognition that education is becoming an endeavour where individual contributors need to work more together. Digital technology is enabling communication to levels where the boundaries of formal, non-formal and informal learning are becoming blurred, so discussion and involvement of parents and guardians is increasingly important for the success of outcomes for learners. Across the chapter, and in this context, behaviours that are shifting have been described and observed. A summary of these shifting behaviours is offered in Table 9.1.

These shifts in behaviours align with educational approaches that are concerned with guidance and policy concerns that are to some extents widely shared across all educational stakeholders, with ongoing professional development associated with all contributing groups. Digital technologies are developing that allow more specific support for the individual, but this support is also enhanced if policy guidance is shared with appropriate indications of recommendations. There are challenges to finding effective means for developing in this direction. All learning still needs to be carefully considered and managed, and online access needs to accommodate provision that ensures safety and protection for all concerned. But with shared guidance and policy, this appears to be more likely to be secured.

Table 9.1 Behaviours associated with digital technologies that relate to policy and guidance contexts

Form of technology	Policy behaviours	Guidance behaviours
Desktops and policy and guidance behaviours	Whilst different procurement models can be in place, it is important to explore cost effective solutions such as the value of bulk purchase, minimum specification levels and provision of social support	If desktops are to be used in school or at home, guidance on most appropriate ergonomic design would be beneficial for long-term wellbeing
Subject influences and policy and guidance behaviours	Different subjects and topics might well be suited to uses of different devices and operating systems, which should be discussed	Guidance about subject and topic uses within and outside school could be of benefit to all involved
Information technology and policy and guidance behaviours	Policy decisions on access to peripherals is likely to lead to activities that go beyond consumer approaches	Guidance for those outside schools, about the ways that peripheral devices may be supporting data gathering through the IoT, would be of value
The internet, communications technologies, networking and policy and guidance behaviours	For those without regular broadband access, curated content downloaded for offline use may offer facilities to support learning	Guidance on coping strategies when Internet access fails could positively support all involved
Interactive whiteboards and policy and guidance behaviours	All digital devices are likely to develop rather than stay static, so professional development for all parties will ensure more appropriate and updated practices	Guidance should indicate, where possible, the frequency of professional development that is needed for each digital device or resource
Mobile devices and policy and guidance behaviours	Policies on ownership of mobile devices for use in schools should accommodate specific community contexts	Guidance about developing communities of practice for updating and professional development should be based on technical and pedagogical features
Specific software and policy and guidance behaviours	Policy about specific software and apps should be considered for all involved, whether learners, teachers, parents and guardians, or educational advisers	Guidance on software and apps that do not feature distractions may well support learning endeavours more effectively

Chapter 10
Making a Difference for All: Enabling Behaviours that Can Match Wider Individual Needs

Abstract It is well recognised that individuals who, for a wide range of reasons might find engaging with education and learning more difficult than others, often rely upon support from specific individuals and agencies. Those with specific needs where this might be the case have been defined by Passey (2013). In this chapter, the range defined in that text will be explored in terms of how current and future digital technologies are and might be impacting educational behaviours, both positively and negatively.

Keywords Enabling behaviours · Behaviours and cognitive disabilities · Behaviours and those with limited opportunities · Behaviours and physical disabilities · Behaviours and those not physically present in classrooms or schools · Behaviours and emotional challenges · Behaviours and attitudinal challenges · Behaviours and challenging dispositions · Behaviours and social challenges · Behaviours and those where geography poses challenges · Behaviours supporting excluded populations

10.1 Learners with Cognitive Disabilities

Learners with cognitive disabilities often present severe, profound or multiple disabilities. In some cases, this might mean that those individuals are non-verbal, and that expressing themselves, their ideas and their thoughts to others, can be a challenge. Digital technologies have been seen to support learners with cognitive difficulties, and indeed digital technologies to support engagement with education and learning have been more widely developed over the past 20 years, and they have been focusing increasingly on the needs of specific learner needs and groups. In terms of non-verbal learners, for example, eye-tracking technologies have been deployed to allow individuals to choose and select outputs that can be shared, or to create artwork that is visible to themselves and others. Eye-tracking is also used to support learners with other specific needs, such as those with dyslexia (Chan et al., 2022).

D. Passey, *Shifting Educational Behaviours*,
https://doi.org/10.1007/978-3-032-18942-4_10

An example of how these digital technologies have been used to support engagement and expression in a special school in Northern Ireland, is described in the ICT Excellence Awards 2024–2025 Report (Smith & Anderson, 2025):

> Students can do things they previously could not: Eye gaze technology allows non-verbal students to communicate their preferences and has been instrumental in helping them to select activities, choose meals, and pick colours for their artwork. Additionally, AI-powered word recognition software enables students to describe their desired creations, which AI then helps to bring to life. This approach not only supports their communication but also fosters creativity and self-expression. One notable example is a student who used word recognition software and AI to create a picture inspired by her grandfather's fishing stories. Despite her fine motor skill difficulties, she was able to design and construct her own image, expressing her fondness for her grandfather and the precious time they share. This experience filled her with pride and boosted her emotional wellbeing, as she felt listened to, invested in, and valued. (p.n.p.)

Supporting those with cognitive difficulties, however, requires levels of support intervention that are often quite specific, involving others beyond the educational institution itself perhaps attending for specific time periods. The digital technologies involved may be specific to support the needs of individuals or groups, but increasingly the linking of apps and functionalities is enabling application of digital technologies within specific educational settings to be more easily accessible and applied. This can mean that access and use can go beyond the educational institution itself; parents and guardians, for example, can have access to specific apps and functionalities, but in these cases, awareness and understanding of how to apply these applications is clearly fundamentally important. The widening of applications and functionalities is requiring a widening of understanding—from within schools to beyond schools. In some schools, teachers and leaders are enabling parents and guardians to gain wider understanding and to be guided in the forms of digital technology that will support their young people. These individual cases lead to the need to question whether such applications and understandings should become a recognised part of the wider educational system, so that education ministries and departments consider and take on board the need to develop platforms and mechanisms to widen awareness and understanding to parents and guardians. Having access to such facilities in homes could well enable important features of communication and expression, for example, to support these qualities within home as well as in educational settings.

10.2 Learners with Limited Opportunities

Learners may in some cases be presented with situations where they have limited opportunities to engage in standard school activities. For example, some learners may be caring for others. Digital technologies have been seen to support learners in these circumstances, sometimes involving teachers in running online access during class sessions for those individuals. However, to enable this to be in place, it requires the learners to have access to hardware and software that they can use. Some learners may not have this access, or they have access to facilities that are themselves limited in functionality and capacity. In some cases, ministries and education departments support the provision of specific digital technologies for school and home use, but in other cases, support is provided by local communities or charities.

In the case of young carers, there is growing recognition that behaviours need to evolve that involve the wider educational system. For example, as Schweiger (2025) states:

> The issue of young carers in highly developed countries is multifaceted, encompassing both moral and social dimensions. Our analysis reveals that young carers often face significant burdens and injustices, which are amplified by economic and social inequalities, moral blackmail, manipulation, and structural exploitation. However, it is essential to acknowledge that these young individuals are not merely helpless victims; many exhibit substantial capacities for reflection and agency, capable of articulating their own desires and ideas. Nevertheless, it remains imperative to provide these young carers with better support to ensure they have equal opportunities for social inclusion and personal development. (pp. 12–13)

Limited opportunities may also mean that individuals can only gain and use educational provision at certain times or on certain days. In these cases, asynchronous facilities may be better suited to the needs of the individual. Video recordings, audio recordings, and uses of text forums have been used in such cases. But this requires facilities to be available, and an understanding of how these facilities can be used, both by teachers or tutors, and by the learners themselves. Shifting behaviours in these cases requires professional digital development and learning to be in place and available.

Digital technologies have the potential to support communication and educational provision for young carers and those not able to take full opportunity of attendance in school locations. Taking forward implementation to support these individuals is likely to require a systemic shift in behaviours—for those in policy, practice and for users.

10.3 Learners with Physical Disabilities

Physical disabilities can cover motor, visual and auditory disabilities, for example. In all of these cases, practice and research has shown that digital technologies can support positive shifts in educational behaviours. A part of the success of uses of digital technologies in these instances has been down to the expanding functionalities and facilities that have been developed. Research has shown that individuals can access and use digital technologies to support their engagement in cases of motor, visual and hearing disabilities (Karagianni & Drigas, 2023).

During the past 20 years, there has been increasing focus on supporting digital access for those with disabilities. Access to digital technologies and text files through voice activation, and textual transcription of audio files, for example, are now commonly used and accessible. However, there are many individuals who still require access to such facilities outside educational institutions. If informal, non-formal and home learning are to be of value and successful for those individuals, then parallel facilities are required, and these facilities are known to be required across school, local, national and international contexts.

As Taylor and Yuknis (2023) state:

> Assistive technology that is specific to the student, such as assistive listening devices set at ear level, has the capacity to make communication more effective in a distance learning setting. Most assistive listening devices provided by the school district have the capacity to be either hardwired or wirelessly connected to a laptop, Chromebook, or tablet. Often, these devices are left at school; however, for effective communication and per federal guidelines, the devices must be sent home for use with distance learning. (p. 51)

Given that this statement referred to a recent situation evidenced in a well-developed country (the United States of America), it is clear that concerns about systemic approaches to shifting behaviours regarding digital technologies and their applications to education need to be moved from a view that the school is the only institution where education occurs, towards a view that educational through digital technologies needs to be considered at a wider systemic level.

10.4 Learners not Physically Present in Classrooms or Schools

For those learners not physically present in classrooms or schools, a systemic approach could be argued to be of value. Whether physical absence is due to illness or unforeseen circumstances, digital technologies can provide access to educational provision. Examples of how learners have accessed education when they are ill, for instance, have been recognised for some time, since the time when uses of the Internet were initially explored.

As Maor and Mitchem (2015) stated in this context some years ago:

> There is also a pragmatic need to examine the use of off-the-shelf devices rather than one-use specific devices. Investing resources for professional development and technical assistance support for hospital and original schoolteachers using mobile devices would likely be more cost-effective, accessible, portable and efficient than developing and providing support for specially designed applications. Careful consideration of educational and social needs of hospitalized youth who experience isolation and disrupted schooling is an area that deserves further research and attention. Mobile technologies may provide part of the solution in supporting these vulnerable youth to overcome their social exclusion and promote their educational and well-being needs. (p. 703)

In this context, there is need to consider not just the digital technology requirements and the educational requirements, but also the social and emotional requirements, indicating further the need for a wider systemic approach. Shifting behaviours in this context involves adequate consideration of those in the caring environment as well as those providing the educational content and support in educational institutions.

10.5 Learners Presenting Emotional Challenges

Digital technologies have been effectively used to support learners with emotional challenges. The fact that the digital technologies are often regarded by young people as offering neutral responses enables a much greater chance of engagement through the facilities provided via the digital technologies. However, emotional challenges can also arise if there is a high level of reliance on digital technologies, or from high levels of screen use, and from access to resources that exacerbate issues rather than addressing them.

In this context, there is clearly a balance to be had; creating one challenge from solving another does not necessarily provide a positive outcome for the learner. Uses of digital technologies to support emotional challenges need to be considered in terms of how they might affect the longer-term; for example, an important step is putting in place a plan that considers the longer-term goals and possible mid-point outcomes.

In the context of support through use of GenAI, Dray and Symons (2025) stated from their review of studies that:

> Findings of this review highlight the transformative potential of GenAI tools in delivering scalable, engaging, and tailored mental health interventions for children and young people. By integrating co-design methodologies, these tools have demonstrated significant usability and acceptability, particularly among children and young people. However, challenges such as technical limitations, resource-intensive development processes, and the need to improve inclusion of underrepresented groups remain. Advancing AI capabilities and streamlining participatory design processes will be essential for achieving greater inclusivity and effectiveness in future research. As digital mental health continues to evolve, future research should focus on co-design and on rigorously evaluating these tools' long-term impact, scalability, and adaptability to ensure they meet the complex needs of children and young people in real-world settings. (p. 11)

Emotional challenges of learners in educational settings can of course present themselves as emotional challenges for other learners and for teachers. In this context, teachers have considered how to use digital technologies to help to address emotional challenges that are presented in different ways. In one example, a teacher in Northern Ireland adopted the use of a Learning by Questions[1] scheme in mathematics and found that this scheme, where learners needed to answer questions and compete with others in the class, supported engagement and reduced the emotional challenges that the teacher had felt previously. However, shifting behaviours with digital technologies are not always fully anticipated; in this case, the teacher was not aware for some time that the shifting of behaviours of some learners was also shifting behaviours for the teacher.

[1] https://www.lbq.org/.

10.6 Learners Presenting Attitudinal Challenges

Attitudinal challenges can be associated with other challenges that are discussed in this chapter. However, in this sub-section, attitudinal challenges that concern disengagement and disenfranchisement are the main focus. Disengagement is sometimes only recognised when early school leaving (ESL), sometimes referred to as 'dropout', happens. As Montero-Sieburth and Turcatti (2022) stated, reasons for ESL can vary widely, across three main categories: non-academic (for example, concerned with family or friends); academic (for example, concerned with bullying or school friendships); and cognitive, behavioural and socio-emotional (for example, arising from lack of cognitive challenge or lack of a sense of belonging).

If digital technologies can address ESL, clearly the reasons for the disengagement need to be understood. How digital technologies might be deployed in a family issue situation may be quite different from how they would be deployed in a school bullying situation. Whilst the digital technologies might be able to support some aspects of the disengagement, other aspects are likely to require different approaches that would involve individuals or agencies beyond the school itself. The digital technology might be able to support levels of communication and interaction, but direct engagement may also be needed.

As Montero-Sieburth and Turcatti (2022) stated in their paper:

> From day one, schools need to open to parents by inviting them to regular school gatherings and parent-teacher conferences. Equally important is the establishment of a communication system that allows teachers and parents to effectively communicate with each other, by parents having access to the Internet, if schools communicate with parents through a digital portal. If parents or families do not have access to the Internet, schools and educators need to think about alternative ways to communicate with parents, using WhatsApp, or smartphones. (p. 149)

The role of digital technologies in this context is clear in this example, but it is also clear that shifting behaviours is not concerned with shifts in uses of digital technologies alone, but it is also concerned with more systemic shifts (involving parents and guardians to greater extents in this example). In essence, schools and teachers are being asked to engage with wider social and psychological issues, using digital technologies to support this shift in behaviour. In this regard, the realm of education is widening across the social and psychological arenas as well as across the systemic arena.

10.7 Learners with Challenging Behaviours

Aggressive behaviours by young people, both towards peers and towards teachers, is reported to be increasing. Harger (2019) gathered evidence in the USA to indicate that aggressive behaviour was being increasingly normalised, with shared understanding and acceptance between young people and adults arising, creating wider stigmatisation of those not accepting aggressive behaviours. Martos Martínez et al. (2021) confirmed this result in their later study, concluding that:

> The results showed that parental support for the use of nonviolent strategies for resolving conflicts, as well as higher levels of cognitive and affective empathy, are related to more favorable adolescent beliefs in pacific solutions. Students who did not use violence on their classmates, and who acted when in the presence of bullying of another student had higher levels of empathy.
>
> There is therefore a need to train parents in alternative nonviolent conflict resolution techniques so that the education youths receive at home is based on peaceful socialization. Moreover, school violence prevention programs based on training in individual variables, such as empathy, could be options promoting identification of students with their peer group. Thus, violence toward other students would be reduced and action by those who witness this type of action encouraged, creating a network of support and protection of victims of school violence. (p. 583)

The use of digital technologies to positively support aggression intervention strategies has been shown through meta-analysis to have been successful in cases that were studied (Esposito et al., 2024). In this review, the authors identified positive uses of digital technologies in the forms of interactive games, online activities, and video training programs, as well as virtual and immersive reality functionalities. The forms of focus of these programs were on conflict resolution, emotional regulation, positive social attitudes, and positive self-efficacy, so that young people were better able to understand ways to challenge their or others' aggression and to avoid developing situations that might lead to violence.

The evidence from research suggests that addressing these forms of disruptive and aggressive behaviours through digital interventions needs to be considered at a wide systemic level. Where young people and adults alike have access to digital resources and applications that can support the normalisation of disruptive and aggressive behaviours, these require a similar systemic approach to ensure that normalisation is concerned with developing non-disruptive and non-aggressive thinking and actions. In this context, shifting behaviours is likely to require positive involvement of those involved in developing and broadcasting digital news and resources, developing policies that concern adults as well as young people, and enhancing digital interventions that support non-aggressive behaviours.

10.8 Learners with Social Challenges

Social challenges are also being reported to be increasing in learner populations in school settings. Santos et al. (2023) explored the existing research relating social and emotional competencies to engagement by learners. They defined social and emotional competencies as abilities to recognise and regulate one's emotions and behaviours, abilities to solve problems, abilities to make ethical and responsible decisions, and abilities to create relationships with others that are positive and caring, but also abilities to avoid negative behaviours. In conclusion, they stated that research evidence shows the positive relationship between social and emotional competencies and learner engagement.

Social challenges can arise for a number of reasons, and low self-efficacy can be one of those reasons. Research has shown that digital interventions can support the enhancement of self-efficacy for young people who are in low socio-economic situations, and within linguistically diverse contexts (McNaughton & Jesson, 2023). In another context, in the USA, a study (Flynn et al., 2024) found that a digital technology intervention supported the development of positive social and emotional competencies, with the authors concluding that:

> The purpose of this study was to determine the impact of Adventures on third graders' social-emotional competencies. The results indicated that Adventures was positively and significantly associated with gains across a variety of social-emotional competencies as measured through direct student measures. Communication, cooperation, empathy, emotion regulation, impulse control, and social initiation were assessed via Zoo U with an effect size of .60 (Hedges G) and emotion recognition, social perspective-taking, social problem solving, delay of gratification, and frustration tolerance were measured by SELweb with an effect size of .41 (Hedges G). Additionally, the results indicated that the intervention was positively and significantly associated with gains in students' interpersonal strength as measured by teacher ratings using BERS-2 (Hedges G = 0.19). A subgroup analysis of students who were identified as having social-emotional challenges by their teachers at the beginning of the study revealed a similar pattern of findings for Zoo U (Hedges G =.68, p = <.000) and SELweb (Hedges G =.44, p =.001). These findings build on our current knowledge about the potential benefits of using technology to effectively address SEL in schools and across instructional contexts. (pp. 9–10)

Whilst studies have shown that digital interventions have supported the development of positive social behaviours, it is also clear that widening these interventions to support parents and communities could also have positive effects. A wider systemic approach at community level is suggested as a worthwhile next step.

10.9 Learners Where Geography Poses Challenges

There are many parts of the world where geography poses challenges for learners. An early means to address some of these problems was developed in Australia, through a mechanism called School of the Air. Originally supported by radio, the School of the Air still functions but now uses telephone and satellite-linked Internet communication. The School of the Air was established in 1951, and still allows young people access to education in remote areas where it would not be possible to locate viable schools due to travel distances involved for individual young people who might attend.

In other settings, online learning has been used as a means to support those who are geographically remote. However, the success of online learning is not universally reported. In a meta-review by Akpen et al. (2024), the authors concluded from reports of effects of remote emergency online learning during the Covid-19 pandemic that:

> The switch to online learning had both its advantages and disadvantages. The flexibility and accessibility of online platforms have played a major role in the enhancement of student performance, yet the decline in engagement underscores the need for more efficacious strategies to promote engagement. Online learning had a positive impact on student performance, most of the students reported either an increase or no change in grades when they changed to learning online. Only three studies stated a decline in student performance. Overall, students felt with online learning, they could not engage with their peers, teams, and teachers. They had a feeling of social isolation and felt more engagement would have improved their performance better. Schools and policymakers must develop strategies to mitigate the challenge of student engagement in online learning. This is necessary to prepare institutions for potential future pandemics which will compel reliance on online learning, this is critical for maintaining student satisfaction and overall learning outcomes. (p.n.p.)

Online learning is now regarded as a means of providing education for those in areas where geography poses challenges. However, online learning through web-based functionality requires access to the Internet, or access to download facilities that can be used, perhaps at specifically agreed times. Statistica (2025) provides an idea of how many individuals by geographic region do not currently use the Internet: 747.3 million in Southern Asia; 382.5 million in Eastern Africa; 267.9 million in Western Africa; 164.2 million in Eastern Asia; 147 million in Middle Africa; 120.2 million in South-Eastern Asia; 75.4 million in Western Africa; 73.4 million in Northern Africa; 71 million in Southern America; 37.2 million in Central America; and 25.8 million in Northern America. If online learning is to be a central tenet of moving towards inclusive education, then these data clearly show an issue that needs very wide systemic action. Whilst the International Telecommunications Union (ITU) and the World Summit for the Information Society (WSIS) are exploring how to move forward in this respect, it is clear that continued activity is needed.

10.10 Learners in Excluded Populations

Excluded populations can cover a very wide range of possibilities, including those where there are social and linguistic (migrant populations, for example), economic and cultural inequalities (cultural minorities, for example), as well as those where gender, age, race, income, or capabilities may create exclusion (Passey et al., 2024a, 2024b). As the authors of this latter paper state, it is important to understand the reasons for exclusion and the contexts of the individual populations and individuals in order to be able to identify appropriate digital technologies that can support inclusive practices.

Even in well-developed economies, excluded populations can be recognised. Pierce and Cleary (2024), for example, in their study of digital access and use in schools in the USA, concluded that:

> The findings indicate that a significant proportion of children in the United States do not have adequate access to or use education technology resources or to adult support and guidance in using these resources. This is not surprising given that many families may not have the financial means to acquire computing and Internet resources for their children. In addition,

> adults in many families may have limited time and/or the technical knowledge to help their children optimize the use of computers and the Internet for their education, and some families with these resources report difficulties monitoring their children's use of these technologies. (p. 21)

These findings indicate that behavioural shifts are needed across the wide system. Policy, practitioner and user behaviours need to be developed in order to address the underlying exclusion. This is not simply an 'access' issue'; it asks for social, community, professional and user concerns and capabilities to be engaged in a holistic manner.

10.11 Specific Learning Needs: A Summary

This chapter has demonstrated that digital technologies can support specific learning needs. However, understanding what the specific learning need is, and the context of the learner, are important when considering choices of digital technologies that might be made, whether those be hardware, software, peripherals or underlying networking or communication systems.

Additionally, specific learning needs often involve individuals or agencies in providing support that relies upon expert knowledge and experience. In these situations, all parties need to be both involved and both aware of the options and possibilities. In some cases, for example, specific needs might involve those in a health sector rather than an educational sector. If all parties are to be fully cognisant of the choices available, then wider systemic involvement may well be needed.

The potential for digital technologies to support inclusion has been widely researched and positive examples and successful achievements have been identified. While digital technologies will be developed in the future that continue to address exclusion and to support inclusion, means to effectively share awareness, understandings and means to support inclusive needs, across all stakeholders involved, is likely to offer positive ways forward for all concerned.

Chapter 11
The Future: Continuous and Continuing Inquisitiveness and Critical Concern

Abstract It is well recognised that digital technologies will continue to be developed and will emerge over the coming decades. For education, this means that uses of those emerging digital technologies will need to be explored and identified, as many digital technologies are not created for educational purposes, but are applied once they are accessible to those in education. Finding ways to use future digital technologies is likely to require an increasing systemic approach, as those digital technologies are likely to have the potential to affect ways and places for educational endeavour. Whilst the future holds uncertainties, it is likely that learners, teachers, parents and guardians, and advisers and policy makers will rely upon behaviours that accommodate systemic concerns, thinking about uses and outcomes beyond the digital technologies themselves, and that consider criticality, inquisitiveness, applicability to the individual, being selective, and context.

Keywords Educational behaviours and possible futures · Digital uncertainty and educational certainty · Educational digital competencies and digital skills · Accommodating emerging digital technologies · Future choices and shifting behaviours · Future scopes for learning · Future approaches for teaching and tutoring · Future approaches to home support · Future directions for policy and guidance

11.1 The Contemporary Position

Identifying a contemporary position regarding educational behaviour shifts related to uses of digital technologies is drawn in this chapter from the positions highlighted in previous chapters. However, it should be noted that the shifts in behaviours (shown in Table 11.1) were identified and related in the earlier tables of this text from examples within settings and situations recognised as being developed in terms of the uses of specific digital technologies or a wide range of different digital technologies, in schools and for educational purposes. Table 11.1 considers these educational behaviours as they were identified through uses of a range of digital technologies,

D. Passey, *Shifting Educational Behaviours*,
https://doi.org/10.1007/978-3-032-18942-4_11

whether by learners, teachers, parents and guardians or advisers and policy makers. The behaviours are framed in ways that could be regarded as 'ideal' positions, based on evidence currently accessible and known.

What these behavioural shifts, all identified in current practices show, is that digital technologies are becoming more widely accessible across the learner, teacher, parent and guardian, and adviser and policy maker arenas. Digital technologies are enabling access to resources and practices that were not easily possible at earlier times. Learners can access different digital technologies in schools as well as out of schools; but this is also true for teachers, parents and guardians, and advisers and policy makers.

As an example, the number of educational applications (apps) that were reported to be accessible via mobile Google Play[1] and Apple App[2] stores in 2023 was 389,000 (Business of Apps, 2025). As this site states:

> Study apps are increasingly being used to supplement traditional classroom-based learning, filling the role of private tutoring and parental support, albeit in a less personalised and focused approach. With the coronavirus pandemic, some of these apps began to stand in for in-person teaching and act as a medium for students to complete work and receive feedback remotely. (p.n.p.)

Details on the same site indicate that the most commonly downloaded educational app was a language learning app—Duolingo—with 500 million registered users. These apps are not solely being used within classrooms and schools; they are being used by learners across the age range, by learners outside classrooms and schools, and with tutors who are not associated with specific classrooms or schools. Education through the use of apps has shifted; it has moved from a largely classroom and school-based activity, to one where classroom and school are balanced with outside activity. Beyond the use of apps, the uses of different mobile and peripheral devices such as Digital Versatile Discs (DVDs), Moving Picture Experts Group (MPEG) 4 (mp4) players and Kindles are also blurring boundaries. In this context, which is unlikely to move towards previous forms of access and practices, and is more likely to develop more strongly, how can teachers, parents and guardians, and advisers and policy makers, consider education? The realm of formal learning is shifting; it is becoming balanced, or even overtaken in some instances, with informal and non-formal learning.

11.2 Competencies Versus Skills

A major difference between competencies and skills is concerned with the behaviours that are associated with uses and applications. Skills are often considered as more technical in nature, not involving how behaviours and approaches mediate their use, whilst competencies are concerned with the nature of associated behaviours that can

---

[1] https://play.google.com.

[2] https://www.apple.com/app-store/.

Table 11.1 Educational behaviours associated with digital technologies used in well-developed contemporary settings

Form of technology	Learner behaviours	Teacher behaviours	Parent and guardian behaviours	Adviser and policy maker behaviours
Physical computing and learning and teaching behaviours	Computational thinking should be considered as not always requiring screen time, but recognising the importance in developing computational thinking approaches using off-screen resources through collaborative activity	Computational thinking should not be considered just as an independent, individual learner activity, but involving activities where groupwork, learner interest and wellbeing, and developing future student wellbeing practices are a priority	Whilst observing what is being done is important, discussion about and being involved in activities where suggestions might be made about programming physical computing devices to address particular needs can also be offered	Beyond the need to provide schools and learners with digital devices as a main focus, there should also be thinking about ways that physical digital devices can address specific problems and the needs of users, friends, family and communities
The Internet and learning and teaching behaviours	As well as creating learning outputs as texts, learners can also use the possibilities of multimedia outputs to demonstrate learning outcomes	Whilst the teacher can review resources and details in accessible sources on the Internet, they also consider and share with learners the importance of reviewing how search words, phrases and source legitimacy can address concerns about source validity	As well as considering concerns about online safety for their children, parents and guardians should also consider consulting schools and teachers as they might suggest effective ways to address these concerns	As well as considering developing policy from personal experiences and individual perspectives, online discussion with practitioners, online drafting and practitioner review can also be considered and integrated into practice

(continued)

Table 11.1 (continued)

Form of technology	Learner behaviours	Teacher behaviours	Parent and guardian behaviours	Adviser and policy maker behaviours
Mobile devices and learning and teaching behaviours	As well as relying on memory in specific learning contexts, learners can also use mobile device access for reflection and review of details at later times	As well as providing learners with immediate responses and knowledge, teachers can also provide possible routes including those involving digital resource functions that allow learners to gain knowledge themselves from recognised sources	Whilst parents and guardians may provide their children with digital devices and support at home, schools might also be asked whether out-of-lesson digital resource access might be provided	Whilst learners might access resources through their own digital devices in schools, policy can also distinguish between digital device access for learning purposes and those for purely social purposes
Desktops and learning behaviours	Learners should not only seek a correct answer when undertaking online activities, but seek ways that they can tackle and solve problems	Marking and handing back individual work is balanced with the sharing of completed work so that learners can gain highlights from their and others' work to help subsequent activity	Monitoring of their children's communication in unobtrusive ways can lead to identifying more positive links and safe practices	Supporting unobtrusive monitoring of communication by learners, teachers, parents and guardians and the wider communities can support positive links and safe practices

(continued)

Table 11.1 (continued)

Form of technology	Learner behaviours	Teacher behaviours	Parent and guardian behaviours	Adviser and policy maker behaviours
Subject influences and learning behaviours	Learners balance the need for short-term memorising with longer-term reflection and evaluation	Whilst teachers develop and use activities requiring learners to remember words and phrases through notetaking, for example, they also use digital activities that highlight words and phrases and then lead to discussion and text transcription	Parents and guardians continue to reassure their children, but also seek and gain support through digital means that can further enhance their engagement with their children	Policy not only ensures that digital education within a curriculum is covered, but also ensures and accommodates contextual long-term interests and potential for further development, adaptability and employment
Information technology and learning behaviours	Learners use sources that the teacher suggests, but also develop an understanding of the principles of information literacy	Teachers suggest sources that learners might use, but also support them in understanding processes that enable them to identify useful sources for themselves	Parents and guardians develop ways to monitor situations before involving their children in direct discussions	Whilst local advice and context is important, wider national and international options are also considered
The Internet, communications technologies, networking and learning behaviours	Whilst relying on information from teachers and from online sources, learners at the same time think about questions to ask and how to effectively gather advice from experts through direct online communication	Teaching approaches involve not only the classroom as a focus of interaction, but also integrate an onsite and online shared classroom where activities are undertaken with another teacher and another class	Parents and guardians avoid the challenges of physical attendance at school meetings by moving to online attendance that can suit all parties	Inclusive policy considers all, not just the majority, discussing individual circumstances that show and can lead to specific educational benefits

(continued)

Table 11.1 (continued)

Form of technology	Learner behaviours	Teacher behaviours	Parent and guardian behaviours	Adviser and policy maker behaviours
Interactive whiteboards and learning behaviours	Whilst learners can still work on activities paired with their peers in classrooms, focusing on their notes on desks, they also are involved in open discussions about details that are visible across the class	An individual lecture style is balanced with a multimedia approach that involves different forms of input	Parents and guardians become aware of the changes in forms of interaction in schools, for example, where their children may now be able to physically move items on a large screen	As well as concerns about providing digital technology through pilot projects, later wider implementation focuses importantly also on professional development
Specific software and learning behaviours	Learning tasks are not just recognised as items that need to be completed, but online tasks that are enjoyable and engaging lead to completion of correct answers and results where there may also be positive competition with other learners	Whilst single demonstrations or physical activities continue to be fundamentally important, online activities are recognised as ways to generate a range of results as conditions can be changed	From limited involvement with their children's homework, more direct involvement and monitoring can be supported	Purchase of educational software can be considered more widely, where the software purchase contract is coupled with needs for social practice such as professional development
AI and GenAI	Rather than accepting outcomes generated by AI and GenAI engines, learners are critical of outcomes	Rather than teachers using digital technologies to create an outcome, AI and GenAI generated text are critically reviewed	Rather than parents and guardians recording when a home activity is completed, appropriate supporting and monitoring are encouraged prior to recording	Rather than policy makers needing to spend time on drafting, the focus is shifted to reviewing and refinement of GenAi generated drafts

(continued)

Table 11.1 (continued)

Form of technology	Learner behaviours	Teacher behaviours	Parent and guardian behaviours	Adviser and policy maker behaviours
Robotics	From a position of more limited choice for learner support, choice of support can now include robots whose forms of recognised interactions such as patience and neutrality of social responses are regarded as positive	From a focus on individual work and outcomes, choice of groupwork to enable teamwork including robots and wider social interactions and understanding is now possible	Rather than trying to persuade children to engage, support has shifted to observing, monitoring and encouraging	Rather than relying more on previous existing knowledge, the focus is now more on research-informed approaches, as needed and as they arise
VR	From a reliance on observation, greater visual stimulation is now possible as a choice for learners	From a reliance on text-based and memorisation approaches, greater visually and observationally based approaches can incorporate peer collaboration	From a reliance on being told about certain experiences from memory, first-hand experiences can now be observed and discussed	From a reliance on ad hoc feedback, informed research-based approaches can now detail specific features and factors
AR	From having to rely on abilities to abstract outside unknown contexts, visualisation in context is now possible	From offering a limited range of direct observations, a wider range of related observations in contexts is now possible	From a focus on ensuring completion, parent and guardian focus can now be shifted to monitoring when and how to support engagement to greater extents prior to recording outcomes	Relying only on previous knowledge, plans and directions can now be informed more readily by short-term research feedback on specific details of interest

apply skills in specific situations. From the shifts in educational behaviours that are highlighted in this text, it is clear that competencies are now becoming involved to a much greater extent than skills. Those competencies are concerned with the ways that skills are considered, when, how and under what circumstances there might be implications.

The need for educational behaviours being developed across the educational system that involve active 'thinking' is clear. Learners are being asked to question more, to consider legitimacy of details that they are encountering. Teachers are being asked to develop questioning in learners, through collaboration, peer and teamwork, and through problem solving. Parents and teachers are being asked to develop support and monitoring practices that offer reassurance, but that these also do not interfere with the development of independent competencies for learners. Advisers and policy makers are being asked to question the development of policy at different levels, to involve wider evidence, that is more often reassessed and reviewed.

In this context, competencies are much more concerned with the application beyond the immediate activity. They are concerned with application in other situations, application at different times and in different circumstances. This means that activities that are longer in duration, that involve teamwork, collaboration and review, are much more likely to support the development of competencies that will be of benefit for the longer-term. Short-term activities and learning outcomes may be useful in some situations, but the application of these is now vitally important if longer-term learning outcomes are to benefit learners for the future.

11.3 The Place of Digital Skills

There is an important place for digital skills. However, it should be recognised that the digital skills of today may not be the entire range of digital skills that are needed in 5 years' time. We know that some digital technologies disappear, while others are superseded and others are added. Digital skills, therefore, need to be conceived within a broad framework, that can enable changes in digital technologies over time. Focusing on the digital skills associated with a single software, for example, will not on its own offer digital skills that are necessarily those needed for the future. With major shifts in digital technologies roughly every 5 years (exemplified by the introduction of the desktop computer, later the worldwide web, then mobile devices, and cloud computing later) and more minor shifts every 18 months (for example, new apps being developed, updates being made to existing software, and new multimedia versions arising), digital skills need to move beyond the skills needed to operate at these levels, and to consider the wider applications of these functionalities.

Different education institutions, ministries, departments and agencies have addressed this need in different ways. As an example, Northern Ireland adopted a cross-curricular framework for its schools called 'Using Information and Communications Technologies' (UICT) (CCEA, 2025), and primary schools and teachers were asked to incorporate seven aspects into their curricula: Computational Thinking and Coding (Interactive Design); Digital Art and Design (Working with Images); Digital Audio (Music and Sound); Digital Storytelling: Film and Animation (Film and Animation); Digital Storytelling: Presenting (Presenting); Digital Storytelling: Publishing (Desktop Publishing); and Managing Data. As can be seen from these titles, these aspects do not identify specific digital technologies or specific skills;

they ask teachers to incorporate these on an ongoing and updating basis. Australia has used an alternative framework termed 'Digital Literacy' (ACARA, 2025), which asks schools and teachers to incorporate four elements that are further sub-divided: Practising digital safety and wellbeing (Manage online safety; Manage digital privacy and identity; Manage digital wellbeing); Investigating (Locate information; Acquire and collate data; Interpret data); Creating and exchanging (Plan; Create, communicate and collaborate; Respect intellectual property); and Managing and operating (Manage content; Protect content; Select and operate tools). Again, these categories do not focus on digital skills but look to the application of those skills.

What is clear from these examples is that they are attempting to be futureproof. They do not identify specific digital skills; they take a broad view of the competencies that are likely to serve for the future as well as for the present.

11.4 Accommodating Emerging Digital Technologies

Emerging digital technologies do not only affect learners; they affect teachers, parents and guardians, and advisers and policy makers as well as learners. Emerging technologies can take a range of forms; they may concern hardware devices, or software, or functionalities. All of these forms of digital technologies can affect learning, teaching, home support and engagement, and guidance and policy.

How often emerging digital technologies should be reviewed and integrated into educational practices is a question that has concerned educators for many decades. Considering that Moore's Law (Kaliski, 2025) still appears to hold to an extent, in that progress in terms of computing capacity is advancing rapidly, then emerging technologies are likely to be seen to arise often. A curriculum that accounts for this is clearly an advantage for learners, but this in itself does not stop the need for review and updating. Supporting the learning of competencies is not in itself divorced from the need to consider the underlying networking and infrastructure, the communications infrastructure, the hardware and the software in place to enable those competencies to be supported.

In some schools, specific digital technicians have responsibility for these reviews, while in other schools ICT co-ordinators take this responsibility, or all teachers are asked to explore this area and to share their findings with others. Whatever management approach is taken in a school, review and updating should ideally be happening regularly; some schools ensure that this issue is placed on their staff meeting agendas every few months. This reviewing and updating is, of course, linked closely with the ways in which schools are managed within a region, authority, jurisdiction or country. There may be financial and security issues that need to be considered when reviews and updating are taking place. Importantly for all parties, whether learners, teachers, parents and guardians, or advisers and policy makers, it is clear that the outcome of any review should very carefully consider how any updating will benefit and positively influence teaching, learning or educational support. Decisions are likely to involve all parties, so how consultation and evidence is drawn to come to decisions is in itself an important concern. Communication across the sectors may well be a necessary and effective requirement so that all parties are aware of what is involved, why, and what might need to be done to accommodate the updating.

11.5 Digital Skills Related to Learning and Teaching Behaviours

Whilst an argument has already been made that digital competencies are of concern for the longer-term, it is also important to recognise that digital skills can be vitally important for the shorter-term. All parties need to know how to access and use digital facilities and functionalities that are in place or that can support learning and teaching. Behaviours need to accommodate at least two specific areas of digital skills: digital skills concerned with using existing digital technologies (what might be regarded as consumer skills); and digital skills concerned with creating usable forms of digital technologies (what might be regarded as computational thinking skills, coding, programming and producer skills).

It has been argued that learners now live in environments where digital technologies are so pervasive that they do not need to learn digital skills (Prensky, 2001). This argument has been widely contested (Mertala et al., 2024), and indeed many teachers report that learners may be able to use a smartphone to communicate with friends through social media, but do not know how to create and edit text on a word processor. It cannot be assumed that learners know the digital skills needed to support their learning, and the provision of digital skills often is accommodated by teachers, sometimes across a school in subject lessons, or sometimes in a more specific digital skills lesson where those skills are then transferred into use and applied in other subject areas.

Whatever approach is taken, it is important that a school is aware of what digital skills are needed by learners at home as well as in school, what digital skills they possess already, and what form of provision is felt to be accommodated in the individual context. It is also important that whichever form of provision is taken, that the development of digital skills is not left as a final objective, but that those digital skills are developed in learning and teaching contexts as digital competencies.

11.6 Digital Skills Related to Educational Behaviours

Digital skills are important to those who are involved in key areas of educational support—parents and guardians, and advisers and policy makers. If learners are increasingly using digital technologies for their learning, and this is happening in homes and in areas outside educational institutions, then those providing educational support also need to be aware of the digital skills that are needed, why they are needed, and how they can be provided.

Some schools provide regular updates to parents and guardians, but updates to advisers and policy makers are seen less often in practice. Some schools provide parents and guardians with videos of what their children are doing in classrooms, what digital technologies they are using, and what the outcomes are. Parents and guardians may also be informed about the sorts of ways that they might best support their children at home. During the Covid-19 pandemic, many parents and guardians found that they needed to try to come to grips with uses of digital technologies that they had not experienced previously. This happened on many jurisdictions world-wide, often asking parents and guardians to develop their digital skills to ensure that videoconferencing could provide lessons from teachers. Not all parents and guardians found this possible, and when they did, they also found that they often did not acquire skills in specific areas, as shown in one study that gathered evidence from parents and guardians in India (Balakrishnan & Charania, 2023):

> The study highlighted the importance of parental digital competence in mediating digital technology use in children. The study found that in the rapidly advancing technological environment, parental participation in mediating the access and exposure to digital opportunities of children was restricted. While parents may be able to purchase digital devices for their children to use, they do not seem to be in a position to provide adequate and appropriate guidance to their children regarding safe, responsible and productive use of these opportunities. Children can be exposed to diverse risks on digital platforms such as cyberbullying, scams, and online frauds. As these threats pose significant risks to their devices and personal data, it is essential to provide children comprehensive education to enhance their device security skills and to recognise and avoid potential threats. (p.n.p.)

If schools are to require their learners to use digital technologies at home, then mechanisms to enable parents and guardians to gain digital skills becomes more important. In this respect, policy makers can play an important part in supporting processes that will enable this to take place.

11.7 Features of Ongoing Educational Behaviours

From the evidence presented in published research and from the analysis in this text, there are at least seven features that ongoing educational behaviours should accommodate, if the future for learners is to enable their uses of digital technologies in the long-term as well as in the short-term.

All parties need to consider learning as a systemic concern. Learners need to consider the balance of formal (in classrooms and in schools), informal (at home and with friends and family) and non-formal learning (in outside venues that might include after-school clubs, museums or visits to industry) that is effective for them. Teachers need to consider the digital skills and competencies of their learners, how their digital skills and competencies are developed, how parents and guardians can be informed, and how they can inform policy makers of their ongoing needs following reviews. Parents and guardians need to consider what their children are doing and using, how they can seek support from outside agencies, schools and teachers, and how their needs might be supported at policy levels. Advisers and policy makers need to consider what learners should be accessing and achieving, what teachers need, to ensure that the curriculum can be completed, and how they can engage with and support external agencies, parents and guardians.

Educational behaviours need to be in some respects independent of digital technologies themselves. Educational behaviours are not digital skills; they are the manifestation of thinking and approach; they are the ways that individuals adopt when considering learning, teaching or educational support. Educational behaviours need to be informed, reassuring, and not overbearing. Examples of parents and guardians not enabling their children to make mistakes takes away a key concept of learning—that we learn through our mistakes. Learners need to be able to handle mistakes and learn from them; digital technologies are not there as a means to take mistakes away. Indeed, school-based project work shows so well how groups of learners pick up mistakes, discuss them and overcome them, consequently gaining important problem-solving abilities.

Inquisitiveness is a requirement for all parties. Learners need to question more than ever before; teachers need to support questioning to greater extents; parents and guardians need to reassure and support through questioning; and advisers and policy makers need to question as far as possible across the system. The importance of inquisitiveness has been identified as a key educational behaviour for those who maintain a sustained use of digital technologies over many years (Passey & Lee, 2020).

Criticality is a growing requirement. The advent of AI and GenAI systems requires all parties to be critical, at a number of levels. Ethics and privacy are certainly concerns at one level, but being critical and questioning outcomes is important at another level. The outcomes of AI and GenAI systems should always be questioned; criticality ensures that acceptance is based on individual choice and informed choice.

A key feature of educational behaviours will be the need to be concerned for the individual. Digital technologies have been and are being developed that can support the individual to greater extents, whether this support accommodates their individual learning needs (for example, the topic they are working on, specific details that they request, or specific contexts that they wish to explore) or their specific needs (for example, whether they have auditory disability, motor disability, social challenges, or are located in a remote geographic area). Learners need to question their needs; teachers need to consider how the digital technologies can support the individual; parents and guardians need to consider the characteristics and needs of their children; and advisers and policy makers need to consider the width of all learners rather than considering the average.

But in this context, being selective is also an important feature. There is a large and growing variety of digital technologies that can be selected, whether this is hardware or software. Being selective is and will be likely to be increasingly important as further digital technologies emerge. How to make choices might well be supported for different educational groups, but all parties will need to explore how to do this.

Learners may need to select apps; teachers may need to select apps for use in specific lessons; parents and guardians may need to select appropriate hardware devices for their children; and advisers and policy makers may need to select networking and infrastructure, communication systems, hardware and software that are appropriate for schools.

Considering context is the last key feature. Contexts are different, whether these be country, jurisdiction, geographical location, home, or school. Digital technologies need to be applied and appropriate to context. The digital technologies required in a home where a child has a visual disability may be different from those in a home where a child has anxiety issues; both can be supported, but both require different digital technology applications. All parties need to consider context, whether it be at the level of school, home or jurisdiction.

11.8 The Future for Learners

The future for learners in terms of educational behaviours is likely to be shaped by educational behaviours that are being seen to be emerging currently, and by the emerging digital technologies that are likely to impact practice over the next 5 years at least. Taking forward the key elements from the previous section offers a way to consider these futures.

Digital skills will continue to be important, but digital competencies are likely to be seen as increasingly important. Digital technologies will continue to emerge, so thinking about approaches and directions will allow learners to shape their learning paths. At the same time, learners will need to engage with productive involvement with digital technologies, ensuring that they connect with and grasp computational thinking so that they can apply their interests and knowledge to solving problems, in teams, collaboratively, and over periods of time that go beyond single lessons.

Inquisitiveness will continue to be a required characteristic if learners are to find the most effective ways to engage with emerging technologies. Being inquisitive about GenAI, VR and AR, for example, will allow the development of understanding to make choices and apply uses. In this context, online sources of support and information will be likely to become more prevalent in some respects.

Criticality will be a growing requirement if sources do become more accessible online. The validity of sources, the ethical nature of those sources, and an understanding of privacy and security, will all be essential when learners engage with the current scenarios that are represented in this text.

At the same time, digital technologies will continue to be developed that are likely to support the individual to greater extents. Personalisation, however, is not likely to be determined by someone sitting on the sidelines; personalisation will involve individuals understanding about their own characteristics, interests and needs, and being supported in the identification of sources to support these. However, focusing on long-term goals will also be a necessity; at the moment, digital technology resources often focus on short-term goals, without enabling the individual to understand where they might position themselves and develop to in 1-, 2-, or 3-years' time.

In this context, being selective will be an important feature. Already, the range of resources, whether hardware- or software-based, is large. This range is not likely to reduce over the coming years, so learners will need to be selective, and to find sources that will help them with those selections. Teachers, parents and guardians, and advisers and policy makers could all play a part in that selection support.

Context will also be an important feature. This will not only be concerned with the individual's current context and understanding how this might direct some selection and choice of uses, but it will also be concerned with the future context that the individual perceives as being a road to travel. In this respect, learner aspiration is important; and again, teachers, parents and guardians, and advisers and policy makers, all can play a vital part in opening up aspirational ideas, of how current activity links to future uses in possible employment.

Figure 11.1 shows the educational behaviours that are suggested currently as those likely to be supportive of learners and learning in settings where digital technologies are used.

11.9 The Future for Teachers

The current evidence about the future for teachers in terms of educational behaviours also highlights some uncertainties in some respects. However, these uncertainties appear to be much more concerned with choices of directions, rather than uncertainty about teaching futures. Even at this fairly early stage, it is becoming clear that discussions about educational uses of GenAI, for example, will increasingly need to rely upon teacher interventions, to ensure that bias and potential discrimination is adequately considered, as the GenAI systems themselves are unlikely to be able to monitor the situation in this way, as a teacher would.

In this sense, educational behaviours for the future will not be described as digital skills. They will be concerned to a greater extent with levels of deep thinking and considerations of appropriate approaches to take. They may well be more concerned at an individual level, as class teaching may to some extent be supported by forms of online provision, whether that be 'delivered' through interactive whiteboards, tablets, or smartphones.

Inquisitiveness will be important. With the width of digital technologies expanding, with wider options for hardware devices and for software resources, inquisitiveness will allow views to be developed about potential. Professional development relies upon inquisitiveness, and the future with digital technologies will provide options that will need to be explored and trialled. Teacher involvement and teacher sharing will be crucial to decision making in these respects.

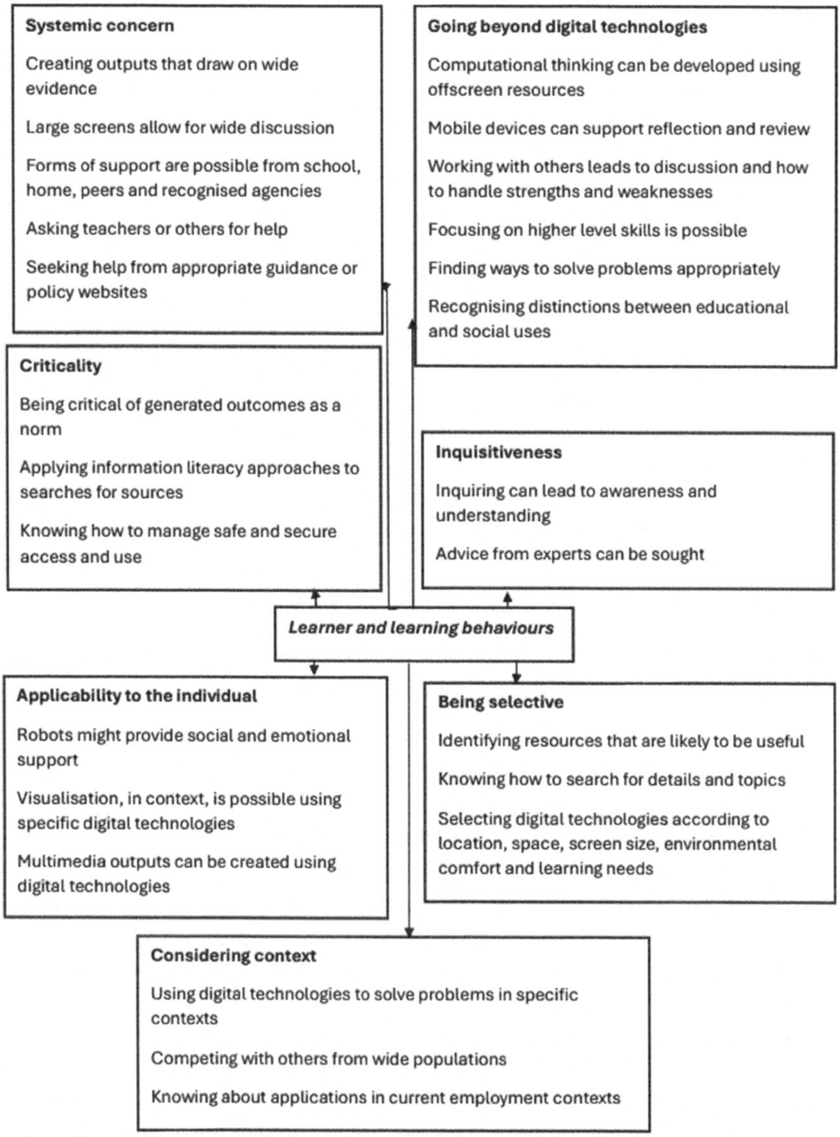

Fig. 11.1 Suggested supportive educational behaviours for learning

Criticality will continue to be a growing requirement. The forms of digital technology that are emerging require teachers to question their outputs, rather than accept them. Supporting others in taking those critical and questioning approaches will be all the more important, and this will need to be considered from young ages and not left until later in the educational process.

At the same time, digital technologies will continue to be developed that can support the individual to greater extents. Teachers may well be in the position where they can take advantage of these facilities, but teachers will also need to be in the position to be able to make choices about specific digital technologies that can apply in specific situations for individuals as well as groups.

But being selective will also apply to selection of settings, approaches and groupings. As online learning becomes more understood and used to increasing extents outside the classroom, teachers will be able to consider what online learning is most appropriate beyond the classroom, perhaps at home, and what forms of learning might be best in the school. For some time, the concept of flipped learning has explored an approach that shifts the earlier parts of topic learning to more individual learning settings, with follow-up concerned more with discussion and analysis. A systemic review article by Rahmatika et al. (2024) identified how flipped learning had positively impacted learners' critical thinking. This form of approach with online learning may well develop further.

Teachers should also be in a position to consider context, not just for the individual but also for the group. Individual context may well determine the selection of one resource rather than another, as well as the provision of digital devices that might be appropriate. Communication with and advice and support from parents and guardians and advisers and policy makers will also be crucial in this respect.

Figure 11.2 shows the educational behaviours that are suggested currently as those likely to be supportive of teachers and teaching in settings where digital technologies are used.

11.10 The Future for Parents and Guardians

Many parents and guardians experienced educational behavioural shifts during the Covid-19 pandemic. There were various reasons why some parents and guardians found it more difficult to adapt to these shifts than others. But, nevertheless, some parents and guardians have recognised that the uses of digital technologies had and can continue to change the educational landscape, and that they can become more involved in aspects of their children's education. In some cases, this involvement has unfortunately led to over-bearing levels of involvement (usually close monitoring and checking), which in turn has not led to positive engagement with teachers; but in other cases the opposite outcome is seen, where positive scenarios have been identified as outcomes.

Many parents and guardians have recognised that educational support behaviours go well beyond having digital skills. Whilst some have highlighted their lack of digital skills, others have gone further, and they have considered the ways that they should approach support for their children.

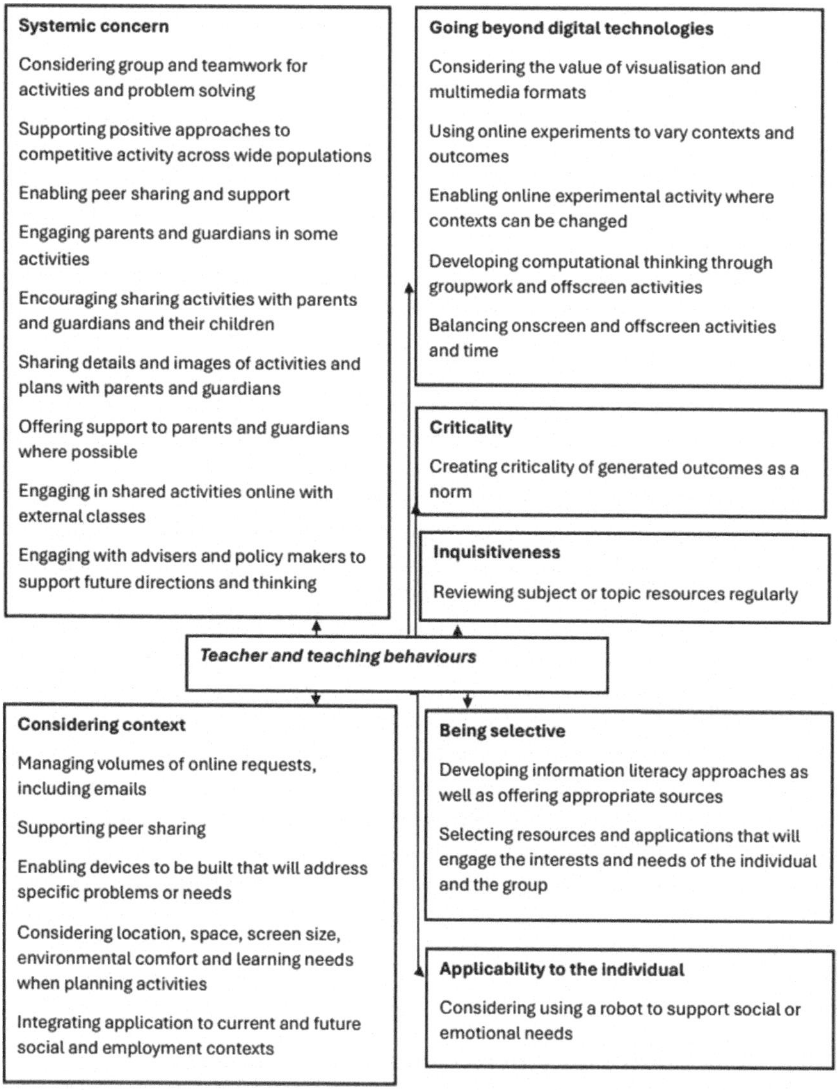

Fig. 11.2 Suggested supportive educational behaviours for teaching

Inquisitiveness has played a key part already in these scenarios. Parents and guardians have shared and questioned, they have sought sources to inform them, and they have set up online and support groups to try to find the most effective answers to their queries. Some parents and guardians have run home learning for their children for many years, and the reasons that they have done this may relate to the educational behaviours that they desire, which wider groups of parents and guardians could consider similarly in the future.

Criticality has been a feature of support for home learning and indeed has been crucial in effectively supporting many remote emergency online learning situations. Criticality has been concerned with what the home can offer, and how it should do this. Criticality has been concerned with decisions about interests, whether those be social interests or cognitive interests. But criticality has also been concerned with ensuring balance; balance between onscreen and offscreen time; balance between educational working time and non-working time; balance between personal interests and future needs.

Whilst digital technologies continue to be developed that can support the individual to greater extents, parents and guardians have already in some cases and are likely in the future to be able to consider how digital technologies can support an effective home learning situation. Whilst they may well be able to identify those resources that might best apply for their children, they also often require support in doing this. Teachers, advisers and policy makers have already been involved in helping in those respects, and it is likely that this trend will continue.

Parents and guardians will need to be selective with regard to a number of features: resources; settings; and approaches to support. Parents and guardians are likely to value support that is effective for all of these features, as they seek to enable their children to aspire to engage in a positive future.

Parents and guardians may well be the best placed to understand or recognise their contexts and those of their children. Educational behaviours for parents and guardians are, in this respect, likely to involve greater communication with schools, with teachers, with agencies and with advisers and policy makers. Some of this will be online, whether searching a website or sending emails, but some is likely to be more face-to-face. Parents and guardians will need to find ways to manage these interactions, and this will be another feature of their future educational support behaviours that is likely to further emerge and develop over time.

Figure 11.3 shows the educational behaviours that are suggested currently as those likely to be supportive of parents and guardians and home support in settings where digital technologies are used.

11.11 The Future for Advisers and Policy Makers

Advisers and policy makers will ideally need to ensure that they maintain a focus on the present and on the future, rather than focusing only on the past. The past may in some ways offer comfortable views of approaches to take, but the pervasiveness of digital technologies is already shaping interactions and interventions that offer different approaches and futures. Today's young people are looking to emerge in a world that is beyond the current; they should be prepared for that world as much as possible.

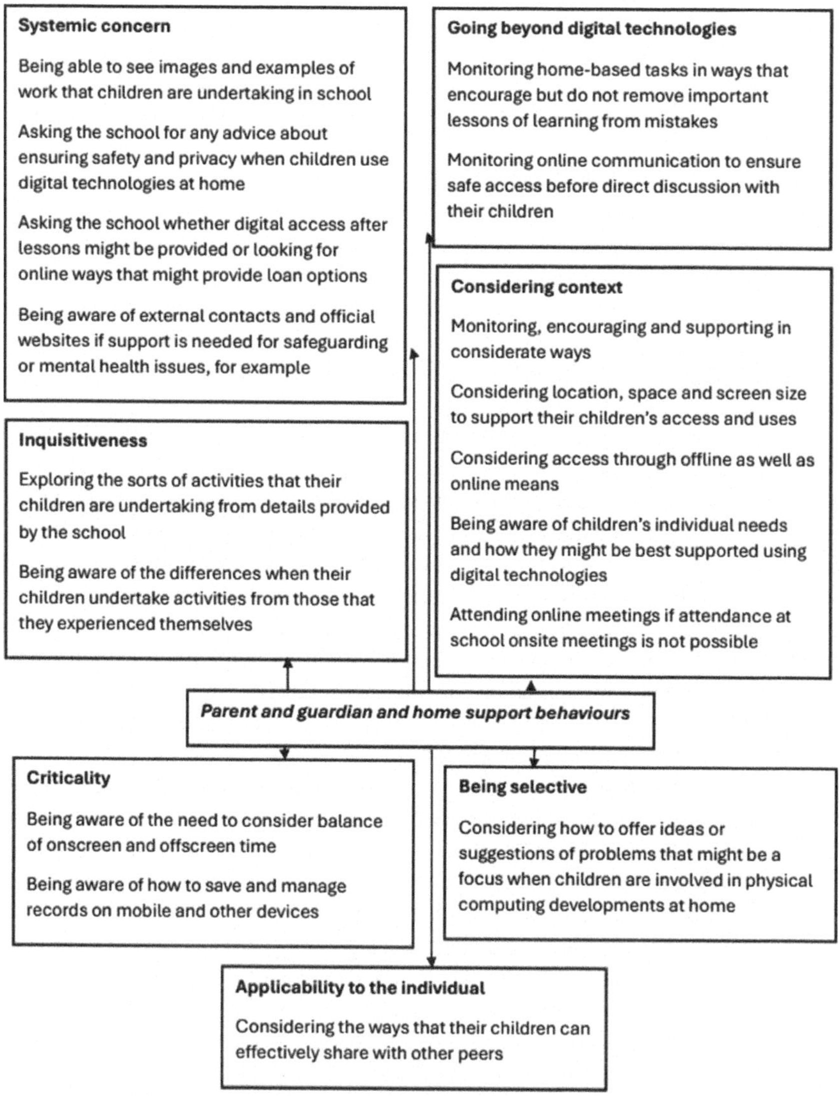

Fig. 11.3 Suggested supportive educational behaviours for home support

Educational support behaviours for advisers and policy makers need to go beyond an approach for support that advocates and instils digital skills. Whilst these will continue to be important, they will themselves shift; the use of word processing and text creation is not the same as it was 20 years' ago, and it will not be the same in 20 years' time.

Policy makers need to be inquisitive. They need to know what is happening today in order to have sight of what might be happening tomorrow. They need to gather evidence that will allow them to gain these perspectives and insights, from those who are developing in current contexts.

Criticality will be crucial. Being critical of what is happening does not mean that it should be dismissed, and different individuals are likely to have different perspectives. But in part, this is the essence of what is at the core of the changes that are happening.

Digital technologies have been and are being developed that support the individual to greater extents. For policy, this is not necessarily a helpful situation. Trying to create policy that can support the individual, as well as all, relies on levels of finer details and an understanding of those involved in putting the policy into practice. Whilst there has been an increase in the levels of details on some policy websites over the past few years, this is likely to be a continued need. As diversity and inclusion to support individuals is more accommodated, the detail on websites is likely to need to be enhanced, covering suggestions and recommendations about more specific needs as new digital technologies and their functionalities emerge.

Supporting appropriate selectiveness with regard to digital technologies and their uses in education is likely to be important not just for teachers and schools, but also for parents and guardians, and for learners themselves. If home learning is being seen as extensions of school learning, both parents and guardians and learners are likely to value advice and support that enables them to gain most effectively.

Considering context is a last feature that is also likely to be vitally important. Advisers and policy makers may be in the best position to understand the wide context, both current and future, and how this can be considered as a means to support learners' aspirations. But whatever the contextual scenario might be, learners are likely to benefit from developing educational behaviours that support their engagement and learning in computational thinking and digital competencies, enabling them to problem solve, for themselves and for others.

Figure 11.4 shows the educational behaviours that are suggested currently as those likely to be supportive of advisers and policy makers for guidance and policy in settings where digital technologies are used.

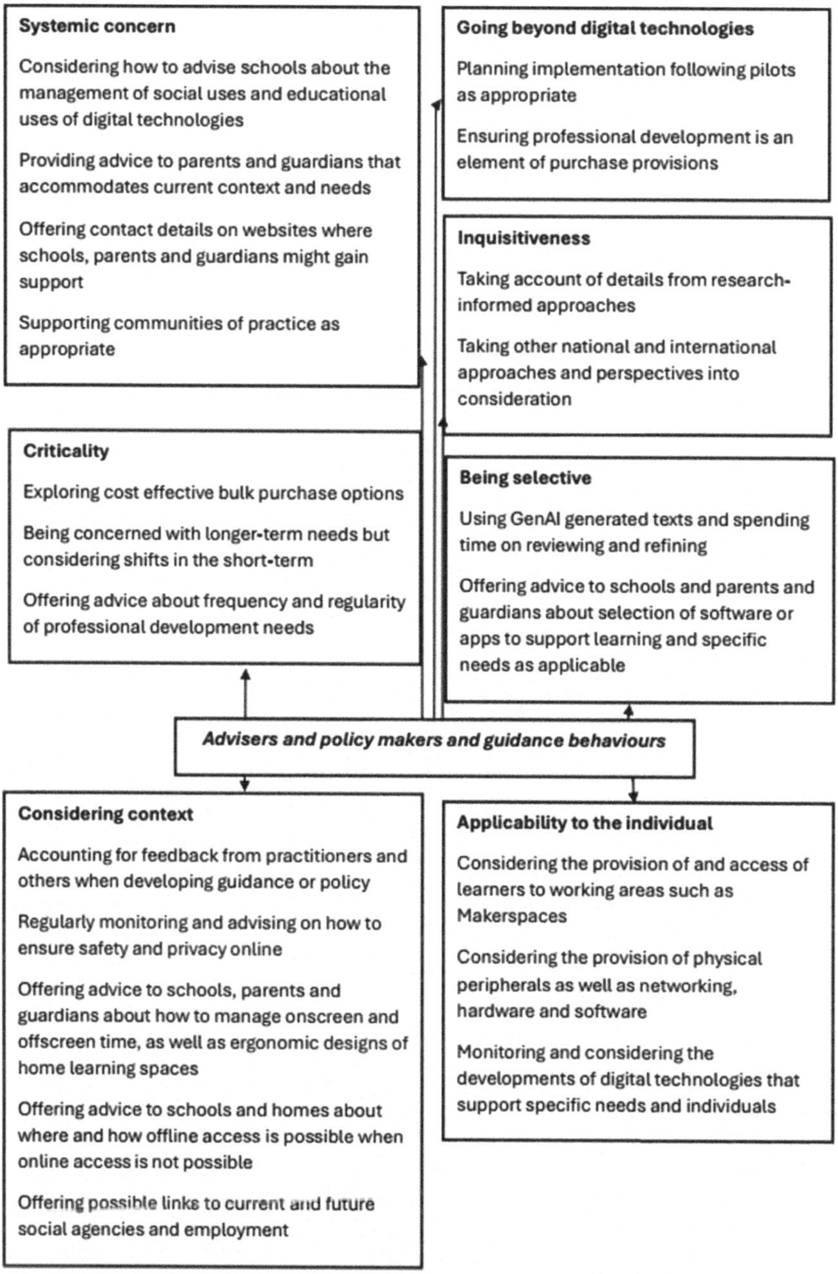

Fig. 11.4 Suggested supportive educational behaviours for policy and guidance

References

Abdulrahaman, M. D., Faruk, N., Oloyede, A. A., Surajudeen-Bakinde, N. T., Olawoyin, L. A., Mejabi, O. V., Imam-Fulani, Y. O., Fahm, A. O., & Azeez, A. L. (2020). Multimedia tools in the teaching and learning processes: A systematic review. *Heliyon, 6*(11), e05312. https://doi.org/10.1016/j.heliyon.2020.e05312

ACARA. (2025). *Understand this general capability: Digital literacy*. https://www.australiancurriculum.edu.au/curriculum-information/understand-this-general-capability/digital-literacy

Agayon, A. J. D., Agayon, A. K. R., & Pentang, J. T. (2022). Teachers in the new normal: Challenges and coping mechanisms in secondary schools. *Journal of Humanities and Education Development, 4*(1), 67–75.

Agbo, B., Morris, C., Osman, M., Basketts, J., & Kyriacou, T. (2024). A systematic literature review on software applications used to support curriculum development and delivery in primary and secondary education. *International Journal of Educational Research Open, 7*, 100385. https://doi.org/10.1016/j.ijedro.2024.100385

Ahmadvand, S., & Khoshchehreh, M. (2023). Theory and practice: Implications of social constructivism in education. *International Journal of Humanities and Social Development Research, 7*, 19–30.

Akpen, C. N., Asaolu, S., Atobatele, S., Okagbue, H., & Sampson, S. (2024). Impact of online learning on student's performance and engagement: A systematic review. *Discover Education, 3*, 205. https://doi.org/10.1007/s44217-024-00253-0

Aksakal, N. (2015). Theoretical view to the approach of the edutainment. *Procedia Social and Behavioral Sciences, 186*, 1232–1239. https://doi.org/10.1016/j.sbspro.2015.04.081

Al Halaibi, H. (2021). *How does professional development affect interactive whiteboard use in public and private international school mathematics teaching in Saudi Arabia?* Doctoral Thesis, Queen's University Belfast, UK. https://pureadmin.qub.ac.uk/ws/portalfiles/portal/235414692/my_thesis_2_1_pdf

Al-Ansi, A. M., Jaboob, M., Garad, A., & Al-Ansi, A. (2023). Analyzing augmented reality (AR) and virtual reality (VR) recent development in education. *Social Sciences and Humanities Open, 8*(1), 100532. https://doi.org/10.1016/j.ssaho.2023.100532

Alharbi, S. (2016). Benefits and barriers: Incorporating assistive technology in an inclusive setting for primary school students with learning disabilities in language arts. *American Research Journal of Humanities and Social Sciences, 2*, 1–11.

Alzahrani, N. M. (2020). Augmented reality: A systematic review of its benefits and challenges in E-learning contexts. *Applied Sciences, 10*(16), 5660. https://doi.org/10.3390/app10165660

Amayou, J., Sadikb, O., & Paul, K. (2025). Exploring teachers' understanding of collaborative learning and teamwork strategies in design and skills-labs. *Journal of Learning and Teaching in Digital Age, 10*(1), 12–32.

D. Passey, *Shifting Educational Behaviours*, https://doi.org/10.1007/978-3-032-18942-4

An, X., Hong, J.-C., Li, Y., & Zhou, Y. (2022). The impact of attitude toward peer interaction on middle school students' problem-solving self-efficacy during the COVID-19 pandemic. *Frontiers in Psychology, 13*, 978144. https://doi.org/10.3389/fpsyg.2022.978144

Andersen, C., Pold, S., & Riis, M. (2014). A dialogue on cassette tapes and their memories. *A Peer-Reviewed Journal about, 3*, 156–167. https://doi.org/10.7146/aprja.v3i1.116095

Anderson, M., Carroll, D., & Cameron, J. (Eds.). (2011). *Drama education with digital technology*. Bloomsbury Academic.

Apps, J., Webb, S., & Hutton, E. (2024). Parents' and carers' attitudes to the use of digital technology and its role in the care of children with complex needs. *British Journal of Occupational Therapy, 87*(7), 452–460. https://doi.org/10.1177/03080226241233112

Arms, W. Y. (2012). The 1990s: The formative years of digital libraries. *Library Hi Tech, 30*(4), 579–591. https://doi.org/10.1108/07378831211285068

Asare, S., Kyenkyehene, S., & Kwadwo, M. (2023). Interactive technology in physical education classroom: A case of a Ghanaian college of education. *American Journal of Education and Information Technology, 7*(2), 51–58.

Asotić, D. (2023). *Interconnected behaviours: Unraveling the internet of behaviours*. Independently Published.

Auerbach, J. (2021). Students as producers, not consumers? Digital capabilities, higher education transformation and the futures of learning in Southern Africa. *International Journal of Critical Diversity Studies, 4*(2), 81–95.

Australian Skills Quality Authority. (ASQA). (n.d.). *Data and reporting requirements*. https://www.asqa.gov.au/resources/faqs/data-and-reporting-requirements

Balakrishnan, R., & Charania, A. (2023). Parental digital competence and influences on parenting mediation. *Studies in Technology Enhanced Learning, 3*(3), 7987.

Balalle, H. (2024). Exploring student engagement in technology-based education in relation to gamification, online/distance learning, and other factors: A systematic literature review. *Social Sciences and Humanities Open, 9*, 100870. https://doi.org/10.1016/j.ssaho.2024.100870

Balan, A. (2024). Examining the ethical and sustainability challenges of legal education's AI revolution. *International Journal of the Legal Profession, 31*(3), 323–348. https://doi.org/10.1080/09695958.2024.2421179

Banko, A., Leoste, J., & Õun, T. (2025). Exploring the impact of social robots on second language learning in primary and elementary schools: Teacher involvement and learning outcomes. *Educational Media International, 7*, 1–18. https://doi.org/10.1080/09523987.2025.2505505

Barron, A. B., Hebets, E. A., Cleland, T. A., Fitzpatrick, C. L., Hauber, M. E., & Stevens, J. R. (2015). Embracing multiple definitions of learning. *Trends in Neurosciences, 38*(7), 405–407. https://doi.org/10.1016/j.tins.2015.04.008

Becker, H. J., & Hativa, N. (1994). History, theory and research concerning integrated learning systems. *International Journal of Educational Research, 21*(1), 5–12. https://doi.org/10.1016/0883-0355(94)90019-1

Belkina, M., Daniel, S., Nikolic, S., Haque, R., Lyden, S., Neal, P., Grundy, S., & Hassan, G. M. (2025). Implementing generative AI (GenAI) in higher education: A systematic review of case studies. *Computers and Education: Artificial Intelligence, 8*, 100407. https://doi.org/10.1016/j.caeai.2025.100407

Berger, P. L., & Luckmann, T. (1966). *The social construction of reality: A treatise in the sociology of knowledge*. Anchor Books.

Bernacki, M. L., Greene, J. A., & Crompton, H. (2020). Mobile technology, learning, and achievement: Advances in understanding and measuring the role of mobile technology in education. *Contemporary Educational Psychology, 60*, 101827. https://doi.org/10.1016/j.cedpsych.2019.101827

Bidaki, M. Z., & Mobasheri, N. (2013). Teachers' views of the effects of the interactive white board (IWB) on teaching. *Procedia Social and Behavioral Sciences, 83*, 140–144. https://doi.org/10.1016/j.sbspro.2013.06.027

Black, A., Warstadt, M. F., & Mamas, C. (2025). It's who you know: A review of peer networks and academic achievement in schools. *Frontiers in Psychology, 15*, 1444570. https://doi.org/10.3389/fpsyg.2024.1444570

Bluhm, H. P. (1986). Local area networks in the school setting. *Educational Technology, 26*(5), 26–31.

Bokhove, C., Jerrim, J., & Sims, S. (2023). How useful are ofsted inspection judgements for informing secondary school choice? *Journal of School Choice, 17*(1), 35–61. https://doi.org/10.1080/15582159.2023.2169813

Böttger, T., & Zierer, K. (2024). To ban or not to ban? A rapid review on the impact of smartphone bans in schools on social well-being and academic performance. *Education Sciences, 14*(8), 906. https://doi.org/10.3390/educsci14080906

Brito, R., & Dias, P. (2020). "Which apps are good for my children?" How the parents of young children select apps. *International Journal of Child-Computer Interaction, 26*, 100188. https://doi.org/10.1016/j.ijcci.2020.100188

Bromcom. (n.d.). *Bromcom MIS for secondary schools*. https://assets.digitalmarketplace.service.gov.uk/g-cloud-11/documents/93515/172233866143787-service-definition-document-2019-05-22-1425.pdf

Brummer, E. C., & Achterberg, M. (2025). *Unplugged and unheard: Dutch youth on smartphone policies in secondary schools*. Open Science Framework. https://doi.org/10.17605/OSF.IO/5RW2V

Burke, P. F., Schuck, S., Burden, K., & Kearney, M. (2025). Mediating learning with mobile devices through pedagogical innovation: Teachers' perceptions of K-12 students' learning experiences. *Computers and Education, 227*, 105226. https://doi.org/10.1016/j.compedu.2024.105226

Business of Apps. (2025). *Education app revenue and usage statistics*. https://www.businessofapps.com/data/education-app-market/

Butler, D., Leahy, M., Charania, A., Gedara, P. M., Keane, T., Laferrière, T., Nakamura, K., Ueda, H., & Bocconi, S. (2024). Aligning digital educational policies with the new realities of schooling. *Technology, Knowledge and Learning, 29*, 1831–1849. https://doi.org/10.1007/s10758-024-09776-9

Butler, N., Quigg, Z., Bates, R., Jones, L., Ashworth, E., Gowland, S., & Jones, M. (2022). The contributing role of family, school, and peer supportive relationships in protecting the mental wellbeing of children and adolescents. *School Mental Health, 14*(3), 776–788. https://doi.org/10.1007/s12310-022-09502-9

Butler, T. (n.d.). *A critical review of digital technology in education that should give policy makers and educators pause for thought*. Cork, Ireland: University College Cork. https://ehtrust.org/wp-content/uploads/Digital-Technology-in-Education-Working-Paper-2019.pdf#:~:text=The%20paper%20highlights%2C%20for%20example%2C%20that%3A%20%281%29%20Screens,needs%20to%20find%20a%20place%20in%20the%20curriculum.

Byrne, J., & Burton, P. (2017). Children as Internet users: How can evidence better inform policy debate? *Journal of Cyber Policy, 2*(1), 39–52. https://doi.org/10.1080/23738871.2017.1291698

Caballero-Julia, D., Martín-Lucas, J., & Andrade-Silva, L. E. (2024). Unpacking the relationship between screen use and educational outcomes in childhood: A systematic literature review. *Computers and Education, 215*, 105049. https://doi.org/10.1016/j.compedu.2024.105049

Cacicio, S., & Riggs, R. (2023). Bridging resource gaps in adult education: The role of generative AI. *Adult Literacy Education, Fall, 2023*, 80–86.

Cadiz, R. G. D., & Guerrero, C. J. J. (2021). Ergonomic design of computer workstations of high school students studying at home. In *Proceedings of the international conference on industrial engineering and operations management Rome, Italy* (pp. 1311–1319). IEOM Society International. https://ieomsociety.org/proceedings/2021rome/498.pdf

Calderón-Garrido, D., Ramos-Pardo, F., & Suárez-Guerrero, C. (2022). The use of mobile phones in classrooms: A systematic review. *International Journal of Emerging Technologies in Learning, 17*, 194–209. https://doi.org/10.3991/ijet.v17i06.29181

Calinescu, A. (2024). The impact of digital technologies on memory and memory studies. *Journal of Contemporary Philosophical and Anthropological Studies, 2*, 2977–5507.

Campbell, M., Edwards, E. J., Pennell, D., Poed, S., Lister, V., Gillett-Swan, J., Kelly, A., Zec, D., & Nguyen, T.-A. (2024). Evidence for and against banning mobile phones in schools: A scoping review. *Journal of Psychologists and Counsellors in Schools, 34*(3), 242–265. https://doi.org/10.1177/20556365241270394

Cascales, A., Pérez-López, D., & Contero, M. (2013). Study on parent's acceptance of the augmented reality use for preschool education. *Procedia Computer Science, 25*, 420–427. https://doi.org/10.1016/j.procs.2013.11.053

Chan, A. S., Lee, T. L., Sze, S. L., Yang, N. S., & Han, Y. M. Y. (2022). Eye-tracking training improves the learning and memory of children with learning difficulty. *Scientific Reports, 12*(1), 13974. https://doi.org/10.1038/s41598-022-18286-6

Chang, H.-Y., Binali, T., Liang, J.-C., Chiou, G.-L., Cheng, K.-H., Lee, S.W.-Y., & Tsai, C.-C. (2022). Ten years of augmented reality in education: A meta-analysis of (quasi-) experimental studies to investigate the impact. *Computers and Education, 191*, 104641. https://doi.org/10.1016/j.compedu.2022.104641

Chara, Y., Machaca, A., Yepez, J., Mendoza, F., & Rucano, F. (2023). Coping strategies for online learning from home. *International Journal of Learning, Teaching and Educational Research, 22*, 359–378.

Cheah, Y. H., Lu, J., & Kim, J. (2025). Integrating generative artificial intelligence in K-12 education: Examining teachers' preparedness, practices, and barriers. *Computers and Education: Artificial Intelligence, 8*, 100363. https://doi.org/10.1016/j.caeai.2025.100363

Chen, C.-H., & Tsai, C.-C. (2021). In-service teachers' conceptions of mobile technology-integrated instruction: Tendency towards student-centered learning. *Computers and Education, 170*, 104224. https://doi.org/10.1016/j.compedu.2021.104224

Chen, J., Jiang, H., Justice, L. M., Lin, T. J., Purtell, K. M., & Ansari, A. (2020). Influences of teacher-child relationships and classroom social management on child-perceived peer social experiences during early school years. *Frontiers in Psychology, 11*, 586991. https://doi.org/10.3389/fpsyg.2020.586991

Cheng, K.-H. (2017). Exploring parents' conceptions of augmented reality learning and approaches to learning by augmented reality with their children. *Journal of Educational Computing Research, 55*(6), 820–843. https://doi.org/10.1177/0735633116686082

Chiu, M. S., & Zhu, M. (2025). Parents' perspectives on using virtual reality for learning mathematics: Identifying factors for innovative technology acceptance. *Education and Information Technologies, 30*, 779–799. https://doi.org/10.1007/s10639-024-12935-1

Chiu, T. K. F. (2023). The impact of generative AI (GenAI) on practices, policies and research direction in education: A case of ChatGPT and Midjourney. *Interactive Learning Environments, 32*(10), 6187–6203. https://doi.org/10.1080/10494820.2023.2253861

Chiu, T. K. F. (2024). Future research recommendations for transforming higher education with generative AI. *Computers and Education: Artificial Intelligence, 6*, 100197. https://doi.org/10.1016/j.caeai.2023.100197

Chiu, T. K. F., Sun, J. C. Y., & Ismailov, M. (2022). Investigating the relationship of technology learning support to digital literacy from the perspective of self-determination theory. *Educational Psychology, 42*(10), 1263–1282. https://doi.org/10.1080/01443410.2022.2074966

Chong, S. C., Teo, W. Z., & Shorey, S. (2023). Exploring the perception of parents on children's screentime: A systematic review and meta-synthesis of qualitative studies. *Pediatric Research, 94*(3), 915–925. https://doi.org/10.1038/s41390-023-02555-9

Chu, S.-T., Hwang, G.-J., & Tu, Y.-F. (2022). Artificial intelligence-based robots in education: A systematic review of selected SSCI publications. *Computers and Education: Artificial Intelligence, 3*, 100091. https://doi.org/10.1016/j.caeai.2022.100091

Chui, H. S., Hui, W. T., & Chui, S. W. H. (2025). Online teaching and learning effectiveness for kindergartens, primary and secondary schools. *Cogent Education, 12*(1), 8067. https://doi.org/10.1080/2331186X.2024.2448067

Cleveland, G., Bebell, D., & Xin, Z. (2024). Parents' use of technology to stay informed about their children's education. *Education and Information Technologies, 29*, 23249–23270. https://doi.org/10.1007/s10639-024-12785-x

Conry, P. T. (2020). *Parental perceptions of mobile device learning for students in special education.* Doctoral dissertation. Walden University College of Education. https://scholarworks.waldenu.edu/cgi/viewcontent.cgi?article=10985&context=dissertations

Council of Europe. (2025). *Linguistic integration of adult migrants (LIAM): Formal, non-formal and informal learning.* https://www.coe.int/en/web/lang-migrants/formal-non-formal-and-informal-learning

Council for Curriculum, Examinations and Assessment (CCEA). (2025). *Using ICT desirable features.* https://ccea.org.uk/learning-resources/using-ict-desirable-features

Cowley, S. (2021). *Learning behaviours: A practical guide to self-regulation in the early years.* Hodder Education.

Csizmadia, A., Standl, B., & Waite, J. (2019). Integrating the constructionist learning theory with computational thinking classroom activities. *Informatics in Education, 18*, 41–67.

Curriculum and Assessment Policy Statement (CAPS) 123. (2023). *Understanding the differences between the CAPS curriculum and other educational frameworks and curricula.* https://caps123.co.za/understanding-the-differences-between-the-caps-curriculum-and-other-educational-frameworks-and-curricula/

Dao, P., Hoang, S. T. T., & Nguyen, M. X. N. C. (2024). Young learners' synchronous online peer interaction: Teachers' beliefs of its benefits and implementation. *Language Awareness, 33*(1), 45–69. https://doi.org/10.1080/09658416.2022.2152828

Darmawansah, D., Hwang, G. J., Chen, M. R. A., et al. (2023). Trends and research foci of robotics-based STEM education: A systematic review from diverse angles based on the technology-based learning model. *International Journal of STEM Education, 10*(12), 400. https://doi.org/10.1186/s40594-023-00400-3

Data Insights Market. (2025). *Online tutoring: Growth opportunities and competitive landscape overview 2025–2033.* https://www.datainsightsmarket.com/reports/online-tutoring-1981349

Dawson, C., Julku, H., Pihlajamäki, M., Kaakinen, J. K., Schooler, J. W., & Simola, J. (2024). Evidence-based scientific thinking and decision-making in everyday life. *Cognitive Research: Principles and Implications, 9*, 50. https://doi.org/10.1186/s41235-024-00578-2

de Barros, E. C. (2024). Understanding the influence of digital technology on human cognitive functions: A narrative review. *IBRO Neuroscience Reports, 17*, 415–422. https://doi.org/10.1016/j.ibneur.2024.11.006

de Jong, L., Meirink, J., & Admiraal, W. (2022). School-based collaboration as a learning context for teachers: A systematic review. *International Journal of Educational Research, 112*, 101927. https://doi.org/10.1016/j.ijer.2022.101927

De Vita, M., Verschaffel, L., & Elen, J. (2014). Interactive whiteboards in mathematics teaching: A literature review. *Education Research International, 316*, 1–16. https://doi.org/10.1155/2014/401315

Dehdary, N., & Meschi, R. (2024). The role of ChatGPT in language education: A study of Omani students' perspectives. *Studies in Technology Enhanced Learning, 4*(1), 5360.

Dennis, J. (2024). Capitalizing networked learning: Connectivism, multiliteracies and the architectonics of pedagogy. *Journal of Contemporary Issues in Education, 19*(1), 138–167.

Department for Children, Schools and Families. (DCSF). (2009). *Your child, your schools, our future: Building a 21st century schools system.* DCSF. https://assets.publishing.service.gov.uk/media/5a75c407ed915d6faf2b582e/21st_century_schools.pdf

Department for Education. (2022). *Meeting digital and technology standards in schools and colleges.* Department for Education. https://www.gov.uk/guidance/meeting-digital-and-technology-standards-in-schools-and-colleges/laptop-desktop-and-tablet-standards

Department for Education. (2024). *NCCIS management information requirement 2025 to 2026.* Department for Education. https://assets.publishing.service.gov.uk/media/6758709c8a1ef8f66413b9c4/NCCIS_Management_Information_Requirement_-_2025_to_2026.pdf

DeSantis, J. D. (2013). Exploring the effects of professional development for the interactive whiteboard on teachers' technology self-efficacy. *Journal of Information Technology Education: Research, 12*, 343–362.

Dias, P., & Brito, R. (2021). Criteria for selecting apps: Debating the perceptions of young children, parents and industry stakeholders. *Computers and Education, 165*, 104134. https://doi.org/10.1016/j.compedu.2021.104134

Digregorio, P., & Lojeski, K. (2009). The effects of interactive whiteboards (IWBs) on student performance and learning: A literature review. *Journal of Educational Technology Systems, 38*, 255–312. https://doi.org/10.2190/ET.38.3.b

Dominke, H., & Steffensky, M. (2025). The quality of parent–child interactions in science and associations with children's science learning: A systematic review. *Review of Education, 13*, e70067. https://doi.org/10.1002/rev3.70067

Downes, S. (2019). Recent work in connectivism. *European Journal of Open, Distance and e-Learning, 22*(2), 112–131.

Downes, S. (2022). Connectivism. *Asian Journal of Distance Education, 17*(1), 623.

Dray, J., & Symons, D. (2025). Review of innovative mental health support for children and young people: Generative AI co-design applications and challenges. *Current Developmental Disorders Reports, 12*(13), 1–13. https://doi.org/10.1007/s40474-025-00328-z

Dron, J., & Anderson, T. (2023). Informal learning in digital contexts. In O. Zawacki-Richter, & I. Jung (Eds.), *Handbook of open, distance and digital education*. Springer. https://doi.org/10.1007/978-981-19-2080-6_84

Du, X., Zhang, M., Shelton, B. E., & Hung, J. L. (2019). Learning anytime, anywhere: A spatio-temporal analysis for online learning. *Interactive Learning Environments, 30*(1), 34–48. https://doi.org/10.1080/10494820.2019.1633546

Durk, J., & Sentence, S. (2025). A positive and inclusive classroom experience: Primary school teachers' perspectives of physical computing. In *Proceedings of the 24th interaction design and children* (pp. 1146–1150). Association for Computing Machinery. https://doi.org/10.1145/3713043.3731552

Dutton, W., Kovaric, P., & Steinfield, C. (1983). Computing in the home: A research paradigm. *Computers and the Social Sciences, 1*(1), 5–18. https://doi.org/10.1177/089443938500100102

Education Scotland. (n.d.). *Inspection and review*. https://education.gov.scot/inspection-and-review/

Ellis. S., & Tod, J. (2018). *Behaviour for learning: Promoting positive relationships in the classroom*. Routledge.

Entwistle, N. J. (2012). Approaches to learning and studying. In N. M. Seel (Ed.), *Encyclopedia of the sciences of learning*. Springer. https://doi.org/10.1007/978-1-4419-1428-6_652

Esposito, C., De Masi, F., Dragone, M., & Bacchini, D. (2024). Technology-based interventions for preventing youth violence: A systematic review of programs, tools, and evidence. *Adolescent Research Review, 9*, 165–192. https://doi.org/10.1007/s40894-023-00222-y

Evans, M. (2009). *Foreign language learning with digital technology*. Bloomsbury Academic.

Farangi, M. R., Nejadghanbar, H., & Hu, G. (2024). Use of generative AI in research: Ethical considerations and emotional experiences. *Ethics and Behavior, 21*, 1–17. https://doi.org/10.1080/10508422.2024.2420133

Farooqi, M. T. K., Siddique, Z., & Awan, S. M. (2024). The effectiveness of educational software and applications for primary students' learning outcomes: A systematic review. *Journal of Excellence in Social Sciences, 3*(4), 347.

FE Online. (2024). *GenAI era: New report says over 70% parents admit their kids use AI for educational purposes*. https://www.financialexpress.com/jobs-career/education-genai-era-new-report-says-over-70-parents-admit-their-kids-use-ai-for-educational-purposes-3603881/

Fernández-Batanero, J. M., Montenegro-Rueda, M., Fernández-Cerero, J., & García-Martínez, I. (2022). Assistive technology for the inclusion of students with disabilities: A systematic review. *Educational Technology Research and Development, 70*, 1911–1930. https://doi.org/10.1007/s11423-022-10127-7

Ferraz, R., Cortiz, D., & Xavier, H. (2025). A brief history of images on the web. In *Companion proceedings of the ACM web conference 2025 (WWW Companion '25)* (pp. 833–836). ACM. https://doi.org/10.1145/3701716.3716839

Finney, J., & Burnard, P. (2010). *Music education with digital technology*. Bloomsbury Academic.

FitzGerald, E., Kucirkova, N., Jones, A., Cross, S., Ferguson, R., Herodotou, C., Hillaire, G., & Scanlon, E. (2018). Dimensions of personalisation in technology-enhanced learning: A framework and implications for design. *British Journal of Educational Technology, 49*, 165–181. https://doi.org/10.1111/bjet.12534

Flynn, K. S., Li, L., Huang, C.-H., Patel, T., Luttgen, K., Yang, S., & Chow, E. (2024). Leveraging technology to address social-emotional learning during the pandemic: Findings from an efficacy trial. *Social and Emotional Learning: Research, Practice, and Policy, 4*, 100045. https://doi.org/10.1016/j.sel.2024.100045

Fung, K. Y., Fung, K. C., Lui, T. L. R., Sin, K. F., Lee, L. H., Qu, H., & Song, S. (2025). Exploring the impact of robot interaction on learning engagement: A comparative study of two multimodal robots. *Smart Learning Environments, 12*(12), 362. https://doi.org/10.1186/s40561-024-00362-1

Garcia, J. (2016). *The impact of peer support on homework completion*. Masters dissertation. Rowan University, USA. https://rdw.rowan.edu/cgi/viewcontent.cgi?article=2412&context=etd

Garzón, J., Kinshuk, C., Burgos, D., & Tlili, A. (2024). Advantages and challenges associated with mobile learning in education: A systematic literature review. *Journal of Computers in Education, 24*, 342. https://doi.org/10.1007/s40692-024-00342-x

Gath, M. E., Monk, L., Scott, A., & Gillon, G. T. (2024). Smartphones at school: A mixed-methods analysis of educators' and students' perspectives on mobile phone use at school. *Education Sciences, 14*(4), 351. https://doi.org/10.3390/educsci14040351

Ghavifekr, S., & Rosdy, W. A. W. (2015). Teaching and learning with technology: Effectiveness of ICT integration in schools. *International Journal of Research in Education and Science, 1*(2), 175–191.

Ghoshal, S., & Upadhyay, A. (2023). The effect of internet on students' studies: A review. *International Journal of Multidisciplinary Research, 9*(7), 38–42.

Giannoukos, G. (2024). Main learning theories in education. *European Journal of Contemporary Education and E-Learning, 2*(5), 93–100.

Gill, T. G. (1995). Early expert systems: Where are they now? *MIS Quarterly, 19*(1), 51–81.

Giraldo, J-P., Jenkins, R., & Tungatarova, A. (2022). *The case for edutainment: Rethinking how we can enable multiple pathways to learning for all children*. UNICEF. https://www.unicef.org/blog/edutainment-multiple-pathways-learning

Gondwe, F. (2021). Technology professional development for teacher educators: A literature review and proposal for further research. *SN Social Sciences, 1*, 200. https://doi.org/10.1007/s43545-021-00184-9

González Crespo, R., & Burgos, D. (2019). Advanced sensors technology in education. *Sensors, 19*(19), 4155. https://doi.org/10.3390/s19194155

Goodyear, V. A., James, C., Orben, A., Quennerstedt, M., Schwartz, G., & Pallan, M. (2024). Approaches to children's smartphone and social media use must go beyond bans. *British Medical Journal, 388*, e082569. https://doi.org/10.1136/bmj-2024-082569

Grau, M., Indri, L., Bello, L., & Sauter, T. (2021). Robots in industry: The past, present, and future of a growing collaboration with humans. *IEEE Industrial Electronics Magazine, 15*(1), 50–61. https://doi.org/10.1109/MIE.2020.3008136

Grillenberger, M. (2023). Why and how to teach physical computing: Research and practice in computer science education at secondary schools. In T. Keane, & A. E. Fluck (Eds.), *Teaching coding in K-12 schools*. Springer. https://doi.org/10.1007/978-3-031-21970-2_15

Guo, L., Wang, D., Gu, F., Li, Y., Wang, Y., & Zhou, R. (2021). Evolution and trends in intelligent tutoring systems research: A multidisciplinary and scientometric view. *Asia Pacific Education Review, 22*, 441–461. https://doi.org/10.1007/s12564-021-09697-7

Gür, D., Schäfer, N., Kupnik, M., & Beckerle, P. (2020). A human–computer interface replacing mouse and keyboard for individuals with limited upper limb mobility. *Multimodal Technologies and Interaction, 4*(4), 84. https://doi.org/10.3390/mti4040084

Gür, D., & Türel, Y. K. (2022). Parenting in the digital age: Attitudes, controls and limitations regarding children's use of ICT. *Computers and Education, 183*, 104504. https://doi.org/10.1016/j.compedu.2022.104504

Haleem, A., Javaid, M., Qadri, M. A., & Suman, R. (2022). Understanding the role of digital technologies in education: A review. *Sustainable Operations and Computers, 3*, 275–285. https://doi.org/10.1016/j.susoc.2022.05.004

Hammond, M. (1995). Learning from experience: Approaching the research of CD-ROM in schools. In *World conference on computers in education VI: WCCE 1995*. Springer. https://doi.org/10.1007/978-0-387-34844-5_29

Harger, B. (2019). A culture of aggression: School culture and the normalization of aggression in two elementary schools. *British Journal of Sociology of Education, 40*(8), 1105–1120.

Harris, A., & Goodall, J. (2007). *Engaging parents in raising achievement: Do parents know they matter?* DCSF. https://dera.ioe.ac.uk/id/eprint/6639/1/DCSF-RW004.pdf

Harverson, J., Paatsch, L., Anglim, J., & Horwood, S. (2025). Digital technology use and well-being in young children: A systematic review and meta-analysis. *Computers in Human Behavior, 168*, 108660. https://doi.org/10.1016/j.chb.2025.108660

Hasnain, S. G. M., & Rafi, F. A. (2019). Windows, Linux, Mac operating system and decision making. *International Journal of Computer Applications, 177*(27), 11–15.

Hatteberg, S. J. (2020). A tale of many sources: The perceived benefits of significant other, similar other, and significant and similar other social support. *Sociological Perspectives, 64*(1), 37–57. https://doi.org/10.1177/0731121420908885

Hattie, J., & O'Leary, T. (2025). Learning styles, preferences, or strategies? An explanation for the resurgence of styles across many meta-analyses. *Educational Psychology Review, 37*, 31. https://doi.org/10.1007/s10648-025-10002-w

He, J., Wang, Q., & Lee, H. (2025). Enhancing online learning engagement: Teacher support, psychological needs satisfaction and interaction. *BMC Psychology, 13*, 696. https://doi.org/10.1186/s40359-025-03016-0

Health-Europe, T. L. R. (2023). Embracing generative AI in health care. *Lancet Regional Health-Europe, 3*(30), 100677. https://doi.org/10.1016/j.lanepe.2023.100677

Hennessy, S., & London, L. (2013). *Learning from international experiences with interactive whiteboards: The role of professional development in integrating the technology*. OECD. https://www.oecd.org/content/dam/oecd/en/publications/reports/2013/03/learning-from-international-experiences-with-interactive-whiteboards_g17a2281/5k49chbsnmls-en.pdf

Hennessy, S., Dragovic, T., & Warwick, P. (2017). A research-informed, school-based professional development workshop programme to promote dialogic teaching with interactive technologies. *Professional Development in Education, 44*(2), 145–168. https://doi.org/10.1080/19415257.2016.1258653

Henry, L. (2005). Information search strategies on the internet: A critical component of new literacies. *Webology, 2*(1), 9.

Hermann, E., & Puntoni, S. (2024). Artificial intelligence and consumer behavior: From predictive to generative AI. *Journal of Business Research, 180*, 114720. https://doi.org/10.1016/j.jbusres.2024.114720

Higgins, S., Baumfield, V., & Hall, E. (2007). *Learning skills and the development of learning capabilities: Technical report*. EPPI-Centre, Social Science Research Unit, Institute of Education, University of London. https://www.researchgate.net/profile/Steven-Higgins-4/publication/232607684_Learning_skills_and_the_development_of_learning_capabilities/links/0046352133d61a947f000000/Learning-skills-and-the-development-of-learning-capabilities.pdf?_tp=eyJjb250ZXh0Ijp7ImZpcnN0UGFnZSI6InB1YmxpY2F0aW9uIiwicGFnZSI6InB1YmxpY2F0aW9uIn19

Higgins, S. E. (2010). The impact of interactive whiteboards on classroom interaction and learning in primary schools in the UK. In *Interactive whiteboards for education: theory, research and practice* (pp. 86–101). Hershey. https://www.igi-global.com/gateway/book/37282

Ho, H.-R., White, N., Hubbard, E., & Mutlu, B. (2023). Designing parent-child-robot interactions to facilitate in-home parental math talk with young children. In *Interaction design and children (IDC '23), June 19–23, 2023, Chicago, IL, USA*. ACM. https://doi.org/10.1145/3585088.3589358

Hollingworth, S., Mansaray, A., Allen, K., & Rose, A. (2011). Parents' perspectives on technology and children's learning in the home: Social class and the role of the habitus. *Journal of Computer Assisted Learning, 27*, 347–360. https://doi.org/10.1111/j.1365-2729.2011.00431.x

House of Commons Education Committee. (2024). Screen time: Impacts on education and well-being. HC. https://committees.parliament.uk/publications/45128/documents/223543/default/

Howard, S. K., & Mozejko, A. (2015). Considering the history of digital technologies in education. In M. Henderson & G. Romero (Eds.), *Teaching and digital technologies: Big issues and critical questions* (pp. 157–168). Cambridge University Press.

Hsu, C., Lopez, O., & Raj, S. Y. (2020). Considering parental perceptions on mobile learning systems with in-app advertising: Taiwan case study. *International Journal of Advanced Science and Technology, 29*(7s), 2437–2471.

Hu-Au, E., & Lee, J. (2018). Virtual reality in education: A tool for learning in the experience age. *International Journal of Innovation in Education, 4*, 12691. https://doi.org/10.1504/IJIIE.2017.10012691

Hughes-Roberts, T., Brown, D., Burton, A., Shopland, N., Tinney, J., & Boulton, H. (2023). Digital game making and game templates promotes learner engagement in non-computing based classroom teaching. *Technology, Knowledge and Learning*. https://doi.org/10.1007/s10758-023-09654-w

Hugh-Jones, S., Pert, K., Kendal, S., Eltringham, S., Skelton, C., Yaziji, N., & West, R. (2022). Adolescents accept digital mental health support in schools: A co-design and feasibility study of a school-based app for UK adolescents. *Mental Health and Prevention, 27*, 200241. https://doi.org/10.1016/j.mhp.2022.200241

Hwb. (n.d.). *Curriculum for wales*. https://hwb.gov.wales/curriculum-for-wales

İnan, B., & Güldenoğlu, B. (2025). The use and future of social humanoid robots in special education: A systematic review. *International Journal of Sciences: Basic and Applied Research (IJSBAR), 75*(1), 45–67.

International Telecommunication Union Development Sector. (2020). *Guidelines for parents and educators on child online protection*. ITU Publications. https://www.itu.int/dms_pub/itu-s/opb/gen/S-GEN-COP.EDUC-2020-PDF-E.pdf

Jacob, U. S., Ologbosere, O. A., Onyemah, T. N., & Eniolorunda, J. T. (2024). Assistive technology in special education: Current practices and emerging trends. *International Journal of Research in Special Education, 4*(1), 30–38.

Jeffs, T. L. (2009). Virtual reality and special needs. *Themes in Science and Technology Education, 2*, 253–268.

Johnson, M., Rodrigues, A., & Brady, J. (2025). Community and collaborative learning in online schools: Students' and teachers' perspectives. *E-Learning and Digital Media, 13*, 8590. https://doi.org/10.1177/20427530251348590

Kadel, R., Babarenda-Guruge, D., Aziz, S., Karagiannidis, V., & Paudel, K. (2021). Mobile learning approaches and its impact on student's education: A survey. *International Journal of Information and Education Technology, 11*, 1546.

Kafai, Y. B., & Burke, Q. (2015). Constructionist gaming: Understanding the benefits of making games for learning. *Educational Psychologist, 50*(4), 313–334. https://doi.org/10.1080/00461520.2015.1124022

Kalelioglu, F., & Sentance, S. (2020). Teaching with physical computing in school: The case of the micro:Bit. *Education and Information Technologies, 25*, 2577–2603. https://doi.org/10.1007/s10639-019-10080-8

Kaliski, B. (2025). Moore's law. In S. Jajodia, P. Samarati, & M. Yung (Eds.), *Encyclopedia of cryptography, security and privacy*. Springer. https://doi.org/10.1007/978-3-030-71522-9_420

Kamoyo, M., Masamha, T., & Chikazhe, L. (2025). Remote e-learning model in the post COVID-19 era; building a resilient higher education strategy. *Cogent Education, 12*(1), 8854. https://doi.org/10.1080/2331186X.2025.2498854

Kampylis, P., Bacigalupo, M., Punie, Y., Redecker, C., Langer, L., Rasmussen, M., Conrads, J., Winters, N., & Geniet, A. (2017). *Digital education policies in Europe and beyond: Key design principles for more effective policies*. EU Publications Office. https://doi.org/10.2760/462941

Kanbach, D. K., Heiduk, L., Blueher, G., Schreiter, M., & Lahmann, A. (2024). The GenAI is out of the bottle: Generative artificial intelligence from a business model innovation perspective. *Review of Managerial Science, 18*, 1189–1220. https://doi.org/10.1007/s11846-023-00696-z

Kaplan-Rakowski, R., Grotewold, K., Hartwick, P., & Papin, K. (2023). Generative AI and teachers' perspectives on its implementation in education. *Journal of Interactive Learning Research, 34*(2), 313–338.

Karagianni, E, & Drigas, A. (2023). Using new technologies and mobiles for students with disabilities to build a sustainable inclusive learning and development ecosystem. *International Journal of Interactive Mobile Technologies (iJIM), 17*, 57–73. https://doi.org/10.3991/ijim.v17i01.36359

Kastner-Hauler, O., Tengler, K., Sabitzer, B., & Lavicza, Z. (2022). Combined effects of block-based programming and physical computing on primary students' computational thinking skills. *Frontiers in Psychology, 13*, 5382. https://doi.org/10.3389/fpsyg.2022.875382

Katterfeldt, E.-S., Cukurova, M., Spikol, D., & Cuartielles, D. (2018). Physical computing with plug-and-play toolkits: Key recommendations for collaborative learning implementations. *International Journal of Child-Computer Interaction, 17*, 72–82. https://doi.org/10.1016/j.ijcci.2018.03.002

Kaur, H., Ahmad, B., Rajoo, M., Singh, B., Manan, N. Z. A., & Arshad, B. (2022). Research on the effects of mobile learning on student education. *International Journal of Health Sciences, 6*(S6), 1155–1168.

Kay, R. (2018). Creating a framework for selecting and evaluating educational apps. In *Proceedings of INTED2018 conference, Valencia, Spain*. https://doi.org/10.21125/inted.2018.0106

Kemp, P., Wong, B., Hamer, J., & Copsey-Blake, M. (2024). *The future of computing education: Considerations for policy, curriculum and practice*. https://www.kcl.ac.uk/ecs/assets/kcl-scari-computing.pdf

Khatter, A., Thalaachawr, K., & Blyth, M. (2024). Student engagement and fostering ownership of learning. *Journal of Applied Learning and Teaching, 7*(1), 291–302.

Khosrowi, D., Finn, F., & Clark, E. (2024). Engaging the many-hands problem of generative-AI outputs: A framework for attributing credit. *AI Ethics, 24*, 440. https://doi.org/10.1007/s43681-024-00440-7

Kirkpatrick, M., Rivera, G., & Akers, J. (2022). Systematic review of behavioral interventions using digital technology to reduce problem behavior in the classroom. *Journal of Behavioral Education, 31*, 69–93. https://doi.org/10.1007/s10864-020-09406-1

Koohang, A., Springer Sargent, C., Nord, J. H., & Paliszkiewicz, J. (2022). Internet of Things (IoT): From awareness to continued use. *International Journal of Information Management, 62*, 102442. https://doi.org/10.1016/j.ijinfomgt.2021.102442

Kooli, C., & Chakraoui, R. (2025). AI-driven assistive technologies in inclusive education: Benefits, challenges, and policy recommendations. *Sustainable Futures, 10*, 101042. https://doi.org/10.1016/j.sftr.2025.101042

Kostyrka-Allchorne, K., Cooper, N. R., & Simpson, A. (2017). The relationship between television exposure and children's cognition and behaviour: A systematic review. *Developmental Review, 44*, 19–58. https://doi.org/10.1016/j.dr.2016.12.002

Kuldas, S., Sargioti, A., Staksrud, E., Heaney, D., & Norman, J. O. (2024). Are confident parents really aware of children's online risks? A conceptual model and validation of parental self-efficacy, mediation, and awareness scales. *International Journal of Bullying Prevention, 6*(3), 252–266. https://doi.org/10.1007/s42380-023-00157-x

Kurni, M., & Srinivasa, K. G. (2025). *Ethics on the use of IoT in education.* Springer. https://doi.org/10.1007/978-3-031-67387-0_13

Kurum Tiryakioğlu, G. (2024). Roles of the parents in online learning during the COVID-19 pandemic: A phenomenological study. *Asian Journal of Distance Education, 19*(1), 120–141. https://doi.org/10.5281/zenodo.10674551

Kveselava, K., Bochorishvili, I., & Jikidze, L. (2024). Multimedia in education: what do students think? *Georgian Scientists, 6*, 2.

Lao, Y. (2025). The effect of peers' parent-child relationships on student academic performance. *Acta Psychologica, 257*, 105083. https://doi.org/10.1016/j.actpsy.2025.105083

Laretive, J. (2019). Information literacy, young learners and the role of the teacher librarian. *Journal of the Australian Library and Information Association, 68*(3), 225–235. https://doi.org/10.1080/24750158.2019.1649795

Latifi, F., & Kasumi, H. (2022). Teachers' perspectives on innovative and interactive teaching methods: Perspective of mobile learning. *International Journal of Interactive Mobile Technologies, 16*, 73–83. https://doi.org/10.3991/ijim.v16i23.36217

Laumann, D., Krause, M., Kremer, F., Leibrock, B., Ubben, M., Forthmann, B., Janzik, R., Masemann, D., Reer, F., Denz, C., Greefrath, G., Heinicke, S., Marohn, A., Quandt, T., Souvignier, E., & Heusler, S. (2024). Mobile learning in the classroom: Should students bring mobile devices for learning, or should these be provided by schools? *Education and Information Technologies, 30*, 9463–9496. https://doi.org/10.1007/s10639-024-13213-w

Lavric, A., Beguni, C., Zadobrischi, E., Căilean, A. M., & Avătămăniței, S. A. (2024). A comprehensive survey on emerging assistive technologies for visually impaired persons: Lighting the path with visible light communications and artificial intelligence innovations. *Sensors, 24*(15), 4834. https://doi.org/10.3390/s24154834

Lee, A. SH., & Passey, D. (2019). Sustaining uses of digital technologies among educational and business communities. In A. Tatnall (Ed.), *Encyclopedia of information and communication technologies.* Springer. https://doi.org/10.1007/978-3-319-60013-0

Lee, H. J. (2023). Comparison of suppliers and consumers' choice factors in the online education market. *Applied Economics, 56*(21), 2585–2598. https://doi.org/10.1080/00036846.2023.2288047

Leeder, T. M. (2022). Behaviorism, skinner, and operant conditioning: Considerations for sport coaching practice. *Strategies, 35*(3), 27–32. https://doi.org/10.1080/08924562.2022.2052776

Leong, W. Y., Leong, Y. Z., & Leong, W. S. (2023). Virtual reality in education: case studies and applications. In *IET international conference on engineering technologies and applications (ICETA 2023), Yunlin, Taiwan* (pp. 186–187). https://doi.org/10.1049/icp.2023.3332

Levido, A., Matthews, S., Amery, P., & Cross, E. (2025). Parent perspectives of digital media for learning at home. *Children and Society, 16*, 1–10. https://doi.org/10.1111/chso.12979

Levin, H. I., Egger, D., Andres, L., Johnson, M., Bearman, S. K., & de Barbaro, K. (2021). Sensing everyday activity: Parent perceptions and feasibility. *Infant Behavior and Development, 62*, 101511. https://doi.org/10.1016/j.infbeh.2020.101511

Li, Y., Hu, T., Ge, T., & Auden, E. (2019). The relationship between home-based parental involvement, parental educational expectation and academic performance of middle school students in mainland China: A mediation analysis of cognitive ability. *International Journal of Educational Research, 97*, 139–153. https://doi.org/10.1016/j.ijer.2019.08.003

Lipson, S. K., Zhou, S., Abelson, S., Heinze, J., Jirsa, M., Morigney, J., Patterson, A., Singh, S., & Eisenberg, D. (2022). Trends in college student mental health and help-seeking by race/ethnicity: Findings from the national healthy minds study, 2013–2021. *Journal of Affective Disorders, 306*, 138–147. https://doi.org/10.1016/j.jad.2022.03.038

Liu, Y., & Zhu, C. (2025). The use of deep learning and artificial intelligence-based digital technologies in art education. *Science Reports, 15*, 15859. https://doi.org/10.1038/s41598-025-00892-9

Liu, Z. (2023). The attitudes of students' parents towards their children's information-based learning under the background of the combination of large-scale online learning and multimedia technology. *International Journal of Web-Based Learning and Teaching Technologies, 18*(2), 1–15. https://doi.org/10.4018/IJWLTT.320519

Lloyd, L. (2020). *Policy making in a digital world: How data and new technologies can help government make better policy.* Institute for Government. https://www.instituteforgovernment.org.uk/sites/default/files/publications/policy-making-digital-world.pdf

Lodge, J. M., & Harrison, W. J. (2019). The role of attention in learning in the digital age. *The Yale Journal of Biology and Medicine, 92*(1), 21–28.

Loveys, M., & Butler, C. (2023). Teachers' and students' perspectives on the extent to which assistive technology maximises independence. *British Journal of Visual Impairment, 43*(1), 156–174. https://doi.org/10.1177/02646196231212736

Luo, J. (2024). A critical review of GenAI policies in higher education assessment: A call to reconsider the "originality" of students' work. *Assessment Adn Evaluation in Higher Education, 38*, 1–14. https://doi.org/10.1080/02602938.2024.2309963

Male, T. (2016). Digital technologies and implications for education in 21st century digital technologies: Implications for educational organisations and settings in the twenty-first century. *Educational Futures, 7*, 5–25.

Mao, S., Wang, D., Tang, C., & Dong, P. (2022). Students' online information searching strategies and their creative question generation: The moderating effect of their need for cognitive closure. *Frontiers in Psychology, 13*, 877061. https://doi.org/10.3389/fpsyg.2022.877061

Maor, D., & Mitchem, K. J. (2015). Can technologies make a difference for hospitalized youth: Findings from research. *Journal of Computer Assisted Learning, 31*, 690–705. https://doi.org/10.1111/jcal.12112

Martos Martínez, Á., Molero Jurado, M. D. M., Pérez-Fuentes, M. D. C., Simón Márquez, M. D. M., Barragán Martín, A. B., & Gázquez Linares, J. J. (2021). The complex nature of school violence: Attitudes toward aggression, empathy and involvement profiles in violence. *Psychology Research and Behavior Management, 19*(14), 575–586. https://doi.org/10.2147/PRBM.S313831

McNaughton, S., & Jesson, R. (2023). How a digital intervention in schools contributed to students' social and emotional skills, and impacted writing. *New Zealand Journal of Educational Studies, 58*, 361–377. https://doi.org/10.1007/s40841-023-00296-1

Meletiadou, E. (2025). *How educators can use Gen AI to promote inclusion and widen access.* SRHE blog.com. https://srheblog.com/2025/05/16/how-educators-can-use-gen-ai-to-promote-inclusion-and-widen-access/

Mello, J., Santos, C., Chaves, J. B., & Fernandes, P. H. (2021). Lego education and use of STEAM methodology in teaching history. *American Journal of Engineering Research, 10*(8), 158–164.

Mendez-Reguera, E. A., & Lopez, M. (2021). Using a digital whiteboard for student engagement in distance education. *Computers and Electrical Engineering, 93*, 107268. https://doi.org/10.1016/j.compeleceng.2021.107268

Mertala, P., López-Pernas, S., Vartiainen, H., Saqr, M., & Tedre, M. (2024). Digital natives in the scientific literature: A topic modeling approach. *Computers in Human Behavior, 152*, 108076. https://doi.org/10.1016/j.chb.2023.108076

Meyer, M., Zosh, J. M., McLaren, C., Robb, M., McCafferty, H., Golinkoff, R. M., Hirsh-Pasek, K., & Radesky, J. (2021). How educational are 'educational' apps for young children? App store content analysis using the four pillars of learning framework. *Journal of Children and Media, 15*(4), 526–548. https://doi.org/10.1080/17482798.2021.1882516

Meylani, R. (2024). Innovations with schema theory: Modern implications for learning, memory, and academic achievement. *International Journal for Multidisciplinary Research, 6*(1), 13785.

Milková, E., Kaliba, M., & Ambrožová, P. (2022). Internet addiction in university students—Czech study'. *Journal on Efficiency and Responsibility in Education and Science, 15*(2), 94–102. https://doi.org/10.7160/eriesj.2022.150204

Mohammed, A. (2017). The role of language laboratory in English language learning settings. *English Language Teaching, 10*(2), 86–93. https://doi.org/10.5539/elt.v10n2p86

Mohr-Schroeder, M., Jackson, C., Cavalcanti, M., Jong, C., & Speler, L. (2017). Parents' attitudes toward mathematics and the influence on their students' attitudes toward mathematics: A quantitative study: Parents' attitudes toward mathematics. *School Science and Mathematics, 117*, 214–222. https://doi.org/10.1111/ssm.12225

Mokoena, M. M., Simelane-Mnisi, S., & Mji, A. (2022). Challenges and solutions for teachers' use of interactive whiteboards in high schools. *Universal Journal of Educational Research, 10*(1), 36–47.

Momani, M. A. K. A., Alharahasheh, K. A., & Alqudah, M. (2023). Digital learning in sciences education: A literature review. *Cogent Education, 10*(2), 7007. https://doi.org/10.1080/2331186X.2023.2277007

Monserate, C. A. (2018). Impact of technology on the academic performance of students and teaching effectiveness. *International Journal of Interdisciplinary Research and Innovations, 6*(1), 47–87.

Montazami, A., Pearson, H. A., Dubé, A. K., Kacmaz, G., Wen, R., & Alam, S. S. (2022a). Why this app? How parents choose good educational apps from app stores. *British Journal of Educational Technology, 53*(6), 1766–1792. https://doi.org/10.1111/bjet.13213

Montazami, A., Pearson, H. A., Dubé, A. K., Kacmaz, G., Wen, R., & Alam, S. S. (2022b). Why this app? How educators choose a good educational app. *Computers and Education, 184*, 104513. https://doi.org/10.1016/j.compedu.2022.104513

Montero-Sieburth, M., & Turcatti, D. (2022). Preventing disengagement leading to early school leaving: Pro-active practices for schools, teachers and families. *Intercultural Education, 33*(2), 139–155. https://doi.org/10.1080/14675986.2021.2018404

Montuori, C., Gambarota, F., Altoé, G., & Arfé, B. (2024). The cognitive effects of computational thinking: A systematic review and meta-analytic study. *Computers and Education, 210*, 104961. https://doi.org/10.1016/j.compedu.2023.104961

Mora, T., Escardíbul, J.-O., & Di Pietro, G. (2018). Computers and students' achievement: An analysis of the one laptop per child program in Catalonia. *International Journal of Educational Research, 92*, 145–157. https://doi.org/10.1016/j.ijer.2018.09.013

Morris, P., & Sarapin, S. (2020). Mobile phones in the classroom: Policies and potential pedagogy. *Journal of Media Literacy Education, 12*(1), 57–69.

Moss, G., & Jewitt, C. (2010). Policy, pedagogy and interactive whiteboards: What lessons can be learnt from early adoption in England? In *Interactive whiteboards for education: Theory, research and practice* (pp. 20–36). IGI Global. https://doi.org/10.4018/978-1-61520-715-2.ch002

Motene, R. F. (2022). *Influencing rural school teachers' use of mobile devices for teaching and learning*. Doctoral thesis. University of Pretoria, South Africa. https://repository.up.ac.za/bitstreams/f55dc0bc-5ac3-4282-85ab-ca4ef8787bde/download

Moura, A., & Carvalho, A. A. (2007). Learning anywhere, anytime through a laptop: A pilot study in a secondary school. In *IADIS international conference mobile learning* (pp. 184–188). https://www.academia.edu/579406/Learning_anywhere_anytime_through_a_laptop_a_pilot_study_in_a_secondary_school

Mourin Moral, F. J., & de Marcos Ortega, L. (2014). Perceptions and attitudes toward interactive whiteboards and classroom response systems. In *Proceedings of the 2014 IEEE 6th international conference on adaptive science and technology (ICAST), Ota, Nigeria* (pp. 1–5). https://doi.org/10.1109/ICASTECH.2014.7068132

Mouza, C., & Barrett-Greenly, T. (2015). Bridging the app gap: An examination of a professional development initiative on mobile learning in urban schools. *Computers and Education, 88*, 1–14. https://doi.org/10.1016/j.compedu.2015.04.009

Muhammad, N., Sidhu, G., & Srinivasan, S. (2020). Effect of the instruction time of the day on student learning. *International Journal of Pedagogy and Teacher Education, 4*, 43070.

Murcia, K., & Sheffield, R. (2010). Talking about science in interactive whiteboard classrooms. *Australasian Journal of Educational Technology, 26*(4), 417–431.

Myeong, S., & Choi, Y. (2010). Effects of information technology on policy decision-making processes: Some evidences beyond rhetoric. *Administration and Society, 42*, 441–459. https://doi.org/10.1177/0095399710362724

Ng, I. Y. H., Lim, S. S., & Pang, N. (2023). Making universal digital access universal: Lessons from COVID-19 in Singapore. *Universal Access in the Information Society, 22*, 1073–1083. https://doi.org/10.1007/s10209-022-00877-9

Niraula, K. B. (2023). School students' experience of using the internet. *International Journal of Studies in Education and Science, 4*(2), 124–136.

Novković-Cvetković, B., Arsić, Z., & Cenić, D. (2022). Attitudes of teachers to using information and communication technology in teaching: Advantages and obstacles. *International Journal of Cognitive Research in Science, Engineering and Education, 10*(2), 69–76.

Nur-Fitria, T. (2024). Using interactive whiteboards (IWB) in the English classroom as supporting technology in the teaching and learning process: Opportunities and challenges. *Journal of English Language and Pedagogy, 2*, 74–91.

Ó-Dochartaigh, N. (2007). Searching the keyword search engines. In *Searching the keyword search engines* (pp. 78–97). Sage. https://doi.org/10.4135/9781849209304.n5

Office for Standards in Education (Ofsted). (2004). *ICT in schools 2004: The impact of government initiatives five years on.* https://dera.ioe.ac.uk/id/eprint/4977/7/The%20impact%20of%20government%20initiatives%20five%20years%20on%20%28PDF%20format%29_Redacted.pdf#:~:text=The%20combined%20impact%20of%20government%20initiatives%20for%20ICT,mask%20continuing%20difficulties%20of%20access%20for%20individual%20departments

Office for Standards in Education (Ofsted). (2022). *Research review series: Computing. Ofsted.* https://dera.ioe.ac.uk/id/eprint/39245/1/computing%20-%20GOV.pdf

Oldnow, A., & Knights, C. (Eds.). (2011). *Mathematics education with digital technology.* Bloomsbury Academic. https://doi.org/10.5040/9781472553119

Ong, S. G. T., & Quek, G. C. L. (2023). Enhancing teacher–student interactions and student online engagement in an online learning environment. *Learning Environments Research, 26*, 681–707. https://doi.org/10.1007/s10984-022-09447-5

Organisation for Economic Cooperation and Development. (OECD). (2015). *Students, computers and learning: Making the connection.* OECD Publishing. https://doi.org/10.1787/9789264239555-en.#

Organisation for Economic Cooperation and Development. (OECD). (n.d.). *Digital divide in education.* OECD Publishing. https://www.oecd.org/en/topics/digital-divide-in-education.html

Orhani, S. (2023). Robots assist or replace teachers in the classroom. *Journal of Elementary and Secondary School, 1*, 29–41.

Outhwaite, L. A., & Van Herwegen, J. (2023). Educational apps and learning: Current evidence on design and evaluation. *British Journal of Educational Technology, 54*, 1268–1272. https://doi.org/10.1111/bjet.13360

Ozturk, H. T. (2015). Examining value change in MOOCs in the scope of connectivism and open educational resources movement. *International Review of Research in Open and Distributed Learning, 16*(5), 806.

Pakdee, S., & Sengsoon, P. (2021). Immediate effects of different screen sizes on visual fatigue in video display terminal users. *Iranian Rehabilitation Journal, 19*(2), 137–146.

Palada, B., Chandan, V. S., Gowda, C. P., & Nikitha, S. (2024). The role of augmented reality (AR) in education. *International Journal for Research in Applied Science and Engineering Technology, 12*(3), 1400–1408.

Palines, K. M. E., Moreno, J. M. U., Tatlonghari, A. G., & Ortega-Dela Cruz, R. A. (2025). Integrating information and communication technologies to enhance high school students' research capabilities. *Journal of Educational Research and Practice, 15*, 1–12. https://doi.org/10.5590/JERAP.2025.15.1952

Palmqvist, L., & Danielsson, H. (2020). Parents act as intermediary users for their children when using assistive technology for cognition in everyday planning: Results from a parental survey. *Assistive Technology, 32*(4), 194–202. https://doi.org/10.1080/10400435.2018.1522523

Papadakis, S., & Kalogiannakis, M. (2017). Mobile educational applications for children: What educators and parents need to know. *International Journal of Mobile Learning and Organisation, 11*(3), 256–277. https://doi.org/10.1504/IJMLO.2017.10003925

Papert, S. (1980). *Mindstorms: Children, computers, and powerful ideas*. Basic Books.

Papert, S., & Harel, I. (1991). *Constructionism*. Ablex Publishing.

Passey, D. (2013). *Inclusive technology enhanced learning: Overcoming cognitive, physical, emotional and geographic challenges*. Routledge. https://doi.org/10.4324/9780203073742

Passey, D., Hawkins, G., & Clift, D. (2016). Fathers and male guardians are important stakeholders in children's education: Do *Lego* building and *Scratch*-like programming activities hold a key to involving them more? In T. Brinda, N. Mavengere, I. Haukijärvi, C. Lewin, & D. Passey (Eds.), *Stakeholders and information technology in education*. Springer.

Passey, D., & Lee, A. S. H. (2020). Blending learning provision for higher education: Planning future professional development. In N. V. Varghese, & S. Mandal (Eds.), *Teaching learning and new technologies in higher education* (pp. 101–116). Springer. https://doi.org/10.1007/978-981-15-4847-5_8

Passey, D. (2025a). *IFIP task force on 'sustaining relevant digital inclusive education for young people (5–18 years of age)': Northern Ireland case study*. IFIP. https://doi.org/10.52545/2-9

Passey, D. (2025b). *IFIP task force on 'sustaining relevant digital inclusive education for young people (5–18 years of age)': Computational thinking and computing linked to problem-solving across the primary curriculum—groggan primary school, Northern Ireland case study*. https://ifip.hal.science/IFIP-EPUBLICATION/hal-05126562

Passey, D. (2025c). *IFIP task force on 'sustaining relevant digital inclusive education for young people (5–18 years of age)': Computational thinking and computing linked to problem-solving across the post-primary curriculum—St Malachy's school, Northern Ireland case study*. IFIP. https://ifip.hal.science/IFIP-EPUBLICATION/hal-05126544

Passey, D. (2000). Developing teaching strategies for distance (out-of-school) learning in primary and secondary schools. *Educational Multimedia International, 37*(1), 45–58.

Passey, D. (2010). Mobile learning in school contexts: Can teachers alone make it happen? *IEEE Transactions on Learning Technologies: Special Issue on Mobile and Ubiquitous Technologies for Learning, 3*(1), 68–81.

Passey, D. (2014). Intergenerational learning practices: Digital leaders in schools. *Education and Information Technologies, 19*(3), 473–494. https://doi.org/10.1007/s10639-014-9322-z

Passey, D. (2021). Possibilities, benefits and limitations of embedding technology enhanced and remote teaching and learning in compulsory education—and not just because of Covid-19. *Malta Journal of Education, 2*(1), 6–20.

Passey, D. (2024). Lessons from learner home engagement prior to and during Covid-19—are parents and guardians prepared for future crises? *Journal of Information Processing, 32*, 53–61. https://doi.org/10.2197/ipsjjip.32.53

Passey, D., Ntebutse, J. G., Ahmad, M. Y. A., Cochrane, J., Collin, S., Ganayem, A., Langran, E., Mulla, S., Rodrigo, M. M., Saito, T., Shonfeld, M., & Somasi, S. (2024a). Populations digitally excluded from education: Issues, factors, contributions and actions for policy, practice and research in a post-pandemic era. *Technology, Knowledge and Learning, 29*, 1733–1750. https://doi.org/10.1007/s10758-024-09767-w

Passey, D., Taggart, S., Leow, S., & Lee, C. E. (2024b). Generative artificial intelligence and education: Research, policy and practice. *Studies in Technology Enhanced Learning, 4*(1), 82.

Passey, D., & Zozimo, J. (2016). Developing mobile learning practices through teacher education: Outcomes of the MLEARN pilot. *Interactive Technology and Smart Education, 13*(1), 36–51. https://doi.org/10.1108/ITSE-01-2016-0002

Pearson, H. A., Montazami, A., Dubé, A. K., Kacmaz, G., Wen, R., & Alam, S. S. (2021). Why this app? How educators choose good educational apps. In *AERA 2021*. https://doi.org/10.3102/1686123

Peng, H., Ma, S., & Spector, J. M. (2019). Personalized adaptive learning: An emerging pedagogical approach enabled by a smart learning environment. *Smart Learning Environments, 6*, 9. https://doi.org/10.1186/s40561-019-0089-y

Perifanou, M., Economides, A., & Nikou, S. (2022). Teachers' views on integrating augmented reality in education: Needs, opportunities, challenges and recommendations. *Future Internet, 15*(1), 20. https://doi.org/10.3390/fi15010020

Perzylo, L. (2006). The application of multimedia CD-ROMs in schools. *British Journal of Educational Technology, 24*, 191–197. https://doi.org/10.1111/j.1467-8535.1993.tb00073.x

Phillips, D. C. (2012). Behaviorism and behaviorist learning theories. In N. M. Seel (Ed.), *Encyclopedia of the sciences of learning*. Springer. https://doi.org/10.1007/978-1-4419-1428-6_750

Piaget, J. (1936). *Origins of intelligence in the child*. Routledge & Kegan Paul.

Picton, I., Moisi, I., Jackson T., & Clark, C. (2024). *Parents' support for young children's literacy at home in 2024. National Literacy Trust*. https://nlt.cdn.ngo/media/documents/Parents_support_for_young_childrens_literacy_at_home_in_2024.pdf

Pierce, G. L., & Cleary, P. F. (2024). The persistent educational digital divide and its impact on societal inequality. *PLoS ONE, 19*(4), e0286795. https://doi.org/10.1371/journal.pone.0286795

Polikoff, M., Rapaport, A., & Fast, N. (2025). *What do parents know about Generative AI in schools?* Center for Reinventing Public Education. https://crpe.org/what-do-parents-know-about-generative-ai-in-schools/

Porkundil, A. A. M. (2023). Experiences of parents of pre-primary students on teaching and learning practices using technology during Covid-19. *Studies in Technology Enhanced Learning, 3*(3), 225.

Prensky, M. (2001). Digital natives, digital immigrants, part 1. *On the Horizon, 9*, 3–6. https://doi.org/10.1108/10748120110424816

Puspita, R., & Rohedi, D. (2018). The impact of internet use for students. *IOP Conference Series: Materials Science and Engineering, 306*, 012106. https://doi.org/10.1088/1757-899X/306/1/012106

Radović, S., Marić, M., & Passey, D. (2019). Technology enhancing mathematics learning behaviours: Shifting learning goals from "producing the right answer" to "understanding how to address current and future mathematical challenges." *Education and Information Technologies, 24*, 103–126. https://doi.org/10.1007/s10639-018-9763-x

Rahmatika, N., Hanapi, M., Jendriadi, J., Sariasih, Y., Imami, M., & Uslan, U. (2024). The impact of flipped learning on students' critical thinking: A systematic literature review. *International Journal of Learning, Teaching and Educational Research, 23*, 180–206.

Rajabalee, B. Y., Santally, M. I., & Rennie, F. (2019). A study of the relationship between students' engagement and their academic performances in an eLearning environment. *E-Learning and Digital Media, 17*(1), 1–20. https://doi.org/10.1177/2042753019882567

Rangarajan, S. (2020). Satellite-connected hotspot for offline learning systems (SCHOOLS): An innovative approach for universal education. *International Journal of Education and Psychological Research, 9*(4), 14–17.

Raptis, D., Tselios, N., Kjeldskov, J., & Skov, M. B. (2013). Does size matter? Investigating the impact of mobile phone screen size on users' perceived usability, effectiveness and efficiency. In *MobileHCI 2013—proceedings of the 15th international conference on human-computer interaction with mobile devices and services* (pp. 127–136). Association for Computing Machinery (ACM). https://doi.org/10.1145/2493190.2493204

Reddy, K., Gharde, P., Tayade, H., Patil, M., Reddy, L. S., & Surya, D. (2023). Advancements in robotic surgery: A comprehensive overview of current utilizations and upcoming frontiers. *Cureus, 15*(12), e50415. https://doi.org/10.7759/cureus.50415

Rehman, N. U., Aftab, M. J., & Ali, H. H. (2024). Role of technology integration in educational settings for students with hearing impairment. *Bulletin of Education and Research, 46*(1), 87–105.

Republic of Estonia Ministry of Education and Research. (2022). *National curricula.* https://www.hm.ee/en/national-curricula

Ribeiro, J., Lima, R., Eckhardt, T., & Paiva, S. (2021). Robotic process automation and artificial intelligence in industry 4.0: A literature review. *Procedia Computer Science, 181*, 51–58. https://doi.org/10.1016/j.procs.2021.01.104

Rizk, J., & Hillier, C. (2022). Digital technology and increasing engagement among students with disabilities: Interaction rituals and digital capital. *Computers and Education Open, 3*, 100099. https://doi.org/10.1016/j.caeo.2022.100099

Rodolico, G., & Hirsu, L. (2023). Virtual reality in education: Supporting new learning experiences by developing self-confidence of postgraduate diploma in education (PGDE) student-teachers. *Educational Media International, 60*(2), 92–108. https://doi.org/10.1080/09523987.2023.2262195

Rodrigues, S., Chittleborough, G., Gooding, A., Papadimitropoulos, T., Varughese, V. K., Kemp, S., Sadler, J., Gilmour, M., McKenna, S., & Helme, S. (1999). Using CD-ROMs in teaching science: Findings from a small scale study. *Australian Journal of Educational Technology, 15*(2), 136–147.

Romanelli, F., Bird, E., & Ryan, M. (2009). Learning styles: A review of theory, application, and best practices. *American Journal of Pharmaceutical Education, 73*(1), 9. https://doi.org/10.5688/aj730109

Rong, Y. (2024). *Behaviorism.* Springer. https://doi.org/10.1007/978-981-99-6000-2_547-1

Rose, S. E., Gears, A., & Taylor, J. (2022). What are parents' and children's co-constructed views on mobile phone use and policies in school? *Children and Society, 36*(6), 1418–1433. https://doi.org/10.1111/chso.12583

Rosell-Aguilar, F. (2015). Podcasting as a language teaching and learning tool. In *10 years of the LLAS elearning symposium: Case studies in good practice* (pp. 31–39). Research-publishing.net. https://doi.org/10.14705/rpnet.2015.000265

Roser, M. (2023). *This timeline charts the fast pace of tech transformation across centuries.* World Economic Forum. https://www.weforum.org/stories/2023/02/this-timeline-charts-the-fast-pace-of-tech-transformation-across-centuries/

Ruipérez-Valiente, J. A., Martínez-Maldonado, R., Di Mitri, D., & Schneider, J. (2022). From sensor data to educational insights. *Sensors, 22*(21), 8556. https://doi.org/10.3390/s22218556

Ružić, I., & Balaban, I. (2023). The use of social robots as teaching assistants in education: Literature review. In *Proceedings of the central European conference on information and intelligent systems* (pp. 205–212). https://archive.ceciis.foi.hr/public/conferences/2023/Proceedings/ELA/ELA5.pdf#:~:text=This%20literature%20review%20examines%20the%20impact%20of%20social,social%20robots%20mostly%20in%20preschool%20or%20primary%20education

Ryan, R. M., & Deci, E. L. (2000). Self-determination theory and the facilitation of intrinsic motivation, social development, and well-being. *American Psychologist, 55*(1), 68–78. https://doi.org/10.1037/0003-066X.55.1.68

Şahin, A., & Özenç, E. G. (2021). The use of educational software in teaching initial reading and writing. *International Journal of Progressive Education, 17*(4), 373–389.

Şahin, F., Kızılaslan, A., & Şimşek, Ö. (2024). Factors influencing the acceptance of assistive technology by teacher candidates in the context of inclusive education and special needs students. *Education and Information Technologies, 29*, 12263–12288. https://doi.org/10.1007/s10639-023-12383-3

Saleem, A., Kausar, H., & Deeba, F. (2021). Social constructivism: A new paradigm in teaching and learning environment. *Perennial Journal of History, 2*, 403–421.

Samson, S., & Millet, M. S. (2003). The learning environment: First-year students, teaching assistants, and information literacy. *Research Strategies, 19*(2), 84–98. https://doi.org/10.1016/j.resstr.2004.02.001

Santos, A. C., Simões, C., Melo, M. H. S., Santos, M. F., Freitas, I., Branquinho, C., Cefai, C., & Arriaga, P. (2023). A systematic review of the association between social and emotional competencies and student engagement in youth. *Educational Research Review, 39*, 100535. https://doi.org/10.1016/j.edurev.2023.100535

Sato, S., Moreno, E., Rubio-Zarapuz, A., Dalamitros, A., Yañez-Sepúlveda, R., Tornero-Aguilera, J., & Clemente-Suárez, V. (2023). Navigating the new normal: Adapting online and distance learning in the post-pandemic era. *Education Sciences, 14*, 19. https://doi.org/10.3390/educsci14010019

Saville, M., Beswick, K., & Callingham, R. (2014). The use of interactive whiteboards in education. In *The future of educational research: Bold visions in educational research* (pp. 203–216). SensePublishers. https://doi.org/10.1007/978-94-6209-512-0_17

Sawant, N., & Naik, S. (2022). Is online education leading to technology addiction? *International Journal for Research in Applied Science and Engineering Technology, 10*(2), 338–343.

Schiavetto, S., & Schnaider, K. (2024). Agency and signification in learning with digital technologies: A theoretical approximation of actor-network theory and representational perspectives. In J. Jaldemark, M. Håkansson Lindqvist, P. Mozelius, L. M. Öberg, M. De Laat, N. B. Dohn, & T. Ryberg (Eds.), *Proceedings for the thirteenth international conference on networked learning 2022*. https://doi.org/10.54337/nlc.v13.8527

Schulz, L., Kürzinger, A., & Böttinger, T. (2025). Communication and collaboration in digital learning environments in elementary schools: Findings from a videographic research project. *Learning Environments Research, 28*, 271–287. https://doi.org/10.1007/s10984-025-09537-0

Schweiger, G. (2025). The vulnerability and injustices faced by young carers in developed societies. *Societies, 15*(4), 101. https://doi.org/10.3390/soc15040101

See, B. H., Gorard, S., El-Soufi, N., Lu, B., Siddiqui, N., & Dong, L. (2020). A systematic review of the impact of technology-mediated parental engagement on student outcomes. *Educational Research and Evaluation, 26*(3–4), 150–181. https://doi.org/10.1080/13803611.2021.1924791

Seymour, T., Frantsvog, D., & Kumar, S. (2011). History of search engines. *International Journal of Management and Information Systems (IJMIS), 15*, 5799.

Shadiev, R., & Wang, X. (2022). A review of research on technology-supported language learning and 21st century skills. *Frontiers in Psychology, 13*, 897689. https://doi.org/10.3389/fpsyg.2022.897689

Sharpe, R., Beetham, H., & de Freitas, S. (2010). *Rethinking learning for a digital age: How learners are shaping their own experiences*. Routledge.

Shucksmith, J., Jones, S., & Summerbell, C. (2010). The role of parental involvement in school-based mental health interventions at primary (elementary) school level. *Advances in School Mental Health Promotion, 3*, 18–29. https://doi.org/10.1080/1754730X.2010.9715671

Shulman, L. S. (2005). Signature pedagogies in the professions. *Daedalus, 134*(3), 52–59.

Siemens, G. (2004). Connectivism: A learning theory for the digital age. *International Journal of Instructional Technology and Distance Learning, 2*(1), 525.

Silva, M. J., Rodrigues, M., & Tempera, T. (2024). Framework for a research-based and interdisciplinary use of sensors in elementary teacher education. *Sensors, 24*, 5482. https://doi.org/10.3390/s24175482

Simões, S., Oliveira, T., & Nunes, C. (2022). Influence of computers in students' academic achievement. *Heliyon, 8*(3), e09004. https://doi.org/10.1016/j.heliyon.2022.e09004

Skinner, B. F. (1938). *The behavior of organisms: An experimental analysis*. Appleton-Century-Crofts. https://www.bfskinner.org/wp-content/uploads/2016/02/BoO.pdf

Smale, W., Hutcheson, R., & Russo, C. J. (2021). Cell phones, student rights, and school safety: Finding the right balance. *Canadian Journal of Educational Administration and Policy, 195*, 49–64. https://doi.org/10.7202/1075672ar

Smith, S., & Anderson, J. (2025). *Report on the 2024–2025 ICT excellence awards*. Capita. https://content.capita.com/l/824863/2025-06-26/3r6xq3/824863/1750929287zWaoh28M/C2K_ENni_Excellence_Award_Report_24_25.pdf

Smyth, L., Mavor, K. I., & Platow, M. J. (2017). Learning behaviour and learning outcomes: The roles for social influence and field of study. *Social Psychology of Education, 20*, 69–95. https://doi.org/10.1007/s11218-016-9365-7

Southgate, E., Blackmore, K., Pieschl, S., Grimes, S., McGuire, J., & Smithers, K. (2018). *Short read: Virtual and augmented reality and school education.* University of Newcastle. https://www.education.gov.au/download/4639/short-read-vr-ar/6938/document/pdf

Spratt, J., & Florian, L. (2015). Inclusive pedagogy: From learning to action. Supporting each individual in the context of 'everybody.' *Teaching and Teacher Education, 49*, 89–96. https://doi.org/10.1016/j.tate.2015.03.006

Stanford, J. (2025). How disruptive is AI in students' academic writing in higher education? *Studies in Technology Enhanced Learning, 4*(1), 225.

Statistica. (2025). *Number of individuals not using the internet as of October 2025, by region.* https://www.statista.com/statistics/1378504/people-do-not-use-internet-by-region/

Subramanian, K. (2018). Technology and transformation in communication. *Journal of Advance Research in Electrical and Electronics Engineering, 5*(8), 1–13.

Taggart, S., & Roulston, S. (2025). *Trailblazing NIgenAI in education: A proof-of-concept study in schools in Northern Ireland with MS Copilot.* Ulster University. https://pure.ulster.ac.uk/en/publications/trailblazingni-genaiineducation-aproofofconceptstudyinschoolsinno

Tamim Faruq, M., Neo, K., & Rashid, F. (2023). Music matters: The role of background music in improving students' attention and learning outcomes. *International Journal of Membrane Science and Technology, 10*(3), 1898–1908.

Tang, Y. M., Lau, Y. Y., & Chau, K. Y. (2022). Towards a sustainable online peer learning model based on student's perspectives. *Education and Information Technologies, 27*(9), 12449–12468. https://doi.org/10.1007/s10639-022-11136-y

Tatnall, A., & Davey, B. (2014). *Reflections on the history of computers in education: Early use of computers and teaching about computing in schools.* Springer. https://doi.org/10.1007/978-3-642-55119-2

Taylor, K., & Yuknis, C. (2023). Universal design for learning supports distance learning for deaf students. *American Annals of the Deaf, 168*(3), 41–54.

Teng, M. F. (2021). Interactive-whiteboard-technology-supported collaborative writing: Writing achievement, metacognitive activities, and co-regulation patterns. *System, 97*, 102426. https://doi.org/10.1016/j.system.2020.102426

The Open Innovation Team and Department for Education. (2024). *Generative AI in education: Educator and expert views.* Department for Education. https://files.eric.ed.gov/fulltext/ED649949.pdf

Thornton, P., & Houser, C. (2005). Using mobile phones in English education in Japan. *Journal of Computer Assisted Learning, 21*(3), 217–228. https://doi.org/10.1111/j.1365-2729.2005.00129.x

Throuvala, M. A., Griffiths, M. D., Rennoldson, M., & Kuss, D. J. (2021). Policy recommendations for preventing problematic internet use in schools: A qualitative study of parental perspectives. *International Journal of Environmental Research and Public Health, 18*(9), 4522. https://doi.org/10.3390/ijerph18094522

Toktamysov, S., Alwaely, S. A., & Gallyamova, Z. (2023). Digital technologies in history training: The impact on students' academic performance. *Education and Information Technologies, 28*, 2173–2186. https://doi.org/10.1007/s10639-022-11210-5

Topal, R., & Shargh, F. (2023). Teaching students how to find and identify reliable online sources: A series of exercises. *Journal of Political Science Education, 19*, 1–10. https://doi.org/10.1080/15512169.2022.2163899

Tran, N., Hoang, D. T. N., Gillespie, R., Yen, T. T. H., & Phung, H. (2024). Enhancing EFL learners' speaking and listening skills through authentic online conversations with video conferencing tools. *Innovation in Language Learning and Teaching, 54*, 1–11. https://doi.org/10.1080/17501229.2024.2334809

Traxler, J. (2009). Learning in a mobile age. *International Journal of Mobile and Blended Learning, 1*(1), 1–12. https://doi.org/10.4018/jmbl.2009010101

Trent, S. C., Artiles, A. J., & Englert, C. S. (1998). From deficit thinking to social constructivism: A review of theory, research, and practice in special education. *Review of Research in Education, 23*, 277–307. https://doi.org/10.2307/1167293

Trültzsch-Wijnen, C. W., Velicu, A., & Liubiniene, V. (2021). Robotics for children: National policies and initiatives in three European countries. *Medijske Studije, 12*(24), 3–20.

Tsai, M.-J., & Wu, A.-H. (2021). Visual search patterns, information selection strategies, and information anxiety for online information problem solving. *Computers and Education, 172*, 104236. https://doi.org/10.1016/j.compedu.2021.104236

Ulum, H. (2022). The effects of online education on academic success: A meta-analysis study. *Education and Information Technologies, 27*(1), 429–450. https://doi.org/10.1007/s10639-021-10740-8

United Nations Education, Scientific and Cultural Organization. (UNESCO). (2023). *Guidance for generative AI in education and research*. UNESCO. https://unesdoc.unesco.org/ark:/48223/pf0000386693

Urhahne, D. (2020). Learning approaches. *Educational Psychology, 40*(5), 533–534. https://doi.org/10.1080/01443410.2020.1755503

Van den Broeck, L., De Laet, T., Dujardin, R., Tuyaerts, S., & Langie, G. (2024). Unveiling the competencies at the core of lifelong learning: A systematic literature review. *Educational Research Review, 45*, 100646. https://doi.org/10.1016/j.edurev.2024.100646

Vygotsky, L. S. (1978). *Mind in society: The development of higher psychological processes*. Harvard University Press. https://doi.org/10.2307/j.ctvjf9vz4

Walan, S. (2020). Embracing digital technology in science classrooms—secondary school teachers' enacted teaching and reflections on practice. *Journal of Science Education and Technology, 29*, 431–441. https://doi.org/10.1007/s10956-020-09828-6

Walter, N. (2023). Using audiobooks in elementary education: A study of teacher perspectives. *Studia z Teorii Wychowania, 14*, 199–215. https://doi.org/10.5604/01.3001.0054.1204

Wang, L. (2023). The impact of student-centered learning on academic motivation and achievement: A comparative research between traditional instruction and student-centered approach. *Journal of Education, Humanities and Social Sciences, 22*, 346–353.

Watson, L. (2016). Why should we educate for inquisitiveness. In *Intellectual virtues and education: Essays in applied virtue epistemology* (pp. 38–53). https://doi.org/10.4324/9781315714127-3

Wells, J., & Lewis, L. (2006). *Internet access in U.S. public schools and classrooms: 1994–2005 (NCES 2007–2020)*. U.S. Department of Education. National Center for Education Statistics. https://nces.ed.gov/pubs2007/2007020.pdf

West, M., & Vosloo, S. (2013). *UNESCO policy guidelines for mobile learning*. UNESCO. https://unesdoc.unesco.org/ark:/48223/pf0000219641.pdf

Wing, J. M. (2006). Computational thinking. *Communications of the ACM, 49*(3), 33–35.

Woodhouse, H., Passey, D., & Anderson, J. (2024). Using digital technologies to build connections between families and schools as children transition to school. *Education Sciences, 14*, 520. https://doi.org/10.3390/educsci14050520

World Intellectual Property Organization (WIPO). (2024). *Generative artificial intelligence. Patent landscape report*. WIPO. https://doi.org/10.34667/tind.49740

Wu, D., & Zhang, J. (2025). Generative artificial intelligence in secondary education: Applications and effects on students' innovation skills and digital literacy. *PLoS ONE, 20*(5), e0323349. https://doi.org/10.1371/journal.pone.0323349

Wu, F., Dang, Y., & Li, M. (2025). A systematic review of responses, attitudes, and utilization behaviors on generative AI for teaching and learning in higher education. *Behavioral Sciences, 15*(4), 467.

Wyss, C., & Bäuerlein, K. (2024). Augmented reality in the classroom—mentor teachers' attitudes and technology use. *Virtual Worlds, 3*(4), 572–585. https://doi.org/10.3390/virtualworlds3040029

Yaffe, Y., Roman, N. V., & Alt, D. (2024). Editorial: New directions and trends in parenting research. *Frontiers in Psychology, 15*, 6190.

Yang, X., Wu, J., Ma, Y., Yu, J., Cao, H., Zeng, A., Fu, R., Tang, Y., & Ren, Z. (2025). Effectiveness of virtual reality technology interventions in improving the social skills of children and adolescents with Autism: Systematic review. *Journal of Medical Internet Research, 27*, 845. https://doi.org/10.2196/60845

Yilmaz, K. (2011). The cognitive perspective on learning: Its theoretical underpinnings and implications for classroom practices. *The Clearing House, 84*, 204–212. https://doi.org/10.1080/00098655.2011.568989

Yolcu, V., & Demirer, V. (2023). The effects of educational robotics in programming education on students' programming success, computational thinking, and transfer of learning. *Computer Applications in Engineering Education, 31*(6), 1633–1647. https://doi.org/10.1002/cae.22664

Younas, M., Aldayel, H., Menhas, R., & Qingyu, X. (2022). Learning behavior, digital platforms for learning and its impact on university student's motivations and knowledge development. *Frontiers in Psychology, 13*, 974. https://doi.org/10.3389/fpsyg.2022.933974

Zahedi, S., Jaffer, R., & Iyer, A. (2021). A systematic review of screen-time literature to inform educational policy and practice during COVID-19. *International Journal of Educational Research Open, 2*, 100094. https://doi.org/10.1016/j.ijedro.2021.100094

Zajda, J. (2023). The use of social constructivism to improve learning and performance. In *Globalisation and inclusive schooling. globalisation, comparative education and policy research* (Vol. 36). Springer. https://doi.org/10.1007/978-3-031-24400-1_4

Zhang, L., Basham, J. D., & Yang, S. (2020). Understanding the implementation of personalized learning: A research synthesis. *Educational Research Review, 31*, 100339. https://doi.org/10.1016/j.edurev.2020.100339

Zhang, P. (2021). Understanding digital learning behaviors: Moderating roles of goal setting behavior and social pressure in large-scale open online courses. *Frontiers in Psychology, 12*, 83610. https://doi.org/10.3389/fpsyg.2021.783610

Zhang, X., Ding, Y., Huang, X., Li, W., Long, L., & Ding, S. (2024). Smart classrooms: How sensors and AI are shaping educational paradigms. *Sensors, 24*(17), 5487. https://doi.org/10.3390/s24175487

The manufacturer's authorised representative in the EU is Springer Nature Customer Service Centre GmbH, Europaplatz 3, 69115 Heidelberg, Germany. If you have any concerns regarding our products, please contact ProductSafety@springernature.com

Printed and bound by CPI Group (UK) Ltd, Croydon, CR0 4YY
21/09/2026
02220010-0001